# Massacres

## An historical perspective

# Massacres

## An historical perspective

## ERIC CARLTON

SCOLAR
PRESS

Published by
SCOLAR PRESS
Gower House
Croft Road
Aldershot
Hants GU11 3HR
England

Ashgate Publishing Company
Old Post Road
Brookfield
Vermont 05036
USA


British Library Cataloguing-in-Publication data.

Carlton, Eric
    Massacres: Historical Perspective
    I. Title
    904

Library of Congress Cataloging-in-Publication Data

Carlton, Eric.
    Massacres : an historical perspective / Eric Carlton.
        p.   cm.
    Includes bibliographical references and index.
    ISBN 1–85928–017–X
    1. Massacres.   I. Title.
    D24.C3   1994
    904′.7—dc20       93–41550
                        CIP


ISBN 1 85928 017 X

Phototypeset in 10 point Garamond by Intype, London, and printed in Great Britain at the University Press, Cambridge.

# Contents

# Introduction

War is nasty at the best of times, but when it is also attended by atrocities – and particularly massacre – it can almost become beyond comprehension. For most of us, bestiality in its various forms is the stuff of fiction, a staple of the media – certainly not something which is part of our actual day-to-day experience. Of course, we know it 'goes on', has happened, *is* happening, but except for those unwelcome (or welcome?) images on our screens, it is all very remote and far away. Violence is alien to most of us in the *direct* experiential sense, but *indirectly* – via the media – it is part of our everyday reality. And fictional violence is undoubtedly enjoyed because it brings the vicarious sensation of the act without the guilt of real participation. Sadly, violence has some resonance for us in that it strikes an often unacknowledged cord in our natures. So when we judge – as we must – the acts presented in this book, in a sense we are judging ourselves.

From an unreflective point of view, massacre is just massacre no matter by whom or to whom it takes place. But on reflection it is not quite as simple as this. The empirical data, such as they are, make any classification of massacre rather difficult. Broadly speaking, it may be defined as the indiscriminate killing of unresisting or defenceless people, and can be subsumed under the more general term atrocity which normally refers to some horrible or cruel act. But when we try to analyse exactly what massacre entails, we find that it cannot be classified in terms of any *single* factor. For example, we may wish to look at massacre from the point of view of, say, *motive*, but are we thinking of personal motive such as revenge, or are we thinking of political motive such as expediency? Or we can think of massacre in terms of *type*, which is the method we have adopted in our case studies. This adds colour to the study because it exemplifies the phenomenon in the context of a number of different cultures and situations. But this approach too has its weaknesses. For instance, how are we going to differentiate between massacre as retribution and massacre as punishment? As an alternative we could perhaps look at massacre on the basis of *method*; was it unpremeditated or was it carefully planned? What is most unproductive is to concentrate on the details of what happened; the carnage itself usually tells us nothing about massacre *per se* – although it may tell us a great deal about the nature of inhumanity.

Some might advocate a more *psychological* approach which tries to uncover something of the personalities of the victims and especially those of the perpetrators, yet this can be as fascinating as its conclusions are elusive. Such studies are necessarily retrospective, as neither victims nor perpetrators are available for questioning. It is too late to ask what was in the minds of say, the Vietnamese villagers before they were slaughtered, or exactly what Genghis Khan thought when he butchered unarmed Chinese peasants. This sort of investigation usually ends up by being little more than intelligent guesswork. Complementarily, one could take a more *sociological* stance and ask about the distribution and incidence of massacre. Does it occur in particular environments, and if so to what kinds of people? This involves some intra-group analysis which would look at victims and/or perpetrators in terms of race, class, sex and age, etc.

A further approach would concentrate on the *repercussions* of any particular massacre. What followed from it and what were the reactions to it? Again, this is interesting, but limited in scope. It tells us little about the reasons for the massacre itself. Sometimes the reaction is one of shock and inactivity. On other occasions one massacre may spark off a spate of counter-atrocities as in modern Sri Lanka – all of which makes a political solution more difficult to achieve.

Extremely important in any study of massacre is the complex issue of *reportage*. Who has informed us about the atrocity in question? Was it a survivor? Is it a genuine account, or has it been exaggerated for some covert reason? Has the report been filtered through the media? If so, has it been trivialised or – more commonly – sensationalised for public consumption? The presentation of the 'facts' – insofar as they can be known – is closely allied to the problem of *interpretation*. For example, when Gandhi was assassinated in India in 1947 it gave rise to a wave of rioting and blood-letting and many innocent lives were lost. But can this sort of thing be interpreted as a massacre or must a massacre involve a more calculated cruelty than mob violence suggests?

In this study we are going to begin with a theoretical discussion of the moral issues involved in trying to assess acts of atrocity. In order to do this, we must first of all set aside the problem of whether or not the acts are right *in themselves*, and examine the *criteria* whereby such judgements can be made. Then we will move on to the main body of the book consisting of a series of case studies which examine a number of actual incidents that have taken place, especially during Word War II. There will be a frank appraisal of these acts, but there is no gratuitous concentration on detail. The intention is rather to examine the situational contexts in which these incidents took place in order to appreciate why they happened as they did. So the distinction here is between form and content. Not, of course, that we can ever really know the truth. We can rarely unravel the reasons behind these acts – if indeed, there were clear-cut reasons at all. So many massacres seem to be quite irrational, especially in their actual execution. But we can classify them in a general way, and even offer tentative explanations in some cases. Finally, on the basis of our case studies we may be able to arrive at some theoretical conclusions about the nature of human violence and aggression. It is consideration of problems such as these which shows that the phenomenon of massacre defies any simple analysis.

# CHAPTER ONE

# Morality and Moral Systems

In looking at the moral issues concerning massacre, we cannot really avoid the problem of war itself. The question of whether war can or cannot be justified seems to be almost as old as moral thinking itself. Not everyone would agree with Socrates (d. 399 BC), one of antiquity's keenest thinkers, who – according to Xenophon (*Recollections of Socrates*, 36, 40) – applauds those who are eager 'to grow great through war and [who] wish to be able to liberate [their] friends and overcome [their] enemies'. He also seems to approve, or at least recognise, the right of the strong to rule the weak when he asks an enquirer if he realises that it is 'the brave and powerful [who] enslave and plunder the cowardly and weak . . .'. Such arguments have been rehearsed *ad infinitum*, and have been ably summarised by a number of modern writers, e.g. Walzer (1980) and Fotion and Elfstrom (1986). But they still remain stubbornly inconclusive. What is needed to complement these is a critical appraisal of the general criteria whereby such judgements can be made.

Two initial matters need to be borne in mind from the outset. The first is the distinction between statements of fact and statements of value. There is nothing complex in this. A *statement of fact* is what it says, a declaration or proposition that is purportedly based on empirical evidence. So when we talk about a military atrocity, we are thinking about the facts – or alleged facts – of the case. Did it happen? How did it happen? Who is responsible for it happening? What can be done to see that justice prevails? A *statement of value* is quite different, though in the 'popular mind' it is sometimes confused with a statement of fact. Here some kind of judgement is made in relation to the facts. This judgement expresses a value – often a moral value – about the rightness or wrongness, justification, inexcusability and so forth of the act in question.

The second distinction we must make is between what moral philosophers term Naturalist and Non-naturalist statements. *Naturalists* maintain that moral values can be reduced to non-moral terms. That is to say, certain acts, say atrocities, can be interpreted, even explained, in terms of bio-chemical reactions, or psychological states, or socio-economic determinants of some kind. Some of the arguments offered by Naturalists have an instant plausibility. It is not difficult to see how certain behaviour patterns may have come about in the natural course of things. Fear, for example, my be explained in survival terms. From a socio-biological point of view it can be seen as an emotion that was necessary to our primitive ancestors who had to contend with all manner of daily emergencies just to stay alive. Fear keeps us constantly on the alert, it prepares us to deal with critical situations, whether it has to be by fight or, not uncommonly, by flight. On the other hand, in bio-chemical terms, fear is simply the discharge of adrenalin. But is this all it is? This kind of 'explanation' doesn't tell us anything about the situation which triggers the discharge, or what form the response to that situation takes. No one seriously doubts that a discharge of adrenalin *accompanies* the experience of fear, but the discharge cannot itself be the fear. Complementarily, courage may be seen as an essential part of the human psychological make-up which evolved to enable men to ward off the interminable and often unpredictable dangers that faced them. But even the most superficial glance at the various manifestations of courage will show that it is surely more than this. This type of explanation does not account for the gratuitous exhibitions of courage that we witness in modern society (for example, mountain-climbing, motor-racing, and so forth), nor does it help us to understand in what ways all this is bound up with questions of leadership and social status.

The study of morals and moral behaviour usually comes under the heading of ethics or moral philosophy. And theories of ethics are conventionally divided into (i) teleological theories which stress the consequences of action, the outcome of particular patterns of behaviour, and (ii) deontological theories which emphasise the intrinsic nature of behaviour, that it is good or evil *in itself*, regardless of its consequences. Wartime situations, in particular, are replete with instances of wrong actions that are undertaken for ostensibly good reasons. A suitable rationale for our actions is not usually difficult to find if we are minded to do so. Not only can we sometimes convince others, we can often convince ourselves that we are acting from the very best of motives. We have only to think of the number of wars that have begun – and ended – in this way. As for intrinsic values, how many of us know what these really are? We feel, perhaps rightly, that some values are objective, universal or even eternal, but this is a matter of faith rather than fact. We may be convinced of the ultimate rightness and wrongness of certain things, and also feel that this is inextricably part of our common heritage as human creatures, but the objective nature of values is something which it is impossible to prove.

Quite a useful way of analysing moral theories is by simply dividing them into subjectivist and consensus systems. Both types are particularly pertinent to the kinds of questions we might wish to ask about war and massacre.

There are a number of variants of the subjectivist view, but we are going to consider some of the most fundamental of the arguments in the theory known as Emotivism. This has an interesting provenance and, in one form or another, dates from at least the days of the ancient Greeks. In more recent times, it is particularly associated with the eighteenth-century philosopher, David Hume, and in this century with Bertrand Russell and Alfred Ayer. Emotivists maintain that when we speak of right or wrong we think we are talking about the *quality* of the act, whereas we are really only evincing some measure of approval or disapproval. Russell's opinions changed during his lifetime, but in his earlier writings, he suggests that attitudes to morality are analogous to attitudes about, say, art – its really all a matter of taste. For Ayer, moral propositions were merely 'pseudo-concepts' i.e. they had no *factual* significance. Moral arguments might be interesting, but, strictly speaking, they were meaningless because they could only be matters of opinion, and could never, therefore, be resolved. Human behaviour could not be regarded as *intrinsically* right or wrong; all acts possessed only those properties that we assign to them. So if we choose to think a particular massacre is warranted, given the nature of the circumstances, it is no longer wrong *for us*. Such a view is likely to find us out on a limb as far as the rest of the public is concerned, but – so it is argued – ultimately it is their opinion against ours. There can be no final arbiter because there can be no final answer. In the end it has to be a matter of approbation or disapprobation.

It is only too obvious how directly this relates to acts of war. We will find plenty of examples in our case studies. Emotive theory, if taken seriously, means that almost any act of brutality – not least the launching of war itself – can be justified if opinions or 'feelings' are the only criteria. So if, as has so often happened in enemy occupation situations, the dominant power decides to execute hostages or prisoners of war as an act of retaliation or as an expedient to discourage insurrection, it is all in order if it is effective. I remember once arguing about this with a Jewish student who insisted that the German security-police who had machine-gunned Jewish 'prisoners' to death during World War II were just as 'right', in their own way, as those that they killed. It was all a matter of preference and perspective – a question of personal conviction. But can such a view be right?

Emotivism implies that no opinion is superior to any other opinion. This means that policy decisions become a matter of reconciling different subjectivities. Can something – in our case murder of the defenceless – be both right and wrong depending on the disposition of the observer? What about prejudice? What about pathological mentalities as with, say, serial killers? Surely when we react unfavourably to such acts, it is not *just* a matter of moral repugnance? There is a sense of revulsion, but is this not based upon the judgement that the act is wrong? Emotional reaction may well accompany the judgement, but it is not *in itself* the judgement. Can we simply attribute our moral reactions to our upbringing? If so, why have our forebears decided on these values and not others? Is it just because society works better when we keep the moral rules?

The problem with the subjectivist or individual morality approach is that it can be held to validate any opinion no matter how bizarre or unscientific it appears to be. It is the sort of thing that we see, for instance, in the extreme forms of racism *and* anti-racism (which can also take quite violent forms). The ultimate subjectivist position is that which is based on arguments from conscience. When we think of conscience we think of the small inner voice which checks us when we are about to step out of line. We may think of these warnings as being peculiar to ourselves, but perhaps we are actually dealing with some echo of the norms of society. Rarely are the values we entertain in any way unique – indeed, it is doubtful if there can be such a thing as a completely individual morality. The great snag about arguments from conscience is that they can be so easily rationalised, stifled and even ignored if we are not inclined to obey them. How many times have we all shut our ears to the 'voice' when it was giving us sage advice, or have been plagued by guilt and recrimination after the event? As we shall see, this was not an uncommon experience of those involved in some horrific massacre, especially in Vietnam. Whilst, on other occasions, especially where there has been a strong ideological conviction, the 'voice' has been so conditioned that it either says nothing or actually applauds the act in question.

The consensus approach is quite different. In what is almost certainly its most popular form, Utilitarianism, it maintains that what matters is that we try to bring the greatest happiness to the greatest number of people, and by happiness is normally meant pleasure and absence of pain. This is an extremely persuasive 'doctrine', and one suspects that a great many people are either conscious or unwitting Utilitarians. Certainly, it is the philosophical principle behind democratic systems where it is taken for granted that the majority decision is, *ipso facto*, correct. Utilitarians maintain that other ethical systems are normative in character, that is to say, they put the emphasis on obligatory behaviour and are concerned with the ways in which people ought to act. They insist that Utilitarianism is not like this. It is, they say, concerned not so much with how people ought to act as the ways they *do* act. They do seek – and have always sought – pleasure rather than pain, therefore Utilitarianism must be seen as an empirically substantiated system as it is rooted in actual experience.

The first difficulty with Utilitarianism is that its basic premise is based upon an unverifiable assumption. Although it is psychologically plausible that people seek their own happiness above all else, it cannot be demonstrated in practice. Furthermore, it is not exactly extravagant speculation to suggest that in many actual instances such as crisis situations, many people often put other people's welfare before their own. People are not always totally hedonistic. It must also be noted that Utilitarianism has a marked *quantitative* stress. Even where some Utilitarians have extended the criteria beyond 'happiness', and have included 'greatest truth', 'greatest justice' and so forth, they have still retained the stipulation that it is for the 'greatest number'. But in endeavouring to seek the greatest happiness for the greatest number, we are not told how this happiness should be *distributed* or what *kind* of happiness it should be. After all, happiness means different things to different people. And if we admit – as we surely must – the variability of pleasurable experiences, we have unwittingly introduced *quality* as well as quantity into the equation. There is nothing wrong with this, but it does not accord with Utilitarianism's original premise.

There are difficulties too in trying to apply Utilitarianism to various kinds of social policy. It is not always clear within what *limits* its basic dictum applies. Different societies have been quite happy to extend the franchise to the greatest number, but this did not always mean the majority, it often meant the greatest number within a relatively small, circumscribed, political or ethnic group. On the other hand, where the greatest number does mean the majority, it begs the question of what happens to minorities? Does Utilitarianism lead to hostility and persecution? In practice, Utilitarians have usually been well-intentioned and liberal people, but the Utilitarian *mentality* of serving the interests of the majority, can – and has – led to the ill-treatment of certain proscribed groups – Jews, gypsies, Armenians or whoever.

One particular source of confusion is caused by the failure to distinguish between Utilitarianism as a basis for law-*making* and its application to law-*keeping*. There is a great deal to be said for it as far as law-making is concerned. In fact, it already functions as such in many areas of social life. All kinds of legislation from criminal laws designed to protect the public to laws concerning property, have been based on Utilitarian ideas since long before the term Utilitarianism was coined. But, impressionistically, one might guess that both judges and police actually *apply* the law simply because it *is* the law. They are not primarily interested in how the law was made. Similarly, it is highly doubtful if members of the public pause before, say, breaking the speed limit, and tell themselves that they must think of the greatest happiness of the greatest number.

People generally either observe or break the law for quite other – often self-interested – reasons.

Perhaps the most telling objection to Utilitarianism is that it assumes that individuals can sit down and calmly and dispassionately weigh up all the pros and cons of a situation, and come to an intelligent decision. This assumption discounts the highly charged emotional situations in which many decisions have to be made, and it takes for granted that we can know all the relevant facts *in advance*, and then arrive at a balanced conclusion – something few of us can ever do. The British public, for example, could never know all there was to know about, say the Suez crisis, the Vietnam war, or the Falklands débâcle. Even more relevant is the inability of war-leaders to be able to *predict* what their actions will bring forth, as we shall see from the area-bombing campaign in World War II which was supposed to shorten the conflict – something that has never been proven.

From the foregoing discussion, it would appear that the subjectivist approach to making moral judgements, especially in its Emotivist form, has to be suspect. It does not allow for any kind of objectivity about moral values, but simply relies on an uncertain balance of subjectivities on every issue. One opinion is as good as another, therefore nothing can finally be condemned or applauded. This makes for an extreme relativism (to be explored in the next section) which is in no way consonant with the guilty/guiltless dichotomy that is all too evident in most cases of massacre. By contrast, the consensus approach seems to be much more plausible. The objectivity of moral values is established by the tacit or considered agreement of the society in question. Of course, different societies come to different conclusions on all sorts of issues. But consensus theory does present us with a much more satisfactory state of affairs than unqualified subjectivity, even if, on closer inspection, we have found that this too has its weaknesses which in some cases are really fundamental flaws. In its most popular form, Utilitarianism, it is certainly persuasive, but it can never really be conclusive.

Having said all this, it is difficult to see how one can avoid some application of Utilitarianism in military situations. It is on this basis that some feel that they can defend the notion of the 'just war'. A war to defend others. But is there any sense in which the 'just war' can be equated with the modern concept of 'total war' and all this connotes? Where the primary object is to defeat the enemy, and the immediate aim is to win the battle, the means must sometimes be more than a little doubtful. How are we to rate saturation bombing, the use of poisonous gas, sinking undefended vessels, etc? Surely only in terms of some hypothesised greater good? The realist knows that much modern weaponry is hardly selective, and that the innocent are going to suffer as well as the guilty, if, indeed, these terms have any meaning in a total war situation. The realist may argue with Admiral Lord Fisher that in war moderation is a kind of imbecility, and that the so-called rules of war lie outside the realm of ethics (Fotion and Elfstrom, 1986: 6–10). That, if anything, the rule is that there can be no rules; the enemy is not someone who should be given normal consideration – he may even be regarded as just one more species of vermin to be destroyed (Carlton, 1992).

Harsh as this general view is, can it ever countenance the exercise of gratuitous cruelty? In war, atrocities must always be regarded as a possibility, but must they ever be a necessity? Realists of various persuasions take the view that 'all's fair in love and war', but most of us assume that all humans, even those perceived as the enemy, have certain basic rights, and these include protection from wanton and senseless brutality. In recent times, various agreements, especially the Geneva Convention, have tried to outlaw, or, at least, limit the degree to which ill-treatment of others, particularly the defenceless, takes place. But throughout history there have always been violations of the most rudimentary codes of conduct. These can, in part, be explained in terms of the circumstances obtaining at the time. But this is not entirely convincing as our case studies will show. Perhaps we should think again about the nature of the human animal and his proclivity for violence – especially *irrational* violence. It is one of the persistent myths about humans that they alone of all the life forms kill their own kind. This is not true, but their savagery does outstrip that of others. They will kill *any* creature sometimes from necessity, and often impulsively; and they will also kill for pleasure, and with subtle and calculating ingenuity. In moral terms, humans represent the very best and the very worst of creation.

# CHAPTER TWO

# Massacre as a Military Norm: Mzilikazi and the Matabele

It is something of a truism to say that the horrors of war are directly related to the scale and level of development of society. The obvious implication here is that the worst wars are modern wars where techno-logical advancement has made large-scale carnage possible; the corollary being that the simpler and less developed the society is, the less war is a problem. The difficulty about this is that we cannot examine what actually took place for most of human history when small bands of hunters and gatherers roamed the savannahs and forests in search of game and occasionally came into conflict. But we can get some idea of their way of life from the decreasing numbers of tribal groups with 'Stone Age' economies that still exist. The techniques they used for killing game were extremely primitive but effective. More significantly, these were transferable skills which could be used not just for killing animals but also for killing their own kind. We have no grounds for believing that these early peoples were the amiable social creatures that some writers – on very flimsy evidence – have suggested (e.g. Leakey et al, 1969). They may well have had few inhibitions about killing one another, and it is a reasonable assumption that cannibalism was not that uncommon. The absence of bones on some of the prehistoric habitation sites hardly indicates that they were all confirmed vegetarians. What is significant for our present discussion is that near contemporary analogies indicate that in these societies warfare itself was not a developed art. One writer commenting on Australian aborigine society of the recent past says that warfare – if such it can be called – was a kin-group affair and was largely unorganised and had very few casualties. Unlike much modern warfare it was not usually about either possessions or territory. He adds that

> the Walbiri [did not have a] class of permanent or professional warriors; there was no hierarchy of military command; and groups rarely engaged in wars of conquest . . . [there was] little reason for all-out warfare between communities. Slavery was unknown; portable goods were few; and the territory seized in a battle was virtually an embarrassment to the victors, whose spiritual ties were [elsewhere]. (Meggett, 1960: 245.)

However, as soon as larger groupings of people developed things changed. With more to share in what there was, antagonisms arose and the gravity and magnitude of the killing increased accordingly. So that when we arrive at the stage of the centralised tribal society, we actually have a situation where killing is commonplace, indeed, where – in some cases – massacre became the norm.

Our concern here is with Zimbabwe, the territory roughly co-ter-minus with the area formerly known as Rhodesia, so named in honour of Cecil Rhodes who 'acquired' it for Britain late in the nineteenth century. During our medieval period, Zimbabwe had boasted a Bantu high culture (Great Zimbabwe) but this had become extinct by the middle of the fifteenth century. Not long before it became a British colony, its indigenous peoples were conquered by the Matabele (Ndebele) who were originally the Khumalo, a small clan of the all-powerful Zulu led by a usurper, Shaka, one of the most ruthless rulers in Black Africa.

By 1818, Shaka, formerly regarded as an upstart petty chief from a little-regarded clan, was the most powerful figure in Zululand. He had acquired his impis (regiments), revised their tactics, and popularised the use of the long-bladed stabbing spear which he had personally designed, instead of the more conventional throwing assegai. This new spear was used like a sword, and had a devastating effect in hand-to-hand fighting. The regiments were raised on an age-set basis, and Shaka insisted that all able-bodied men should serve with the military. Warriors could neither marry nor leave the army until Shaka had given them permission. Indeed, at the height of his reign, Shaka really had the power of life and death over his subjects. At an early stage he sorted out the 'greybeards', the older males, and had them executed because they were no longer fit for military service. Previously, the Zulu military policy had been one of subjugation rather than destruction, but Shaka changed all that and trained his warriors to kill without mercy.

The depradations of the Zulu in the nineteenth century have been well-documented (e.g. Morris, 1969; Ritter, 1958). Nothing has been seen like it in the Transvaal either before or since. Neighbouring tribes were attacked without provocation, kraals were burnt, herds confiscated, and families exterminated. The only exceptions were military-age males who were sometimes given the opportunity of augmenting Shaka's regiments. The 'crushing' of all those who resisted incorporation into the Zulu kingdom lasted for some years and, one way or another, probably accounted for some two million lives – far more than anything caused by the British and Dutch invaders. This came about largely because of the knock-on effect on weaker tribes. Zulu expansion generated migratory movements, so that tribes attacked each other just in order to survive.

We can get some idea of the kind of warfare in question from the occasion when a powerful northern tribe, the Ndwandwe, who had already suffered a terrible defeat at the hands of the Zulu, had the effrontery to play the Zulu at their own game. They invaded Zulu territory from the North under the leadership of their war chief, Soshangane, who later became famous as the conqueror of the tribes of Portuguese East Africa. The Ndwandwe were lured deep into Zululand without making direct contact with their opponents. The Zulu evacuated their most important kraals in what appeared to the invaders as an unceremonious and hasty retreat. The Ndwandwe grew tired of the pursuit and were running short of supplies so they abandoned the chase and gradually made their way back to their own lands. Then the Zulu regiments attacked. What followed was near annihilation, and we read of 'the waters [of the river Umhlatuze] red with blood and the banks . . . strewn with corpses' (Becker, 1979: 37). When the survivors eventually reached their own territory, they found that fleet-footed Zulu warriors had already arrived; their kraals had been destroyed and their families butchered or missing.

In the meantime, Mzilikazi, the leader of the Khumalo, a clan situated in the north of Zululand, who had been under threat from the Ndwandwe voluntarily allied himself with Shaka as a vassal chief and asked that his people become part of the Zulu nation. He was welcomed by the king, and he and his warriors played their part in Shaka's military campaigns. For a while all was sweetness and light, and the newcomer was treated almost like a son. Then Mzilikazi became greedy. He too was ambitious and began to entertain notions of grandeur, and after one important raid refused to send the spoils to Shaka. He grew in confidence, and began a series of raids for himself in which he displayed the same indifference to human life as Shaka. He had learned his trade well. But from now on he was theoretically a doomed man, so he moved his people north to what, for the Zulu, was largely unknown territory.

The Zulu were but one of the peoples that comprise what is generically termed the Nguni, and were linked to other tribal groups partly by custom and partly by similarity of language. When Mzilikazi and his warriors moved over the Drakensberg mountains to the north and west of Zululand into what might be termed the 'interior' of South Africa, they found themselves among people of a different language group, the Sotho. These people had many customs in common with the Nguni, not least of all in their methods of socialising young males for a military role in society. They too were trained so that they would be able to endure hunger, thirst, cold, heat, pain and even death without complaining, and taught that they would be invincible especially as their efforts would be supported by supernatural agencies. Their armies had a wider variety of weapons than the Zulu and included battle axes and bows and arrows, but they were not really a militaristic people and lived quite peaceably when compared with the constant fraticidal exchanges among the Nguni.

Mzilikazi successfully eluded Shaka's vengeful regiments, negotiated the mountains, and he and his warriors found their way to the high veldt of the Transvaal where they reconnoitred the territory and attacked Sotho villages one by one. At first, these attacks took place at night which caused tremendous confusion among the inhabitants. But as the Khumalo became emboldened they assaulted the villages during daylight, butchering everyone in sight except young men who were encouraged to join forces with the invaders, and young women who were taken as concubines for Mzilikazi's warriors. Herds and food were confiscated, and the older people who managed to flee were left to starve on the veldt.

The Khumalo waited for some concerted resistance, and when it came they showed their superiority in discipline and technique over their enemies. Sometimes petty Sotho chieftans would offer friendship and provisions in exchange for exemption from molestation, and more often than not these would be accepted after which the benefactors were murdered and their kraals destroyed. It was really a life of brigandage and slaughter for the Khumalo. Every village they encountered was laid waste, and by 1824 'the territory they held was covered with skeletons, and literally no human beings were left in it' (Theal, 1908: Vol. 1, p. 456). Mzilikazi then decided that he would cease this nomadic existence, and settle at what he called the Place of Rest. But this did not stop him from sending out his regiments on campaigns against Sotho tribes further afield. Those that resisted were treated unmercifully; one chief who had the temerity to organise his forces against the Khumalo was duly defeated and then impaled to satisfy Mzilikazi's sense of what was an appropriate punishment for such presumption. In some ways, this does not quite accord with the Zulu respect for bravery. Zulu chiefs often had those guilty of cowardice or failure clubbed to death, drowned, impaled or fed to the crocodiles – forms of death also reserved for witches and unsuccessful rainmakers. Mzilikazi was as unfeeling as Shaka in the administration of what passed for justice among his people. Executioners were always on hand to carry out death sentences, sometimes for relatively trivial offences. He liked to ponder exactly what particularly gruesome death would fit the occasion. Observers found that his subjects accepted their fate with apparent resignation, and thanked the despot for his consideration.

However, the Khumalo did not have everything their own way. Other groups of Nguni who fled from Shaka's regiments also invaded Sotho territory and were no kinder to the inhabitants than Mzilikazi. The situation was further exacerbated by the activities of one of the Sotho tribes known as the Wild Cat People led by a dead chief's widow named Mantatisi. Even before the Zulu incursions, her 'reign' had been punctuated by war and civil strife, but once the troubles had begun in earnest she and her warriors displayed a ruthlessness which matched that of the Zulu. The turmoil produced a succession of massacres and counter-massacres which left village people in a state of abject misery.

By 1825 Mzilikazi decided that he had had enough inactivity. Further-more, his people needed food supplies which were easier to take than they were to produce. His kraal was deliberately destroyed – criminals being left in the burning huts – and the Khumalo migrated to the lands of the Bakwera (the Crocodile People), one of the most prosperous of the Sotho tribes who were attacked without mercy. All resistance was brutally suppressed. The unwanted adults were led out in batches and clubbed to death. Some youths were taken as servants, but if they could not keep up with the regiments who travelled at a trot, they too were put to death. Babies were almost invariably left to starve or be devoured by wild animals (later, children were deliberately killed for fear that one day they might grow up to avenge their parents). By this time, the Khumalo and their allies had become known as the Matabele, the feared aggressors, a term that became virtually synonymous with death for the Sotho villagers.

Like so many aggressors, Mzilikazi found that he had developed a taste for military conquest. He organised the establishment of military kraals on much the same lines as Shaka had done in Zululand. These were effectively training depots where his troops could sharpen their skills preparatory to the next series of onslaughts on Mzilikazi's intended victims. To strengthen his forces, he recruited landless Sotho males, and he was also joined by people from disaffected Zulu clans who had fled from Shaka's tyranny which had now become virtually pathological (hundreds of his own people had been killed simply because they had failed to cry at his mother's death).

Fatefully for Mzilikazi his invasion of Sotholand coincided with the decision of some European colonists in the south to explore the South African interior which, at this time, was virtually unknown to them. Colonists had occupied parts of South Africa for about two hundred years, and by 1825 there were thriving settlements at Delagoa Bay estab-lished by the Portuguese, at Port Natal, an English trading station, and the Cape itself where there were Dutch, German, French and British inhabitants. Mzilikazi was still gathering subjects and expanding his terri-tories when he heard of the white men, and particularly of their weapons which belched a destructive fire. Likewise rumours reached the explorers of the Matabele and their chief who had devastated the Sotho tribes and who had consolidated his power in the Transvaal. Conflict was inevitable. The first clash came when some Matabele regiments moving south to catch up with retreating enemy warriors, encountered some Boers who were awaiting their arrival. The Boers were determined not to let them enter the Cape Colony, and their rifle fire sent the puzzled Matabele scurrying back home. It was merely a foretaste of what was to come.

For a while, the Matabele continued to prosper. They did suffer some reverses at the hands of the Zulu whose new king, Dingane, had conspired in the assassination of Shaka, his half-brother, in 1828. Dingane – no warrior himself – sent his regiments against the 'traitors' with some success. On the other hand, the Matabele did much better in their invasion of Bechuanaland where the inhabitants were treated to the same wanton savagery as the Sotho. But the real problem for the Matabele was the Europeans. In 1836, an understanding was reached with the authorities in the Cape Colony that the Matabele would only go to war if they were attacked. Temporarily the agreement held, but when Boer colonists provocatively trekked into Matabele-held territory, they were attacked by vastly superior Matabele regiments which they successfully repulsed. The natives with all their advantage of numbers had no answer to the rifle. Another treaty was made, this time with Mzilikazi personally who attended the meeting resplendent in leopard-skin tails, a headdress of parakeet feathers and a blue-bead necklace (Becker, 1979: 194). But again the 'contract' broke down and there was fighting and yet again the Matabele were worsted by the Boers. This time the Boers were determined to defeat the Matabele once and for all, and after some of the bloodiest battles in South African history, particularly at Magierskop (Maggot Hill), the native regiments were broken and fleeing warriors were hunted down without quarter.

The remnants of the divided Matabele retreated northwards over the Dwarsberg range to what was later to become Matabeleland (Southern Rhodesia). For a while it was not certain that Mzilikazi was still alive, and tentative plans were made by his indunas (chief advisers) and some of his sons to replace him as king. But when he eventually joined his fellow-tribesmen in 1840, he quickly brought the plotters to trial and all of them were promptly dispatched by his executioners.

The territory was occupied by a miscellany of militarily undistinguished tribes, mainly the Makalanga and the Mashona, and Mzilikazi decided that it was ripe for a Matabele takeover. He added an ex-Swazi queen to his harem of three hundred wives and formed a military alliance with her tribespeople who in language and customs were closely related to the Zulu. The army was reformed and military kraals were established, and within a short time the Matabele were ready for new campaigns of conquest.

Once again it was a story of wholesale butchery, although this time the Matabele exercised a little more prudence – for two main reasons. The first was demographic: certain villages were deliberately left unscathed because Mzilikazi wanted the population to increase in order to supply the needs of his armies. The second was superstitious: the Makalanga in particular had a reputation for the powers of their diviners, and Mzilikazi had a great respect for the supernatural. Generally, the Bantu recognised two main types of religious functionary apart from wizards, witches and sorcerers (who were held responsible for all manner of diabolical practices). These were the witchdoctor who diagnosed witchcraft, and the diviner who practised 'white' magic on behalf of the people and especially the chiefs. These factors apart, however, the onslaught of the Matabele on these relatively non-aggressive tribes was devastating. In time they were subjugated and their people forced to pay tribute to their overlords. The Mashona, in particular, put up a fierce resistance and some of their people escaped to the mountains from whence they carried on a sporadic guerrilla war with the Matabele. There were fearful atrocities on both sides, the worst victims being women who sometimes had their limbs amputated and were then left to bleed to death.

The Matabele still had a voracious appetite for conquest, but when they returned to the Zambesi, effectively their north-western borders, and encountered the powerful Makololo people, they were defeated by a combination of swamp-infested terrain and the cunning of their foes. Some two thousand warriors set out to conquer the Makololo and only a few returned including some of the leaders. Needless to say, despite their privations and loyalty in coming back at all, they were promptly executed for failure.

With the Boers and the Zulu to the south, and unknown enemies to the north, the Matabele decided to settle for what they had. Mzilikazi was no longer a young and vigorous warrior. He had grown corpulent and indolent, and had long been content to stay at home and enjoy the comforts of his seraglio while his regiments were either in training or far afield keeping his empire intact. But he was still very much the master of his own kingdom. He presided over tribal courts and made occasional visits to the various parts of his territory, yet the old expansionist urge had gone, and he was prepared to cultivate the role of tribal patriarch.

Mzilikazi controlled a heterogeneous society made up of various tribespeople who had either joined the Matabele voluntarily or who had been absorbed by conquest. Because of its composition it was also a highly stratified society. The Nguni nucleus were considered the elite, and the subjugated Sotho people became a kind of middle class. The conquered tribes of Southern Rhodesia comprised the lower stratum and were, in effect, little more than serfs. Significantly, these divisions were strictly enforced, and non-Nguni people were not allowed to marry or have sexual relations with the Nguni. Conqueror status was to be preserved.

By 1854 Mzilikazi was a sick man. The symptoms suggest that he was suffering from cirrhosis of the liver and possibly heart disease, neither of which can have been helped by the rich fatty foods that he ate, and the copious amounts of beer that he consumed. Observers were reasonably certain that his obstinate intemperance contributed significantly to his condition. Naturally, his chief advisors did not see it this way. They insisted that witchcraft was being exercised by his senior induna – perhaps it suited their political purposes to think so. After much agonised deliberation, he was reluctantly exiled – a very modest punishment by Matabele standards. Despite his growing frailty – perhaps even because of it – Mzilikazi was as tyrannical and volatile as ever, one moment welcoming Europeans to his kraal, and the next regretting that he had even met them and condemning to extermination one of his tribes that had dared to buy a mere five rifles from them. Despite the ravages to his health, the old king lived on until 1868, just long enough to see his life's work potentially ruined. The cause, quite simply, was gold. The coveted metal had been discovered in Mashona territory, and the inevitable happened – a feverish scramble for wealth ensued. When people in the Cape Colony heard of it they were dazzled by the prospect of adventure and almost instant riches. Mining syndicates were formed, and people poured in from overseas, but concessionary rights were given to very few companies. Mzilikazi's successor, Lobengula, a despot in much the same mould as his father, made the crucial mistake of selling the mineral rights of Matabeleland to settlers who eventually occupied much of the territory. Predictably, war broke out, but the Matabele impis were no match for British machine guns, and after a year of campaigning and the death of Lobengula, the Matabele capitulated in 1894.

Despite the modern tendencies towards what might be termed anthropological revisionism, where known despots have been 're-instated' as legitimate fathers of their people, it can hardly be denied that tribal leaders such as Shaka, Dingane and Mzilikazi were despots with few scruples and even less mercy. Of course, it is easy to say that we cannot apply modern western standards to these people, and that they were simply children of their place and time. But can we take refuge in this kind of cultural relativism? They recognised suffering and fear in themselves, so why not in others? Shaka, for instance, could not understand the idea of punishing someone by incarcerating them in prison. For him, death was preferable. Why then could not Shaka, Mzilikazi and others not feel some pity for *their* victims – especially the non-combatants? Moral sensitivity, as we understand it, seems to have been foreign to their make-up. They were not alone by any means, they were just the worst of a very bad bunch. It was the unpredictability and indifference that made them so frightening. They killed on a vast scale, sometimes quite systematically, sometimes capriciously, without any apparent feeling or remorse. They might spare someone on a sudden whim, but they were just as likely to kill for the novelty of it, as in, say, the case of Mutesa of the Buganda who might execute someone who sneezed in his presence or shoot someone just to try out a new gun. When confronted with this sort of behaviour it is difficult not to feel that values cannot simply be culturally specific, and that these often unimaginable cruelties must always be regarded as wrong. It isn't just a question of thinking that makes it so. Incidents of atrocity tend to confirm the suspicion that no matter how difficult they are to define, there are such things as objective values.

CHAPTER THREE

# Massacre by 'Consent':
# Mass killing as a sacrificial offering

In one sense, this chapter is something of a deviation from the main discussion. Here we are going to think about killings which are perpetrated for ostensibly religious reasons, in effect, sacrifice – albeit a particular form of sacrifice.

Sacrifice – including human sacrifice – can take several different forms and may be carried out for a number of different reasons. It may be *penitential* – offerings to express guilt and regret; *intercessory* – offerings on behalf of others; *placatory* – offerings to appease the anger of the gods; *invocatory* – offerings to implore the gods for bounty such as rain, sun, health etc; *expressions of gratitude* – for blessings received; or simply *piacular* – a means of communion with the gods. Some societies, such as the pre-Columbian Meso-American societies, the Maya, Toltecs and especially the Aztecs, practised ritual killing for all of these reasons (Carlton, 1990). Normally, the victims were prisoners of war, but sometimes they were willing subjects who were feted for a few months and then offered to the gods. The practice of sacrificing *un*willing victims, say, as a thank-offering after victory in battle, was not unknown in the ancient world, and was a feature, for example, of some Carthaginian campaigns, especially in Sicily (Finley, 1980). And the practice of offering human sacrifice in extreme circumstances such as enemy invasion, was certainly known among such people as the Myceneans (Taylour, 1983) and the Phoenicians (Harden, 1971) who did not normally resort to these expedients.

In this section of the discussion, however, we are going to look at the custom of ritual sacrifice for rulers, that is the practice of killing slaves and retainers (less commonly, wives and children) to accompany a 'great man' – king, chief, leader – into the next life; to serve him there, and meet his needs as they had done during their earthly existence. Not all these victims will have been naturally acquiescent, but in the broad sense, the evidence indicates that there was a voluntary aspect to their deaths; that it was, in effect, massacre by 'consent'.

Among non-literate peoples, the best known examples of this practice are to be found in the kingdoms of the west coast of Africa. Many of these states were well developed in constitutional and economic terms, and their institutions were such that many of them survived colonisation without any serious loss of national identity. Some of these peoples, especially the Ashanti of the Gold Coast (modern Ghana) were notably militaristic, and – if anything – became more so after the incursions of the Europeans who were particularly intent on looking for gold. In the sixteenth century, during the hey-day of Portuguese exploration, the Ashanti were divided into a number of small independent kingdoms. These coalesced in the eighteenth century after a series of ferocious wars, and the powerful Ashanti state remained substantially intact until its warriors were defeated by the British in 1874.

Traditionally, the king was regarded as a steward of the ancestors who owned the land. He enjoyed virtually despotic power, and exercised control through his military retainers and subordinate chiefs although, in practice, he was subject to election and continued approval by a Council of Elders. Theoretically, he could be impeached and divested of his authority, but once in office he had the power of life and death over his subjects. Indeed, death was the punishment for most crimes including not only serious crimes such as murder and suicide where the dead person's property was automatically forfeit, but also a range of sex crimes such as incest and intercourse with a menstruating woman, believed to be a source of supernatural danger. Among the most heinous crimes were witchcraft and sorcery, and 'cursing the king' which merited a far worse death than the customary decapitation. Both these types of crime involved the invocation of supernatural powers against the king – something that deserved the direst penalties. It was regarded as an offence against the ancestors if the king failed to apply the rules vigorously, although it is believed that commutations were common if a suitable fine or ransom was forthcoming. Indirectly, crime was a great source of revenue for the state (Service, 1978: 361).

Death among the Ashanti was the occasion for a series of rituals including sacrifices and ceremonial head shaving, to placate the spirit of the deceased, and festivities to celebrate his departure to the next life. The funeral rites for kings, however, were much more elaborate affairs, and involved the whole kingdom. In this case, human sacrifice was customary, and a number of the king's wives were put to death in the aristocratic manner, by strangulation, and other members of his staff were also killed to accompany him to his new realm. The victims were supposed to welcome this opportunity to be with their master, and sometimes they apparently volunteered for the privilege. In addition to this, throughout the kingdom, slaves and criminals, and even 'waylaid strangers' were sacrificed while the king lay in state (Service, 1978: 365).

As far as complex pre-industrial societies are concerned, there is some evidence – which is, admittedly, rather sketchy – that this kind of human sacrifice was in vogue in ancient Egypt where it appears that slaves/

retainers were killed and buried with their king together with various accoutrements that he would presumably require in the next life. Hollywood films notwithstanding, the indications are that this was only done in very early times, in the pre-Pyramid Age, in what is technically known as the Archaic period, i.e. during the first two dynasties (c. 3100–2700 BC). Even in these very remote times, before the practice of mummification, considerable care was taken at the burials of the nobility. The body was placed in a sarcophagus, and on its east side dishes and jars were laid out containing food and drink for immediate use together with further reserve supplies for the future. Also in the burial chamber were chests containing clothes, jewellery, even games, as well as costly ivory-inlaid furniture including chairs and beds.

These first-dynasty tombs were often very elaborate affairs, some measuring as much as 22 × 15 metres consisting of a sub-structure, the burial tomb itself, together with an impressive super-structure which gave the effect of a rather austere and well-constructed temple. Both sub-structure and super-structure contained storage rooms and apartments, although these were not as richly-furnished as the burial chamber itself. Surrounding one tomb, that of the King Udimu, were found 136 'slave burials' of both men and women (Emery, 1972: 80). Whether these people went willingly to their deaths, we do not know. But given what we do know of the later religious ideology of ancient Egypt, it is a reasonable assumption that they did. They probably believed that to be buried with the king would ensure their own eternal well-being, albeit in a menial capacity. Archaeological proof for this practice comes only from the funerary monuments of the kings and nobility, but it is supposed that it may also have been common in the lower echelons of Egyptian society.

It is now authoritatively established that similar practices took place in early China. Before the 1920s it was commonly believed that there was no developed civilisation in China before the Chou dynasty dating from the beginning of the first millenium BC. Even the search for an earlier culture had once been thought of as the pious wishful thinking of nostalgic academics. It is now accepted, however, that the Chou dynasty was preceded by about five hundred years by the still little-known Shang dynasty. In 1928, the Chinese National Research Institute began excavations in north-eastern China, and by 1935, some three hundred graves had been discovered, ten of which were large, elaborate constructions and were obviously royal tombs. Even by 1950, almost all that was known of the Shang – or Yin, as the Chou called them – was derived from their capital at Anyang where they had developed techniques of bronze-making that produced vessels of size and quality that were probably without equal in the ancient world. Since 1952 a hundred or so further sites have been discovered, including Chengchow where there are remains of a city a mile square enclosed by massive walls sixty feet thick at the base, together with potteries, foundries, and what are thought to have been sacrificial halls. There were also more large graves that were richly furnished with ritual vessels of bronze, fine pottery, jade and ivory (Sullivan, 1973: 25). It is clear from these and the scanty remains of the dwellings themselves that the nobility lived in some luxury compared with the peasants who lived in squalor in caves and small huts.

The evidence of the inscriptions, especially on the oracle bones, suggests that Shang social organisation may have been a form of feudalism in which nobles rendered military service in exchange for lands, but there is some uncertainty about this. The Shang seem to have been strongly patriarchal and aggressively militaristic, and powerful enough to command allegiance – and presumably tribute – from other smaller states. The king was an absolute monarch who governed by decree. He claimed descent from the great founding ancestor of the people, Shang-Ti, who was the supreme Shang deity and ruler of the natural world. As a Son of Heaven, he also acted as chief priest and officiated at the most important ceremonies. This combination of sacred and secular functions – if indeed the two can sensibly be separated in this type of society – gave the kings considerable power which they sometimes used in arbitrary and repressive ways. One ruler is said to have neglected his duties for 'perverted pleasures' – perhaps more eccentric than perverted – which included constructing a wine lake to which hundreds of subjects were summoned to drink at the sound of a drum (Yap and Cotterell, 1975: 24).

We know something of the religious system of the Shang from the oracle bones which were used for purposes of divination, though it has to be admitted that only about half of the three thousand or so inscribed and painted characters have so far been deciphered. These were the 'instruments' whereby the king was enabled to discern the will of Heaven in relation to such things as war, agriculture, the weather, and special journeys that he had to undertake. They were especially important in determining the exact nature of the elaborate sacrificial rituals that had to be performed in order to ensure the goodwill and esteem of the ancestors. Some of the tombs were quite spectacular in size and adornment; one had a burial pit with two passages leading from it each about fifty yards long. The mass immolation of victims was common. In one tomb, for example, the king was not only accompanied by his sacrificed pets, there were also in the ramps and main chamber the skeletal remains of twenty-two men and twenty-four women. Some of the skeletons showed no sign of violence, and one presumes that these people, servants and perhaps relatives, may have gone to their deaths on a voluntary basis. More ominously, however, on the outside of the main tomb were pits

containing fifty additional skulls of decapitated victims who may have
been slaves, prisoners of war or even criminals. The Shang rulers presumably divorced themselves from the lower orders of society whose peasant
religion involved sorcerers and magicians to ward off the machinations
of malignant spirits. Consequently, they thought it more efficacious to
have a hierarchy of sacrificial victims. High earthly status was regarded
as more pleasing to the gods; so there were fewer victims in this category;
low status, on the other hand, called for an increase in the number of
victims required. Lesser mortals were obviously of little account. It was
their privilege to accompany an already quasi-divine being to his eternal
rest.

The classic example in early society of massacre by consent is to be
found in ancient Sumeria. This was well-documented in the 1920s by the
late Sir Leonard Woolley after his much-publicised excavations at the city
once known as Ur of the Chaldees in modern Iraq. Still called Mesopotamia ('the land between the rivers'), Iraq has given birth to many civilisations, but none more intriguing than the earliest, that of the Sumerians.
These people may have been indigenous to the area, although it is
strongly suspected that they came from elsewhere – but where, nobody
is quite sure. Even their language – about which quite a lot is now known
– seems to be unrelated to any other known language, living or dead.
The 'advent' of Sumeria, a little before the end of the fourth millenium,
appears quite suddenly on the scene of history – almost like a cultural
'breakthrough' (Covensky, 1966). With it came the flowering of those
features which are commonly associated with a developed civilisation,
written language, organised religion and monumental architecture.

The Sumerians were a major power in Mesopotamia for over a thousand years, and during this period their achievements were quite exceptional. They established an agrarian society based upon a kind of money
economy and a complex division of labour. This included a merchant
class, some of whose members traded as far afield as Egypt and the
primary civilisation of the Indus Valley. They created the form of political
organisation that we know as the city-state, which in very early days
may have operated as autonomous democratic units, but which in historical times were almost invariably controlled by kings. The common hypo-
thesis is that the democracies came to need war-leaders in the on-going
strife between states, and that this practice led, predictably, to the development of monarchies. Power was centred on the temple and the palace,
and each state appears to have been organised on theocratic principles
involving highly structured religious ideas and practices. Some writers
(e.g. Whitehouse, 1977) take the view that a gradual rivalry grew up
between the Temple and the Palace, but there seems to be no clear
evidence for this. Both owned vast estates and workshops, and both

appear to have acted as the main collection and distribution centres, although the Palace seems to have been specifically concerned with tax revenues and especially the recruitment and training of military personnel. In general, however, there seems to have been a complementarity of function between the religious and royal orders.

With the consolidation of the monarchy, a gradual rigidification of the stratification system had taken place, and, as in so many early societies, this gradually crystallised into the traditional pattern of nobility, commoners, and slaves – usually either debtor-slaves or prisoners of war. This, in turn, facilitated occupational divisions which included 'professional' people, doctors, teachers, architects, and the like, besides the mass of common peasantry. Indeed, for such an early society, the Sumerians were an extremely sophisticated people. Unlike their Egyptian contemporaries, they formulated intricate legal codes upon which much later legislation was based. Indeed, their 'legacies' are quite considerable. They developed the sexagesimal system which we still use in the calculation of time and in navigation. In chemistry they identified some hundreds of drugs, and experimented with the process of filtration; in medicine, they were already trying out a number of rudimentary surgical techniques, including trepanning. In architecture, they were not as advanced as the Egyptians who, like themselves, were desperately short of wood but had large reserves of stone. Instead, they cultivated the art of building in brick from which they constructed the incredible ziggurats or flat-topped pyramids that were used for religious ceremonies. They may also have been used for astronomical purposes. This was a major preoccupation of the priests who had computed both the length of the year and the dates of eclipses – achievements which were vital for ritual reasons and to enhance their own prestige.

The Ziggurat at Ur, still one of the best preserved in Iraq, was really a temple tower originally built by the founder of the Third Dynasty of Ur, Ur-Nammu, (c. 2100 BC) in honour of the moon-deity, Nanna. Its base measured 62.5 × 43 metres and it consisted of three stages or galleries rising some 26 metres above the plain. The whole edifice was surmounted by an enclosure or cult-centre which was used at the New Year festival by the king and his consort, possibly a priestess, for a Sacred Marriage. This was really an act of ritual intercourse which – as a symbol of fecundity – was thought to ensure the well-being of the land and its people.

Similar examples of the monumental temple architecture can be found throughout Iraq, all testifying to the importance of religion in the life of the Sumerians. Unlike Egypt, where the pharaoh *was* god, in Sumeria the king was merely the steward of the tutelary deity. Legend had it that all the people – though some more than others – were created as serfs of the gods. They were 'fashioned of clay', and the purpose of their existence, as the later Babylonian god, Marduk, is supposed to have put it, is to be 'burdened with the toil of the gods that they might freely breathe' (Cottrell, 1966: 136). This kind of elevated anthropomorphism was exemplified by the forms of the rituals that were carried out, including the reverential washing, dressing and feeding of the god's image every day, and the meticulous recital of the daily offices. The apparent inconsistencies of all this did not seem to present the priests with any insuperable theological problems; all that mattered was that the gods received their requisite nourishment.

There was a vast pantheon of Sumerian gods, from the creator god Enki and his consort down to all manner of lesser deities who were thought to be responsible for various aspects of life. In fact, there was an assembly – analogous to a royal assembly – of seven gods who 'decreed the fates' and fifty 'great gods', some of whom were regarded as creative and others as non-creative deities. The act of creation held no philosophical terrors for the Sumerian theologian; creation was achieved simply by divine will. The cosmos was as the gods ordained. Again by analogy, as mortals tended and supervised human society, so there must be immortals who governed and controlled that much greater entity, the cosmos. Therefore, they must be obeyed. They were, however, regarded with some ambivalence; the attitudes towards the gods reflected only too well the ambiguities of human experience. For example, Enlil, the god of the air, was seen as a generally beneficent deity who – regrettably – sometimes had to carry out the destructive decrees of other gods (Kramer, 1963: 119). Even in these early days of philosophical speculation, there were obviously attempts to solve the problem of theodicy.

Humans were completely enslaved by the immortals, and had little or no control over their individual destinies. Theirs was a state of helpless dependence. The gods could be capricious, but even they had to obey the rules of the divine order which had been established by the god Enki so that the universe could operate in the proper way. The gods were said to prefer good to evil, although human devotion and obedience do not appear to have counted for a great deal because – according to Sumerian cosmology – all a human had to look forward to was a bleak 'eternity contemplating his wretchedness' (Lansing, 1974: 94–5). He could appeal to his personal god or the city god to intercede on his behalf, but ultimately his fate was determined by rules that he could never change.

Sumerians spent a considerable amount of their time trying to assuage the possible ill will of the gods. Several days were set aside each month for religious rituals and public festivities. These were accompanied by the prescribed sacrifices which were carried out with the most exacting precision, all of which added considerable mystery – not to say, mystification – to the proceedings (Frankfort, 1950). Of all the ceremonies, none was more important than those concerned with death, especially the death of a royal personage, and it was the discovery of some previously untouched graves at Ur that excited so much archaeological interest in the 1920s.

Sir Leonard Woolley first began digging at the mound at al-Ubaid where he found the vestigial ruins of a temple dating to the First Dynasty of Ur, *c.* 2700 BC. He then moved his operations to the south, to the mound of the ancient city of Ur at the site of an early cemetery. In the upper layer he found some eighteen hundred relatively simple graves which had indications of tunnels that had obviously been dug by grave robbers. The tunnels suggested the possibility of treasures beneath the surface; the commoners' graves had served to disguise the wealth underneath. The first real prize came when Woolley unearthed the tomb of someone – who was almost certainly a member of the nobility – who had died about 2500. He had been buried with considerable ceremony; the riches in his grave included stone, copper, silver and gold bowls, an embossed shield, gold-mounted daggers, and a gold alloy helmet of superb workmanship. But there was more to come. Digging further, the excavators came across a sloping trench and a series of limestone blocks which, as it transpired, were part of the lining of what must be a royal tomb. In the trench, they encountered five skeletons adorned with intricately worked gold and lapis lazuli headdresses and necklaces together with the remains of what turned out to be a harp. More and more treasure came to light, together with another six skeletons – obviously soldiers – whose helmets and spears were still reasonably intact. Nearby, there were the skeletal remains of nine women whose valuable jewellery and almost decayed dresses lay among the bones. Woolley described it as a 'death pit' which was literally lined with bodies, and the presence of bowls and drinking cups suggested that they had all shared a ceremonial meal before their communal death (Woolley, 1954).

Adjoining this tomb was another which, quite inexplicably, had been unmolested. It was that of a woman, Shub'ad, who may have been a high priestess, but is generally thought to have been a queen. This burial may date from before the First Dynasty of Ur, perhaps as long ago as the beginning of the 3rd millenium. But there is some debate about this and she may, in fact, have been the wife of the man (king?) in the first tomb, if so, it is difficult to know why this was partly plundered – perhaps by the original workmen – and that of the 'queen's' was not. Whatever, the scene was just as macabre. The tomb was replete with ornaments of gold and semi-precious stones, lapis lazuli, agate, carnelian and chalcadony fashioned into various designs with considerable skill. Again there were the remains of other bodies, presumably the personal attendants of the 'queen' who had accompanied her in death. Indeed, it may be that the 'queen's' death was also 'voluntary'; she had a small chalice by her which may have once contained poison or a narcotic of some kind. Woolley took the view that all the deaths were part of an involved and ghastly ritual in honour of a dead king. The queen, attendants, soldiers and musicians all followed their master to the grave in keeping with customary expectation. The actual ritual must be left to speculation. Possibly they were killed at the graveside, or perhaps – more likely – they were drugged into insensibility and then killed – possibly by the military who were best suited to carry out the grisly task. On the other hand, it has been conjectured that they may have entered the pit singing to the accompaniment of the harp, and voluntarily taken poison and then simply been walled up.

This was not the only death pit to be uncovered. At one, Woolley found the remains of six men and sixty-four women all lining the ramp to the tomb, all waiting to share the future with those they had once served. Their actions must have been in keeping with obligatory ritual imperatives, but just what pressures were brought to bear on these poor creatures to obey them we shall never know. What is clear is that the nobility required their personal attendance for the nobility had their duties too – the gods could not be neglected.

# CHAPTER FOUR

# The Greek Experience I:
# Massacre as a military postscript

It has often been observed that *inter-poleis* (inter-state) warfare was a fratricidal pastime of the Greeks. And if they were not fighting between themselves, or had no dominant power to contend with, such as the Persians, they were often fighting among themselves, that is in *intra-state* conflict (*stasis*). Like so many generalisations, this is somewhat exaggerated – but not *that* exaggerated. When spring came and the better weather made travel possible, especially over the mountainous terrain, the Greek campaigning season began. If genuine reasons for invading another's territory were not to hand, some excuse could always be found, sometimes dating from the remote past – almost anything to justify a military expedition. For example, in the mid-fifth century BC a protracted 'sacred war' began which had a knock-on effect in a number of states. For all its religious associations, it looked suspiciously like a conflict over who was to exercise power in central Greece. States switched allegiances, populations were displaced, revolts were generated, not to mention the casualties and privations caused by the battles themselves. And this was neither the first nor the last of the sacred wars in Greece (Ehrenberg, 1968: 221).

A study of the Aegean world during the Classical Period is interesting for this very reason. We can see it as a microcosm of the way the world is: a kaleidoscope of questionable yet interlocking events. They are all here – inter-state rivalries, the motivations and justifications for highly dubious policies and practices. In so many ways there has probably never been a culture as fascinating as that of the Greeks, not because they are our exemplars, not because they supplied our political prototypes, but because they were so full of contradictions and ambiguities. They speculated about and, in many cases, experimented with variants of just about every political form there is – and still could not get it right. In particular they were preoccupied by the perennial problems of oligarchy versus democracy, of aristocracy versus the laity, of the rich versus the poor – in short, the problem of us and them.

There were at least two hundred theoretically autonomous city-states – we are not sure on this point. What we do know is that although they existed independently, many were linked into coalitions and leagues, and, at various times, petty empires of one kind or another. By an unfortunate circumstance of history, our knowledge of almost all of these states is very fragmentary. Most of what we do know is about Athens and, to some extent, Sparta and this largely because of the invaluable contemporary accounts of Thucydides and Xenophon.

Greek states often had disparate and conflicting interests when they were neighbours. A case in point would be the rivalry between Athens, the chief city-state in the 'county' of Attica, and the vigorous, maritime offshore island state of Aegina – an issue which Athens settled by force in 457 BC. The Athenians tore down the walls of Aegina and compelled the state to become one of their dependencies; later, during the Peloponnesian War, the Aeginetans were so distrusted that men, women and children were expelled from the island, and it was settled by migrant Athenians.

Soon after this, however, the tide began to turn against the Athenians. Their influence in Boiotia – the area north of Attica which was largely dominated by the city of Thebes – was considerably reduced when oligarchic (anti-Athenian) factions took over some cities in 447, though the Athenians captured the city of Chaironia and sold the men of the city into slavery. Athenian democracy had its limits.

The atrocities we are going to look at all took place during the Peloponnesian War between Athens, a radical democracy, and Sparta, effectively an oligarchy, but also notionally a monarchy with democratic elements – certainly as far as the elite were concerned. However, when it came to repression and cruelty there was little to choose between them.

The Peloponnesian War is usually dated from 431 to 404. Actually, it was not *one* war, but a series of engagements punctuated by uneasy truces which extended, on-and-off, for rather longer than this. It was immediately precipitated by a dispute over trading rights between Athens and the city-state of Megara, and a dangerous political situation that was brewing in the island state of Kerkyra (Corcyra/Corfu). But the underlying problem was the enmity between the two most powerful Greek states, Athens and Sparta. They had cooperated – albeit a little uneasily – during the wars with Persia (490–479); after that they had quarrelled spasmodically throughout much of the second half of the fifth century. They agreed on a Thirty Years Peace in 445, but it didn't – perhaps couldn't – last. Both were spoiling for a trial of strength, and eventually the Peloponnesian League, comprising Sparta and her allies including Corinth and Thebes, declared war on Athens and her allies (the Delian League) on the grounds that Athens had imperialistic ambitions and was threatening the independence of other Greek states.

The Spartans were supreme on land, so in order to avoid any direct clash with the Spartan army, the Athenian war leader, Perikles, ordered everyone that could to seek protection within Athens' city walls. Very early in the war the Spartans invaded and despoiled the countryside, but Athens – with considerable difficulty – was able to house and feed her swollen population by bringing in supplies by sea. It was a stand-off situation. Athens probably had the most powerful navy in the Mediterranean world, and the Spartans had the most formidable army in Greece. Each hit the other *in*directly by attacking vulnerable allied states, and this sometimes involved a little anticipatory subversion. In fact, the first phase of the war was actually precipitated by the allies rather than the main protagonists themselves. It is here that the story of atrocity and counter-atrocity really begins.

Thebes wanted complete control of Boiotia which included the nearby city-state of Plataea which had longstanding links with Athens and refused to join the Boiotian League. Plataea was determined to withstand the pressure but the authorities there had not reckoned on the enemy within. A group of Theban sympathisers entered into covert negotiations with Thebes, presumably in the hope of eventually taking up key positions in the intended Plataean oligarchy. Consequently, they planned a *coup*, and arranged for a force of 300 Thebans to be admitted secretly into the city one night in the spring of 431. The traitors urged the Thebans to slaughter their political enemies – not an unknown expedient in classical society – but the Thebans, confident of a positive response, preferred to issue a proclamation to the Plataeans urging them to join the League. The Plataeans were aroused, and in the general confusion of the situation the citizens accepted what they saw as a *fait accompli*. Later, when they saw how small the Theban force was they organised an *ad hoc* militia and killed or captured the Theban troops. But within hours another, more formidable, Theban force arrived, and on discovering what had happened, rounded up the Plataeans who were out working in the fields so that they could use them as hostages in exchange for the captured Thebans in the city. Negotiations began but the Plataean response to the Theban overtures was to demand the immediate evacuation of the territory. Furthermore, they threatened that if the Thebans harmed anybody or anything, they would kill their prisoners. The Thebans, sufficiently intimidated, went away, and the Plataeans brought all their people and stock within the city walls. In the meantime, the Athenians, who had been informed of events, sent a messenger to tell the Plataeans not to kill the prisoners without their express instructions, but he arrived too late. The Plataeans had already broken their word and butchered the remaining 180 captives.

Later in the war, Plataea, which by this time had sent many of its women and children to Athens for safety, was besieged by the Spartans for two years. When the siege had begun in 429, the Athenians had encouraged the remaining inhabitants to resist but actually sent no effective help. The Plataeans were finally compelled to capitulate, and the inhabitants – 225 in all – were executed by their captors.

A cynical view of this relatively minor, yet in some ways important series of incidents, was that the Thebans actually engineered these events because they no longer wanted the already precarious peace with Athens to last but wanted to achieve their own ends by an indirect route. Whoever was really responsible, it succeeded in fomenting a conflict which eventually drew in most of the Greek states on one side or another, and resulted in the most appalling atrocities and lasting ill-feeling on both sides. Each blamed the other for stepping up the level of brutality. The Spartans were particularly ruthless with enemy naval personnel, especially if they were captured during 'commando'-type raids on their territory. Then the Athenians retaliated by threatening to use the same methods as the Spartans who 'butchered as enemies all whom they took on the sea, whether allies of Athens or neutrals' (Thucydides 2, 67). Needless to say, it wasn't long before such practices were extended to land-based encounters as well. What had begun in anger very soon became institutionalised as policy.

The complex alliances of the two predominant powers again led to one of the most hideous occurrences which was only incidentally connected with the war. The island of Kerkyra off the western coast of Greece had been an ally of Athens since 433. Originally, the city-state had been a colony of Corinth, for many years an economic rival of Athens, which was now an ally of Sparta. The Corinth–Kerkyra mother–daughter relationship had long since turned sour, and prior to the formal opening of hostilities between Athens and Sparta in 431, a dispute had arisen over a Kerkyrian colony, Epidamnus, on the Illyrian coast – in effect, a 'grand-daughter' of Corinth – which had been established late in the seventh century. This small city-state, like so many in Greece, was plagued by *stasis* – that perennial problem of antagonisms between the *aristoi* (the 'best people') and the *demos*, the proletariat. In 435, the many had ousted the few who then fled inland and sought refuge and assistance from the less cultured *indigenes* of the interior. Together they organised predatory raids on the city and its citizens. In desperation, the citizens turned to their mother city, Kerkyra, for help but Kerkyra was unresponsive; she had enough trouble of her own and obviously did not want to get embroiled in Epidamnus' domestic squabbles. So Epidamnus resorted to 'grandmother' Corinth – by now a naval rival – whose leaders had become thoroughly disgruntled with what they saw as her colony Kerkyra's independence and arrogance. Corinth sent some ships but Kerkyra resented this interference in *her* colony's affairs. Kerkyra came off better in a minor engagement, but knew that it was only a matter of time before the Corinthians returned with a much stronger force. So it was *they* who now needed help and in this way the distant island state became a member of the Athenian alliance.

Both the Corinthians and the Kerkyrians sent envoys to Athens to explain their respective cases. The Athenians were more sympathetic to Kerkyra, not only because of their traditional rivalry with Corinth but also because they suspected Corinth's aggressive intentions. This resulted in another minor, inconclusive naval engagement which, perhaps intentionally, successfully breached the Thirty Years' Peace. Perhaps it was an opening gambit, a preliminary move by Corinth in what was probably a long-term plan for involving Athens in a war with Sparta.

Some years later in 427, when general hostilities were well underway between Athens and Sparta, there was a hideous sequel to these events. In the earlier skirmishes that had taken place, Corinth had taken a number of Kerkyrian prisoners which she now shrewdly decided to return to their home state in the hope that they would persuade other Kerkyrians to go over to a Corinthian alliance. This led to trouble with the pro-Athenian faction in Kerkyra and further exacerbated the already volatile class relations in the city. Kerkyra had been on the oligarchic side in the earlier Epidamnus affair while Corinth had uncharacteristically favoured the democrats. Now the democrats were in control of the city – perhaps because of Athenian influence. There were accusations and counter-accusations involving the Athenian *proxenos* (a kind of ambassadorial representative from Athens). The democrats had imposed confiscatory fines on some of the wealthier citizens on what sounds suspiciously like trumped-up charges of religious violation. This resulted in an attack by the oligarchic faction on the democratic members of the Boule, the city's administrative council whilst they were actually in session. The *proxenos* was murdered, together with sixty of his followers, whereupon full-scale civil war broke out in the city. None of this was exactly helped by the provocative arrival of both Athenian and Peloponnesian ships; obviously both sides hoped to take what profit they could from the situation.

What happened next is given in some detail by Thucydides (Chs. 3 and 4). The fortunes of the rival forces fluctuated. It is difficult to know now just who was using who. Ostensibly, we are dealing with what we might loosely call a class war – oligarchic supporters in conflict with those who wanted to install a democratic government – though, in fact, it was a good old fashioned power struggle. Neither faction was opposed to escalating the conflict by enlisting the help of the 'great powers', the Athenians and the Peloponnesians, to resolve the struggle in their favour. On the other hand, these powers, too, did not hesitate to take advantage of the situation to further their respective political interests. This did not have to include much in the way of direct involvement. In fact, they were actually a little wary of each other, but their very presence constituted a kind of pressure to the immediate adversaries.

There was obviously a virulent hatred between the few and the many. The poor loathed the rich, and the rich despised the masses – an all too common situation in the Greek world. But not in every state did the outcome compare with that of Kerkyra. If it showed anything at all, it was that, regardless of wealth or poverty and regardless of political allegiance, both sides could be as murderous as each other. A fact which should really surprise no one.

The oligarchic faction established themselves on some high ground and made raids with the help of some mercenary troops. They caused much devastation and brought about a great shortage of food and supplies – something which hardly endeared them to the rank and file. They were coming out better in a few small engagements, but overall their position had gradually become virtually untenable, and eventually they agreed to surrender themselves to the people and trust their futures to the judgement of the Athenian assembly. They were then kept in custody with the apparent intention of sending them back to Athens at the earliest opportunity, the understanding being that if any one of them tried to escape it would nullify the treaty for them all.

What followed was worthy of a modern espionage novel for its cynical duplicity. The leaders of the democratic faction, anxious that the Athenian assembly might take a lenient view of the captives and not put them to death, devised a plan whereby the prisoners – through the persuasion of a third party – were encouraged to escape. This plan was then divulged to the Athenian generals in charge. The prisoners were re-apprehended, handed over to the Kerkyrians and the agreement for an Athenian trial became null and void. The Kerkyrians imprisoned them in a large building, and they were then brought out, bound together in batches of twenty, and made to pass between lines of *hoplites* (heavily armed infantry) and beaten and stabbed. After about sixty had been killed in this way, word got back to the other prisoners as to what was happening. They then barricaded themselves in the building and refused to come out. The Kerkyrians climbed on the building, demolished part of the roof and began an assault on the people below. Thucydides – a contemporary – describes the scene graphically: '[those] below protected themselves as well as they could, though in fact most of them now began to take their own lives by driving into their throats the arrows that were shot at them or by hanging themselves with cords taken from some beds that happened to be there or with strips made out of their own clothing. Night fell on the scene and they were still doing themselves to death by all manner of means, and still being killed by arrows from those on the roof. When it was day the Kerkyrians put them on wagons and took them outside

the city. The women who had been captured ... were sold as slaves'
(Thucydides 4, 46–8).

To all intents and purposes, this was a mindless massacre that took
place as part of a popular rising. Thucydides describes it – though not
with approval – as the culmination of a 'revolutionary struggle', but, in
fact, it may well have been a cynically engineered plot on the part of the
Athenian generals who were on their way to Sicily and just did not want
to be bothered taking prisoners. As for the Peloponnesians, they had left
long before. As in the case of Plataea, the defeated found that it didn't
always pay to trust their friends.

This was only one very nasty incident among many. As the war
continued, massacres and depopulation almost became the order of the
day. For instance, in the campaigns in Thrace, Kleon, a prominent political figure in Athens – of whom we shall hear more later – who was now
acting as a *strategos* (general) led a force to the small city of Torone
which had gone over to the Spartans and which he had heard was too
weak to resist a strong attack. The town was easily taken by the Athenians
and the people, together with a small Spartan garrison, were variously
killed or sold into slavery. A year or so later, the Athenians did much
the same at another city that had revolted. As Thucydides dispassionately
reports it, '... this summer the Athenians reduced Skione. They put to
death the men of military age, made slaves of the women and children,
and gave the land to the Plataeans to live in' (Thucydides 5, 32). As we
shall see (Chapter 5), if you were an ally – an Athenian euphemism for
subject – especially a small and rather weak ally, it did not pay to try to
opt out of your treaty obligations, particularly military and economic
support.

As we have seen from the case of Plataea, the faults were by no
means always on the Athenian side. In this long drawn-out conflict the
advantage went first to one and then the other. Eventually, the misfor-
tunes and misjudgements of the Athenians allowed the Spartans to gain
the upper hand. The issue was finally decided at sea. The Athenians had
predominated in naval warfare, and many of her allies, being island states,
had also been primarily maritime people. The Peloponnesians on the
other hand, had not – except for Corinth – been seafaring specialists, but
had generally made good their deficiencies. Before the ultimate critical
encounter, the Athenians had actually won a great naval battle at Arginusae near the island of Lesbos (406) in which, with a much superior force,
they had sunk or captured 70 Peloponnesian ships for the loss of only
25 of their own. But this victory was also attended by a double tragedy
for the Athenians. Their numbers had become so depleted that their
ships had been manned by almost any able-bodied men they could
muster – even metics (*metoikoi* were resident aliens) and slaves were

recruited. In the battle they lost something in excess of 4,000 men who were shipwrecked and drowned – men that they could ill-afford in these desperate times. The generals in charge were accused of abandoning these men to their fate though, presumably, it had been done to safeguard the rest of the force. Two of the generals evaded recall to Athens, but the eight who returned were put on trial by the assembly. It was apparently something of a farce, and by somewhat doubtful legal procedures they were condemned and executed (Xenophon, *Hellenica*, 1, 7, 1–35). Socrates, who was chairman of the Council that day, tried in vain to help them.

This naval victory had lifted spirits in Athens, but soon afterwards fortunes were reversed when Lysander – one of the most ruthless and able Spartan commanders – was re-appointed to take charge of the Peloponnesian fleet. He assembled a large force off the coast near Ephesus (Asia Minor) and threatened Athenian grain supplies from the Black Sea area. The Athenians sent their fleet to counter these moves; and in order to deter any of their allies or former allies from joining forces with Lysander, who was being surreptitiously financed by Persia in the hope that the Greeks would tear themselves apart, their assembly decreed that captured enemy seamen should have their right hands amputated. Lysander had based himself at Lampsacus (in the area of modern Gallipoli), and the Athenians took up an adjacent position at Aigospotami, but were unable to lure the Peloponnesians into battle. They were actually in a very vulnerable position. After five days of stalemate the Athenians became complacent and their discipline slack, and the Peloponnesians caught them off-guard and won a complete victory.

Only 20 out of possibly 180 ships escaped, and these were under the command of one of their best generals, Conon, who, significantly decided to retreat to Cyprus rather than face the wrath of the Athenian assembly. Possibly he had the Arginusae incident in mind which had taken place a year earlier; he knew that failure could be fatal.

Lysander rounded up all the prisoners and segregated the Athenians from the rest – then the massacre began. Some 3,000 men were summarily put to death. Only one general was spared, reputedly because he had opposed the vote for amputation passed by the Athenian assembly. It was a terrible act of revenge and an inauspicious start to a brief and uncertain period of Spartan rule in the Aegean world.

There is good evidence to support the contention that in the heyday of inter-state hoplite engagements, prior to the Peloponnesian War, massacre after battle was not that common (Hanson, 1989) although the pursuit of the broken and dispersed enemy phalanxes often resulted in the murder of unarmed men who were desperately trying to escape from the victors. The seventh century poet, Archilochus, hints at killing with no accompanying risks, and a near contemporary, Tyrtaios, writes of the fear of the defeated warrior who 'reverses and runs in terror of battle [and] offers his back, a tempting mark to spear from behind' (quoted by Hanson, 1989: 182). Later, killing and enslavement after battle became almost *de rigueur* for the Greeks. Victorious states would not often keep other Greeks as slaves, but it didn't stop them from selling them *abroad* as slaves. The question of social system or political preference hardly mattered. Monarchies, tyrannies, oligarchies and democracies, the Greeks experimented with them all. Nothing made any difference. Common language, common religion, many common institutions such as the Games, were all unifying factors, but they didn't prevent Greeks butchering one another. Internecine warfare and all its attendant evils seems to have been endemic to the Greek experience.

# CHAPTER FIVE

# The Greek Experience II:
# Massacre as a political expedient

We have seen already how Athens reacted to those states that she regarded as disloyal. Secession from the alliance was tantamount to rebellion. It mattered so much because it was an affront to her political pride and, worse still, undermined her political authority. In doing so it set precedents that other disenchanted states might wish to emulate; once the ties were broken, there was nothing to stop them joining or forming new alliances which were alien to Athenian interests. Not least of all it weakened the Athenian (Delian) League at a time of grave emergency by the withdrawal of mandatory contributions of money and/or ships. And there is some evidence that these contributions – perhaps better described as tribute – that were made by the allies had more than doubled after a reassessment of League expenses, and this may have occasioned stirrings of serious discontentment among League members.

The Delian League had been formed originally with the proclaimed intention of forestalling any future Persian invasion. But it had developed – or, depending upon one's perspective, degenerated – into an Athenian hegemony where the allies had virtually become the subjects of Athenian imperialism. It was felt that their contributions were simply being used to build up Athenian power to the detriment of their own prized autonomy, and there was a nagging suspicion that some League monies were actually being used to beautify Athens itself. It was exactly disaffection of this kind which generated revolt in the city-state of Potidea in northern Greece (432 BC). The Potideans wanted to resolve the anomaly of being free but unfree by breaking their alliance with Athens. But the Athenians were having none of it, and sent an army to besiege the city. This force included Socrates and Alkibiades, a man who was to become one of the most unpredictable war leaders in Athens. The siege lasted two years, when, at last, the inhabitants were starved into surrender. The Athenians compelled everyone to leave the city – in the light of future events, an uncharacteristically merciful gesture for which the generals were duly criticised. The deserted city was then occupied by Athenian settlers.

A much more significant incident occurred a little later on the island of Lesbos. In 428, four of the five cities of Lesbos under the leadership of Mytilene revolted from Athens. At first, the Athenian leaders were stunned and could hardly believe that an island which, along with Chios, enjoyed a privileged status within the alliance could contemplate secession. They suspected that Sparta – unable to attack Athens directly – was indulging in a little subversive activity in her colonies in order to reduce their military effectiveness. The Athenians lost no time once they became convinced of the gravity of the situation. They ordered the people of Mytilene to surrender their ships and demolish their walls, but this was ignored by the leaders of the city who promptly sent envoys to the Peloponnesians for assistance. The Athenians sent troops to enforce their decision, and a siege began which continued into the following year. Meanwhile, the Spartans sent a representative who tried to encourage the people and promised that help would come. They sent a fleet but it failed to relieve the city in time. They also launched an attack on the Athenian countryside which acted as a diversion and took some pressure off the island. This was an extremely indirect means of aiding an island people so far away and had a limited effect.

It is at this point that an anomalous and rather complicated situation developed. There was now a serious shortage of food in Mytilene, and the Spartan envoy, the representative of an oligarchic system, surprisingly arranged for the members of the lower classes to be equipped as heavily armed infantry (*hoplites*). This was a privilege normally reserved for the middle classes – but then crises do not always respect the demands of class ideology. The people then took over the city and demanded a fairer distribution of food from the governing oligarchs who, realising that they now had little chance, decided to sue for terms from the Athenian army. But by this time the Athenian commander had learned that the Spartan fleet was in the vicinity and set off in pursuit, leaving part of his force to garrison the city. The Spartans, seemingly unaware of this, and for reasons best known to themselves, had apparently already decided to make for home and were not overtaken by the Athenians. By way of a modest military divertissement, the frustrated Athenian commander, instead of going straight back to Mytilene, decided to make a detour to intervene in the affairs of another city, Notium, where he resolved a further *stasis* situation in a particularly treacherous and blood-thirsty manner.

On returning to Mytilene the Athenian commander determined to take a more rigorous line. He rounded up those he considered most responsible for the revolt and sent them off to Athens where the assembly, infuriated at the behaviour of one of their favoured colonies, and apparently goaded by the influential non-aristocratic demagogue, Kleon, voted for the death of all the Mytilean males and the enslavement of the women and children. A ship was duly dispatched with explicit instructions for this to be carried out. However, the next day the assembly appears to have regretted this hasty and brutal decision, and convened an extraordinary meeting to debate the issue again. Here they revoked the earlier decision, despite the impassioned arguments of Kleon, and sent another ship with instructions to rescind the original order. Fortunately this ship was able to overtake the first ship just in time and a general slaughter was averted.

Interestingly, the arguments put forward by Kleon were largely in terms of political expediency and the arguments offered against him by the advocate Diodotus were likewise – and perhaps cleverly – deliberately non-moral in tone. Diodotus also stressed the importance of political expediency, and pointed out how the extermination of an erstwhile ally would cause more disaffection than it was worth. This argument tipped the scales, but only by a small majority. From what we know of the sequel to these events, it must have been agreed on conditions that brought no credit to the Athenians who had to have some satisfaction. So it was decided that all those 'culpable' Mytileneans who had been brought to Athens were to be put to death – probably something in excess of a thousand people. Later, the walls of Mytilene were destroyed and the city's ships were confiscated. And then the whole island of Lesbos, except for the loyal city of Methymna, was divided into 3,000 lots (kleroi) – including 300 for the gods – for each of which the people had to pay an annual rent. The Athenians also sent special personnel to the island as a kind of occupation force to make sure that the Lesbians complied with these arrangements.

Later in the war, there was a very similar incident to that of Mytilene, but with much more fateful consequences. This took place in 416 after a long interval of uncertain peace, and just prior to the ambitious but ill-fated Athenian expedition to Sicily – a disaster from which she never really recovered.

The Athenians were frustrated by their inability to gain any lasting or decisive advantage over the Peloponnesians, especially on land, so they looked for some easy pickings abroad and decided to exercise their dominance at sea by attacking the small city-state of Melos in the Cyclades, the only island in that part of the Aegean which had eluded their control. Early in the war – according to a still extant but mutilated inscription – the Melians had made some contribution to the Spartan fleet (427), and the following year the Athenian general, Nikias, had made an unsuccessful attempt to capture the island. But now, as far as we can judge, the Melians were trying to stay neutral.

The decision to attack Melos was sponsored by Alkibiades, one of the most interesting and enigmatic figures in classical history. Alkibiades, a friend and companion of Socrates, was a gifted, wealthy and unscrupulous political opportunist who could apparently talk his way out of any situation. There is little doubt about his powers of persuasion; he changed sides more than once and managed to convince everyone of his complete sincerity. There is ample evidence of his oratorical skills in the assembly as his role in the Sicilian fiasco demonstrates. Alkibiades was also an excellent commander, and it was he who led the decisive expedition to Melos. Thucydides insists that before doing any harm to the land, the Athenian generals sent representatives to the Melian authorities who would not let them put their case to the people (Thucydides 5, 84). There followed a discussion which has become known as the Melian Dialogue – one of the most fascinating debates on the use and justification of violence in ancient literature.

It is highly probable that this Dialogue was meant to be a device to add a dramatic and ironic edge to the general narrative. Thucydides, who is about to follow this with an account of the tragic events in Sicily, may well be suggesting to his readers that the consequences of this imprudent and ill-fated venture were no more than just retribution for the Athenian treatment of the people of Melos. The attack on Melos was really an act of unprovoked aggression which was not even supported by a plausible pretext. Thucydides depicts the Athenian generals as displaying a 'might-is-right' attitude to the Melians: 'they that have power exact as much as they can, and the weak must yield to such conditions as they can get'. (5:105) The generals do not pretend that the Athenian empire can be justified morally, but insist that it is deserved by virtue of its strength of arms. The argument is practical and pragmatic. It is reminiscent, in some ways, of Marx's point about the respective roles of the exploiters and the exploited; neither can be blamed morally, both must do what they must in the given structural situation. Neither side is reprehensible, each must wrest as many advantages as they can from each other – this is the only way to survive. Likewise, the Athenians were not prepared to talk about what is 'right', only what was feasible and necessary. This is the nature of things: the weak must subject themselves to the strong.

No counter-arguments of the Melians in terms of honour and justice had any force with the Athenians, but they refused to surrender insisting that they preferred freedom to Athenian domination. The Athenians were obviously scornful about all this. They regarded moral arguments as the last refuge of the weak – simply making virtue of necessity. They believed that the Melians would probably do the same to them if they could; the Melians did not despise strength, and would be quite happy to be rescued by the military might of the Spartans.

But the Spartans didn't arrive, and the siege continued for several months. Siegecraft was very rudimentary, and walled cities were usually only taken by starving the inhabitants, or by bribery and treachery. In this case the city was betrayed by some of its citizens. Further resistance seemed useless, and the Melians 'surrendered themselves to the discretion of the Athenians' (5.116) who then proceeded to slay all the men of military age and enslave the women and children.

However contrived Thucydides' speeches are – or are even thought to be – the Dialogue does convey a sense of the Athenian imperialistic mentality. (There is no dispute about the subsequent slaughter and enslavement of the Melians – the facts speak for themselves.) The speeches are interesting, and in many ways, are quite timeless in the application. The Athenians maintained that arguments based upon justice were irrelevant. In effect, they discounted the idea of 'natural rights'. They really suggest that not only have they the right to rule by virtue of their strength, but that the weaker state would actually benefit by becoming subject to Athens, even if it was by compulsion – a kind of 'slavery is good for the slave' argument. All Greeks prized freedom (*eleutheria*) including the freedom to rule over others.

It is one thing to try to convince a less powerful state that they should ally themselves with a more powerful state, but quite another to abandon persuasion in favour of a threat of outright terror. Former Athenian spokesmen such as Perikles and Kleon had made it clear that Athens had a right to an empire and that this must then be preserved at all costs, arguing that it had been ordained – presumably by the gods – that the weaker should always bow to the stronger. Donald Kagan, in his commentary on Thucydides, reminds us how a powerful Britain attacked Copenhagen in peacetime in 1807 without justification, and when the Danes protested they were reminded that war was war and therefore they had to be 'resigned to these necessities' (Kagan, 1981: 151). The Athenian treatment of Melos was only an extension of the policies that were pursued generally by Athenians and Spartans alike. No one seems to have protested about it; Alkibiades certainly advocated it, and his political opponent, Nikias, who had a reputation for piety, does not appear to have opposed it. Even Aristophanes, the comic poet, made fun of the starving Melians in a play produced two years later (*Birds*, 186). Such events lend themselves to the contention that not only does cruelty breed cruelty, it also breeds an almost numbing insensitivity to the feelings of others.

These events took place, as we have seen, during what was technically known as the Peace of Nikias. During this period there were occasional skirmishes and some indirect but significant confrontations such as the battle of Mantinea (418) when Sparta defeated a coalition of Argives, who were friendly towards Athens, and their allies. In the early days of the truce, both Sparta and Athens seemed to be pleased to have a breathing space; each needed time to recuperate, but before long each appeared to be waiting for the right opportunity to resume hostilities providing the appropriate justifications were on hand. Matters came to a head with the Athenian decision to attack Syracuse, ostensibly to help her Sicilian allies, but more probably, as Alkibiades suggested, with a view to taking over the whole island. The Syracusans were tribally linked to the Spartans, who came to their aid, and in two years the Athenians and their allies lost their entire force – at least half their total fighting strength (413).

The war continued until the catastrophic battle of Aigospotami (405) when the Athenians were defeated and their city was invaded by both land and sea by the Peloponnesians. Ironically, political expediency, in whose interests they had committed unspeakable crimes, now came to their rescue. They tried to negotiate terms whereby they could retain their land and their walls but the Spartans insisted that they must destroy large portions of their long walls, i.e. the protective walls connecting Athens with its port of Piraeus. The Athenian assembly would have none of this, and the siege dragged on while proposals and counter-proposals were made and rejected. Meanwhile conditions in the city were becoming desperate. During the winter many died of starvation whilst the political leaders argued among themselves as to what should be done. Political opinion became increasingly polarised, and the oligarchic faction became powerful enough to have one of the chief opposition spokesmen tried and executed.

After protracted negotiations, it was finally agreed that the Athenians should destroy their long walls, surrender all but twelve of their warships, allow the return of their exiles, and give up all claims to the cities they controlled – in effect, their empire. A number of Sparta's allies wanted much more than this. Corinth and Thebes especially demanded that Athens should actually be destroyed, which meant not only the obliteration of its buildings – among the wonders of Greece – but presumably also the slaughter and enslavement of its population as retribution for what the Athenians had done to others. Sparta, to her everlasting credit, resisted these demands. Tender heartedness may have played a part, although the Spartans had not been significantly merciful during many of their campaigns. Respect for the Athenian past, and for the critical contributions Athens had made during the Persian wars earlier in the century was given as a principal reason for preserving her state. But there is little doubt that a key factor was simple political expediency. Sparta was flexing her hegemonic muscles; she wanted first of all to keep her allies in their place. Furthermore, Sparta could hardly establish her new position as the leading power in Greece by destroying one of its leading cities. Nothing was more calculated to generate disaffection and distrust than wholesale massacre. So the Athenians were both surprised and relieved at Sparta's moderation.

Did Spartan rule really change anything? Xenophon (*Hellenica*, 2, 2,

1–23) writes of those who '[thought] that this was the beginning of [the] freedom of Greece'. But, unsurprisingly, things did not work out like this. Certainly a number of states were more than relieved at the fall of Athens. Besides the obvious beneficiaries on the mainland and in the islands, there were the Greeks of Sicily, especially Syracuse, who could now feel themselves free to pursue their own particular brands of tyranny and despotism, as they did during the following century. And the defeat of Athens must have brought some satisfaction to the North African city of Carthage (modern Tunisia) whose flourishing maritime empire was continually coming into conflict with that of the Greeks from different states.

As far as Athen's subject states were concerned, nothing changed that much. They were merely exchanging one form of domination for another. Lysander ensured that these states were ruled by boards of aristocratic officials (*decharchies*) that were thoroughly sympathetic to Sparta. These men – as far as we are able to judge – often acted overbearingly in their new roles, confiscating property, and sometimes putting popular leaders to death. In Athens itself, subjection to Sparta and the consequent installation of an oligarchic government ushered in a reign of terror. A group of thirty aristocrats was chosen to reorganise the government of the city. Their leader, Kritias, was, like Alkibiades, a one-time 'student' of Socrates who, it must be said, had left Socrates' circle of friends because he felt he had no more to learn about *practical* affairs. His actions in what has come to be known as the 'Rule of the Thirty' were ruthless in the extreme. He accused many prominent democrats of treason and had them executed, and then turned his attentions – somewhat uncharacteristically for an aristocrat – to an organised persecution of many wealthy citizens and resident aliens. Again the object seems to have been primarily confiscation. Aggrandisement was among the principal crimes of the Thirty. They misused their power by enriching themselves at the expense of others, and conferred full citizen rights on a mere 3,000 people who were chosen for their political predictability. But absolute reliability is often rather difficult to achieve, and as is so common in revolutionary situations, whether they are radical or reactionary, leaders fall out among themselves. Either they try to outdo one another in revolutionary zeal or, in some semi-penitential way, they attempt to mitigate the worst excesses of the movement – as in this case – where one of the more sympathetic oligarchs went out on a limb and was forced to commit suicide by his fellow 'tyrants'.

The Athenians who felt themselves endangered or who could not live with the repressive practices of the regime fled to neighbouring cities. Indeed, things became so bad that a radical revolutionary movement was started by some of these *émigré* Athenians, and after a protracted struggle the oligarchic faction was defeated, Kritias was killed, and a new, more moderate, government was formed.

But there were still serious problems, and eventually Sparta was called in to settle matters. Contrary to custom and conviction, the Spartans sponsored a democratic government – probably again out of political expediency. Order was restored (401) and it was agreed, somewhat optimistically, that there should be no recriminations or punishments despite the fact that the Thirty had systematically massacred some 1,500 people.

Once in power, the democrats were much more restrained, although there were still persecutions, most notably that of the aged Socrates who was arraigned on a charge of 'impiety'. This was a rather ludicrous allegation in the light of Plato's account of his defence. Perhaps what his accusers could not forgive was the spirit of free-thought that he encouraged which had produced such diverse characters as the philosopher Plato, the political renegade Alkibiades, and the ruthless cynic Kritias. Perhaps Athenians held him to be indirectly responsible for the travail it had endured under the Thirty. He was sentenced to death by suicide, yet could probably have avoided taking the hemlock if he had been ready to accept help from his friends. But he insisted that he had always lived by the law of the state, and was not prepared to change course now that the law had condemned him. In Greece, and certainly in Athens, people did not fare any better under a democracy than an oligarchy; both could be equally unforgiving in their own ways.

Athens and Sparta still had extremely important parts to play in the subsequent history of Greece, but their great days were now past. They had rather chequered histories from now on. Both became enmeshed in the interminable inter-state wars that continued to plague Greece, and both flirted with the idea of military revival either with or without the help of Persia. Sparta in particular suffered a serious set-back in a conflict with Thebes (371), and both fell under the shadow of Macedonian power later in the fourth century. Finally, like all Greece, they succumbed to the power of Rome in the second century – an experience from which they never recovered.

Perhaps we should not judge them too harshly. Perhaps, in justice both to them and to ourselves, 'we need to see the Greeks as they were, taking full advantage of the perspectives afforded by our... greater knowledge' (Muller, 1967) – in other words, as children of their time. The Athenians in particular were pioneers of freedom and democratic traditions. There were no satisfactory precedents to guide them, and perhaps it is a wonder they achieved so much in such a relatively short time. Possibly it is unjust to moralise about their sins. After all, they reconciled imperialistic ambition with the idea of the self-governing city-state with some success. Perhaps there never was a people, certainly not in the ancient world, that tried so hard to make equality a living reality. But it must be stressed that this was only for its citizens; it excluded aliens and slaves who together – though we are not at all sure about numbers – may have equalled the free population. Furthermore, although they clung tenaciously to the principle of democracy, in the actual pursuit of the ideal, they paradoxically denied it to those who would not cooperate with them. In creating what they held to be a superior culture, they came to believe that their task – indeed their mission – was to rule others, Greeks and non-Greeks alike. This conviction was then used to justify the most repressive measures, even methodical massacre and enslavement especially if it was thought to be a necessary lesson to others. They subscribed ardently, like so many of the Greeks, to a belief in autonomy, but not to the autonomy of belief.

# CHAPTER SIX

# Roman Slavery I:
# Massacre as social retribution

Slavery was a given institution in the ancient world where it had virtually a universal distribution. It was not regarded as a moral offence and, with one or two exceptions, did not generate the righteous indignation that it does today. We can say, too, that it was not a feature of any *one* kind of social structure or political ideology. It is probably true to say that none of the pre-classical societies was economically dependent on slave labour, although, as in Classical society, most came increasingly to rely on slaves as slave numbers increased through poverty and debt, and especially military conquest. A Mesopotamian king, Rimush (*c.* 2300 BC), claimed after one of his expeditions that he had killed 17,000 men and taken another 4,000 prisoner. Of these he dedicated (sacrificed?) six to the god Enlil, and put the rest to work as slave labourers (Saggs, 1989: 42). Later, also in Mesopotamia (Iraq), labour camps were organised to accommodate the increasing influx of slaves. In ancient Egypt too there are records from at least the Fourth Dynasty in the middle of the third millenium BC boasting of conquests that brought in large contingents of slaves, and these too increased with the expansionist policies of the New Kingdom in the second millenium. In both Mesopotamia and Egypt there was a considerable amount of domestic slavery – as there was also in the near-contemporary Minoan culture of early Crete – but this was always exceeded by the numbers working on state and temple estates. It was particularly common in Classical society; in fact, there is no known state of affairs in either Greek or Roman society when it did not exist, though in both societies it did have more and less developed forms.

In some ways slavery is actually difficult to define. M. I. Finley has argued that in the ancient world there was no such thing as freedom, as we understand it, only varying degrees of unfreedom. Furthermore, he has shown that ancient society was made up of a spectrum of statuses from free man to slave with varying degrees of dependence between. In Greek society alone at least six different types of slavery can be identified ranging from debt-bondsmen and household servants through to the most abysmal forms of chattel slavery (Finley, 1964: 72).

Arguments, therefore, about the 'causes' of slavery are rather fruitless because its origins are quite unknown, though, it would not be difficult to speculate about how it arose. We know that it was feared by the free as an ever-present threat because under certain conditions such as war, piracy, debt, etc., they were always open to the possibility of enslavement. Slaves could, of course, also be obtained by breeding though this tended to be discouraged when there was a glut of slaves as there was, for instance, in Rome during the late Republic. Home-bred slaves were expensive especially where the slave-master had also to maintain the slave's wife and children who were usually regarded as less productive. Consequently, wives were often not allowed although certain 'irregularities' did take place. Breeding was only favoured, therefore, when demand exceeded supply or where a slave was highly skilled and his sons might serve as apprentices. A law passed in Rome in 52 AD decreed that offspring of slaves and free women – presumably something of a rarity – automatically remained in servitude.

What concerns us here is how slavery actually functioned, and this involves two main issues, how slaves were employed and what their rights were. Slaves were used for a multitude of tasks, some of which were highly skilled such as the Greek-tutor slaves often favoured by the Romans, or highly responsible such as the Scythian slave-police employed by the Athenians. Much slavery was really domestic labour, work in manufacturing, and even commerce. At the lowest end there was the relatively unskilled work in mining and quarrying. This was slavery at its worst; the men – often criminals and captives – were usually chained and branded, and made to live out their short, miserable lives in wretched conditions. Also unskilled was most of the work on small-holdings and the huge agricultural estates (*latifundia*) which were found in Italy and Sicily. In a society where there are only small margins over subsistence, and there is little or no technology to speak of, achievement in the public sector is only possible with a plentiful supply of cheap labour. Little wonder that it was the *latifundia* that became the main breeding grounds for dissension and revolt. Some Roman writers (e.g. Cato) suggest that the slaves were treated very callously on these plantations. They often worked in irons and at night were housed in underground prisons. Their brutal treatment really came to light in the first Sicilian slave war which broke out in 135 BC. In this struggle some 70,000 slaves revolted and defied all attempts to suppress them for three years.

Slavery, therefore, was not conditioned by the *kinds* of work which slaves were called upon to do, as these could be similar to, and, in some cases, the same as those of freemen. Slaves must be defined by status; slavery was conditioned by the rights – or lack of them – which slaves enjoyed. Essentially, they were *non*-citizens: they had no political rights and certainly not the right to change their own status; they had no legal rights and had to be represented in law by their masters. Furthermore, they had no rights to military service – a privilege in the ancient world

– although in emergencies they were sometimes used in war, usually in some menial capacity such as rowers in the fleet.

The development of slavery in Rome followed a familiar pattern. There were probably very few slaves in early Rome, although creditors had the right to sell their debtors into slavery – a practice that was almost abolished by c. 300 BC. Agriculture seems to have been carried on mainly by free labour, but this began to change about 200 BC with the increased wealth that flowed in from the wars with Carthage and Rome's further conquests in Greece and North Africa. The actual numbers of slaves are unknown, but we can get some idea from particular instances. In 167 BC, for example, the senate ordered the enslavement of the captive population of Epirus (north-west Greece) amounting to some 150,000 people. Earlier in 177 BC, in Sardinia, we find that 80,000 people were killed or enslaved. Perhaps at the height of her power about 30–35 per cent of Rome's population were slaves.

Slave numbers have always been a problem for the modern researcher; all that can be done is to make intelligent inferences from a limited number of recorded instances. For example, in the late Republic, we find that a farm of 50–100 acres might have about fifteen slaves. During the civil wars between Caesar and Pompey (mid-first century BC) a son of Pompey mobilised some 800 slaves for war service. We know too that some rich people owned hundreds of slaves, one C. Isidorus (d. 8 BC) had 4,116 employed mainly on his estates.

As we have seen, with the slowing down of Roman expansionism, the influx of slaves decreased with a consequent rise in their value. In the early Empire, a slave cost 8–10 times his purchase price to maintain for a year. This may be compared with fourth-century Athens where the cost of keeping a slave for a year was about the same as the initial purchase price. There is obviously nothing new about inflation.

Slaves could be privately or publicly owned, and their employment varied considerably. For instance, at one point the staff for the various Roman aqueduct projects included 700 slaves. Similarly, Crassus, perhaps the wealthiest man of his time (mid-first century BC), had a staff of 500 architects and masons who were mainly slaves. At the other end of the scale, the Roman *publicani* (state contractors) employed some 40,000 slaves in the Spanish mines where life was notoriously brutal and short. And in the mid-range, we have the slave gladiators who were employed in schools or circuses for the entertainment of the Roman crowd (see Chapter 8).

As far as slave rights were concerned, Roman policies were much in line with current practice. In legal terms, slave rights were virtually nil. The owner had the power of life and death over his slaves, but just how often these were exercised in extreme forms, we have no idea. In one particularly infamous case in 61 AD, where a slave had killed his master, the law was invoked for the execution of all the dead man's household slaves because of the (understandable?) presumption that others must have been implicated. There was a public outcry and even a debate in the senate, but in the end the law took its course, and 400 slaves including women and children were executed.

Runaway slaves might be ruthlessly treated when recaptured. In earlier Mesopotamian society, for instance, it was not uncommon for a runaway to be maimed in such a way that he was permanently disfigured – perhaps by cutting off the nose or ears – but not otherwise impaired from carrying out his duties. Such a punishment had a psychological function in that it was an inescapable reminder to the slave himself; it had a social function inasmuch as it was a deterrent to others, and it had an indirect economic function in that it did not detract from the slave's working efficiency. One suspects on the limited evidence available that Roman treatment of slaves was not significantly better. In many situations, escape was relatively simple, but if caught, the Romans could often be less than generous. The Emperor Augustus once proclaimed that one of his principal achievements during the civil wars of the late Republic was the returning of 30,000 slaves to their masters for punishment, and it is worth noting that those for whom no master could be found were duly impaled. Augustus fails to mention the 20,000 slaves he 'redirected' to serve in the navy, or the 6,000 that he had crucified (Finley, 1980: 110). Little wonder that some of the escapees actually pleaded to be allowed to return to their masters and take their chances (Hopkins, 1978: 121).

If a criminal – slave or otherwise – was a Roman citizen, it did not necessarily pay dividends. Not all were as fortunate as the apostle Paul whose punishment was at least delayed when he appealed to the Emperor as citizens were allowed to do. In another roughly contemporary case in the early Empire, a murderer who appealed to the provincial governor that he was a Roman citizen was merely given a higher cross on which to be crucified (Hopkins, 1978: 222).

Slaves did, however, have a certain amount of religious freedom and could, therefore, attend certain festivals such as the Saturnalia. This was allowed on the assumption that religious worship was a relatively harmless exercise which could in no way endanger the state, and could, incidentally, act as a kind of soporific in that it might be a source of consolation to the slave and keep him quiescent. On the other hand, it gave slaves, in effect, the right of assembly, thus providing a venue for possible discussion and conspiracy.

Of course, masters could always manumit slaves if they wished, and at particular times this was done on an appreciable scale, so much so, in fact, that Augustus had to pass laws to limit it. Freedom could be given as a reward for services, or by payments form the slave's restricted earnings – the price of manumission being predictably in excess of the original purchase price. As freedmen the slaves became citizens, though with restricted rights.

There *were* kind masters, and there was even a status infrastructure among slaves in relation to their masters. But, generally speaking, the life of the slave was, at best, unenviable, and, at worst, brutal and precarious. Thus is comes as no surprise that revolt and thought of revolt were always simmering under the surface. This was especially so on the large *latifundia* where so many slaves were herded together in intolerable conditions. Thus there occurred one of the most serious slave rebellions in Roman history. It lasted nine years (140–131 BC), and was particularly difficult to deal with because it took place in Sicily which, although adjacent to the Italian mainland, had an indigenous population which did not easily subscribe to Roman domination.

Of the huge importations of slaves from the provinces during the Roman wars of conquest, a huge percentage were settled on the *latifundia*. Wealthy Sicilians and the often unwelcome Roman immigrants collaborated in the organisation and administration of these estates – a situation reminiscent of the French in Algeria prior to the 1960s. Although a certain degree of circumscribed 'freedom' was given to the slaves to fend for themselves – which in itself, provided a basis for possible armed insurrection – in general, they were treated with considerable cruelty and neglect. The story is told of one especially wealthy landowner, Damophilus (presumably of Greek extraction), who ordered naked slaves to be whipped when they asked for clothes. And it was apparently this particular incident which helped to precipitate the revolt.

Among the slave population was a shrewdly gifted Syrian named Eunus who gained a reputation as a magician and a medium, and even as a prophet. He was said to be able to go into trances and breathe fire – a trick certainly, but one that obviously stood him in good stead with his gullible devotees. In this way too he gained entry into Romano–Sicilian society, and entertained people at feasts with his legerdemain and his prophecies. More ominous for the overlords, he claimed to be in communication with a goddess who had told him in a vision that one day there would have to be a revolt and that he would become king. Eventually, he was able to convince other slaves of his mission, and assured them that the revolt was divinely ordained, and that the whole enterprise was certain of success.

Revolts necessarily require the right pre-conditions if they are going to succeed: good leadership, efficient organisation, access to arms, a medium of communication, and, where possible, an inspirational and unifying ideology – in this case, a prophetic religion. In some ways, this was rather similar to the recent Cargo cults of Melanesia (Worsley, 1968), although, in the main, the Cargo cults were much more pacifistic in orientation. The insurrection, which was made that much easier by the Roman practice of leaving only a minimum of troops to garrison the island, began with a general massacre which was carried out with particular callousness. Initially, sympathetic owners were unmolested, but later many were killed as the rebellious slaves roamed the countryside looting, killing and taking revenge indiscriminately on those who were in any way associated with their enslavement and humiliation. The slaves occupied the town of Enna and tried to set up a *polis*-like structure with a popular court. But many were impatient and some slave masters, including Damophilus, were killed before they could be officially tried. Eunus, who had assumed a near-messianic posture was established as king and organised an assembly which decreed the execution of their prisoners with the exception of those who had treated him well in the past. He took a wife whom he made queen, recruited a bodyguard, and began minting his own coins. One feels that his followers should have read the signs: they were about to exchange one form of bondage for another. Eunus was astute enough to spare skilled freemen who could act as armourers and so forth in his anticipated clash with the legions which he knew would inevitably be sent to quell the uprising.

Another revolt broke out in the south-west of the island and the rebels joined forces until eventually they had some 200,000 supporters. Almost by symbiosis, further revolts occurred in other parts of the Roman world, notably on the Aegean island of Delos, but these were quickly suppressed by the legions. The Sicilian affair was another matter. Here the rebels had some spectacular early successes against the various contingents sent against them, but after a protracted struggle, the Roman commander, Rupillus, destroyed the rebellion on a piecemeal basis, separating the rebel forces and dealing with each in turn. The superior training and discipline of the legions was too much for the slave armies; they were completely defeated, and Eunus was captured and imprisoned. There he died of 'worms', and his death was said at the time to be a fitting end seeing that he had skulked away from the battlefield leaving about a thousand of his followers to commit suicide rather than suffer the horrendous treatment that the Romans reserved for rebellious slaves.

From incidents such as these, we can draw certain tentative conclusions about this particular revolt and about slave rebellions generally. The freeborn – in this case the Sicilians – actually exulted over the suppression of the revolt. They neither saw the slaves as fellow proletarians nor the Romano–Sicilian owner elite as their allies. Really, they were on nobody's side but their own. They helped to suppress the revolt but, at the same time, often pillaged the property of the previous landowners, partly out of greed but largely out of a pent-up resentment against the rich. In a society where slaves farmed estates to provide food for Rome's poor, the free poor in Sicily had as much, if not more, to gain from slavery as the rich. The very existence of a slave population not only relieved them from actual and potential toil, it also reaffirmed their own social position; at least they were one rung up in the social hierarchy. They may, in the Marxist sense, have been as far removed as the slaves from the ownership of the means of production, but they enjoyed quite a different *status* and more extensive privileges than slaves who were without rights and who had very little hope that anything would ever change. So if anyone profited from slavery, it was the ordinary citizen. It gave him increased status and economic assistance. It freed him for war service, and it acted as his 'technology' in a pre-scientific society.

The slave, on the other hand, desperately wanted to change his own status. And this is why it is almost certainly a misnomer to speak of the slave rebellions as though they were revolutions. If the term revolution is taken to mean violent conflict between sections or strata of a state in order to bring about a permanent change in the social structure of society, then we cannot speak of slave revolutions. Slaves were not intent on *changing* society; they were not trying to abolish slavery, merely to escape from being slaves. Indeed, when revolts were successful it was not uncommon for slaves to make slaves of their erstwhile superiors.

# CHAPTER SEVEN

# Roman Slavery II:
# Massacre as condign punishment

This section of our study has been divided into two: firstly, a discussion of massacres *by* slaves, and, secondly, massacre *of* slaves. These obviously complement one another. The treatment of Roman slaves was often brutal in the extreme, particularly if they were recalcitrant or rebellious in any way. It thus becomes at least understandable – as we have seen – that on the rare occasions when they had the upper hand, they, in turn, acted equally harshly to others, especially their former masters.

The gladiatorial schools in Rome were the one place where the free and unfree met on a more or less equal footing. Many, perhaps most, of those engaged in the 'killing-for-entertainment' industry were slaves who had been bought in for the purpose, although there was a healthy proportion of freemen who enrolled either for money or excitement, or both. We have already noted the harsh conditions which existed in many of these schools, and the often unscrupulous way in which the gladiators were sometimes exploited. Perhaps some men actually enjoyed their work; certainly it brought a few of them a measure of fame and notoriety, and even relative wealth. But for others it was a life they could do without. It wasn't that the future was uncertain. That was the problem. The future was quite certain for most – it was a predictable matter of extinction. Perhaps this contest, or maybe the next . . .

Rome's attitude to slaves did not normally have a narrow racial dimension, as we have come to understand it. Certainly the question of colour appears to have been quite irrelevant to the matter of servitude. This attitude also extended to the wider issue of culture. In fact, those who were culturally closest to the Romans – the Greeks – were often their favourite slaves. On the other hand, if we think in broad political terms, we can say that, generally speaking, Romans were reluctant to hold other Romans as slaves. This was not an ethnic issue but one of citizenship; Roman citizenship was regarded as a highly-prized possession.

It is incidental, therefore, that many, possibly most, of Rome's gladiators were not Romans. Spartacus, the leader of one of the most serious revolts Rome ever experienced, was, in fact, a Thracian, as were many of his followers. Actually, Thracians were one of the more popular 'breeds' of gladiator, and were often depicted in fighting poses in Roman art. We are told that Caligula favoured Thracians and chose Thracian gladiators to officer his German bodyguard. The Emperor Titus had a liking for Thracians, but this was not shared by his successor, his brother Domitian. Such was the partisanship in the Games. It is difficult to know exactly what determined the likes and dislikes of the crowd towards any individual. As far as gladiators were concerned, various epigraphic references, graffiti, etc., suggest that there was almost certainly a sexual dimension to the popularity of particular contestants, and that their prowess and demonstrable macho qualities generated an unhealthy eroticism in both males and females alike. It follows, therefore, that gladiators were very much at the mercy of the mob. If they put up a good display, they could do no wrong, but if they made a few mistakes, particularly if they evinced any sign of weakness, they could very easily become the butt of ridicule and abuse. The public was extremely fickle in its affections. A gladiator could be the darling of the crowd one moment and an inconsequential has-been the next. The Roman crowd could be very unforgiving when they did not get what they wanted. A defeated gladiator had to maintain his poise – and his pose – even in death, all for a contemptuous public that had no more need for his services.

One of the most famous of the gladiatorial schools was that of Capua in Campania south of Rome. It was here in 73 BC that Spartacus and about seventy gladiators – mainly Thracians, Germans and Celts – broke out of their barracks taking numerous slaves with them. The whole story is not known because the near-contemporary description of the revolt has been lost, and has had to be pieced together from accounts written about two hundred years after the event. But the main details can be recovered with reasonable confidence. Spartacus, it appears, had once served in the Roman army but had deserted and for a while had survived in the countryside as little more than a bandit. When he was recaptured by the Romans he was sold into slavery, and eventually ended up at the gladiatorial school in Capua. Conditions were so harsh and the future so bleak that he and his fellow conspirators obviously felt that things could get no worse if they made a risky bid for freedom.

The account of the gladiators' subsequent struggle has all the ingredients of high adventure. Their desperate resistance against superior forces is now generally acknowledged as a feat of considerable heroism. But it did have its darker side. Once they were unfettered, their treatment of others often left a great deal to be desired, although it is perhaps understandable that they should give way to the resentment that had built up over the years. At first, there was no clear plan. They just wanted to get away. The only weapons they had were the knives they had stolen from the school's kitchens. With these they were able to repulse their warders, and later defeat a small contingent of troops from whom they obtained the kind of weaponry that armed resistance required. Spartacus had two fellow leaders, Gauls named Crixus and Oenomaus, and together, they and their recruits made their way to the believed extinct crater of Mount Vesuvius, and waited the inevitable Roman onslaught.

This came in the form of an inadequate force led by an over-confident amateur, Cladius Glaber, who thought of this as a routine tidying-up operation from which he would emerge with an established reputation. Needless to say, he was wrong. These enemies might be slaves, but they were very competently-led slaves with a core of contest-hardened veterans. The Romans were surprised and routed by stratagems which they had not anticipated. The slave army's reputation was enhanced and it was joined by hordes of poor herdsmen and agricultural labourers who, though free, were obviously not entranced by Roman overlordship, and who were only too willing to join forces with those who might improve their lot.

More Roman armies came to challenge them, and they too suffered equally humiliating defeats. Even a force led by the praetor, Varinus, who had sent Glaber in the first place, was repulsed, and this enabled the gladiators to embark upon a wider and more ambitious scheme of operations. The slave army was now a large, unwieldy force, and it was at this point that its internal structure began to exhibit certain weaknesses. Discipline became more difficult because some sections of the army were mainly intent on plunder and their recent victories had left them free to pillage at will. Spartacus apparently urged restraint, and tried to curb the wilder elements, but inevitably, it came to a parting of the ways. Crixus, one of his fellow leaders, became a kind of independent war-lord and took most of the Germans and Gauls and continued to ravage the countryside. Spartacus, who realised that anything he could do against Rome was merely temporary, planned to avoid any direct confrontation with the legions, and take the remainder and head north towards the Alps. Eventually he hoped to disband the army and let the men disperse to their own homes. But he hesitated, and decided to winter in Italy where he was joined by the flotsam of Roman society, disgruntled peasants, runaway slaves and sundry malcontents who saw some vestigial hope for themselves as part of this burgeoning rebellion.

By this time Spartacus had amassed an army of about 90,000 and the Roman senate became thoroughly alarmed. Four legions were sent to counter the rebels and this time they were led by two consuls who were both experienced commanders. They quickly overcame Crixus' brigand army, and Crixus himself was killed. But when they encountered Spartacus it was a different story. By the very nature of the challenge, the Romans had to take the war to Spartacus and he chose his ground very carefully on the heights of Picenum. This encouraged the Romans to divide their forces in order to dislodge the rebels from a tactically advantageous position. In this way, Spartacus was able to take on each consul in turn and defeat him. After the battle was over, Spartacus decided to add insult to injury by forcing three hundred of his captives to fight gladiatorial combats as a way of ridiculing Roman justice.

Just what happened next is uncertain and *why* it happened is even more in doubt. By all accounts, after further victories in northern Italy, Spartacus made what turned out to be a fateful decision and left the safety of the highlands and moved south, possibly in the hope of enlisting the aid of pirates who might evacuate his army to Sicily. We are not sure just what went wrong. Perhaps the pirates, traditional enemies of Rome, thought better of it, or possibly negotiations broke down over the question of rewards. Whatever, the rebels turned back and burst through the Roman fortifications which threatened to trap them in the peninsula, and again found themselves in a vulnerable position in the open countryside.

They were now confronted with the legions led by Crassus, one of the wiliest of Roman politicians, a seasoned commander, who also happened to be particularly anxious for military glory. He had already had one or two setbacks, and was very keen to bring the slave rebellion to an end. This would not only enhance his military reputation but would also assuage his sense of pique that an impatient senate had instructed its most eminent soldier, Pompey, to bring *his* legions to help him in the task. The two men had a long-standing and unseemly rivalry, and Crassus was anxious that Pompey should not acquire even more fame by being in at the kill. To add to Spartacus' problems, a third Roman army under the proconsul, Lucullus, was due to land by sea at Brundisium (Brindisi), and this threatened to trap the rebel army on three sides. So Crassus was galvanised into action, and in a series of hard fought battles defeated the rebels who by now were outclassed and potentially outnumbered.

But Crassus still had to share the honour with Pompey, albeit the honour of a massacre, although by the Romans it was seen as a necessary and salutary punishment. It was carried out in two phases. As Pompey did not reach the battle zones in time to get a share of the main action, he was anxious that he could still partake in the victory. In this the fates were kind, because on his way south from Rome he met up with some 5,000 fugitives who had escaped from Spartacus' defeat. For Pompey this was highly fortuitous; he could still rescue something from the chaos at no expense to himself or his men. His troops quickly rounded them up and executed them. He then pre-empted Crassus by sending an urgent dispatch to the Senate in which he recorded the success of his mission, and claimed that while Crassus was, with difficulty, occupied with the gladiators, he had neutralised all possible further resistance.

The two would-be dynasts never quite trusted one another after this, but they did manage to cooperate in the second phase which the perpetrators regarded as an exemplary, if gratuitous, postscript to the war. They were intent on teaching the slave population an unforgettable lesson, regardless of the property rights of the slave-owners (Finley, 1980: 98–9). So they decided to exterminate their prisoners. When their troops had finished their grisly work, the road from Capua to Rome was lined with 6,000 crucified rebels.

The rebellion had taken over two years to suppress. It just may have brought about some mild amelioration in the working conditions of slaves, but it is certainly inaccurate to label Spartacus and his followers as social revolutionaries, as some Marxists have done. The rebellion failed for four main reasons. Firstly, and obviously, the rebel army was eventually confronted by well-trained, superior forces. No other army had proved ultimately successful against the Romans at this time, it was therefore highly unlikely that a courageous but rag-tag rebel force was going to do any better. It was certainly not going to hold out against them indefinitely. Realistically, their days were always numbered. Secondly, the rebels were divided among themselves. The leadership was not always agreed on what should be done next. There was no consistent common policy. True, they had a cause but there was no coherent sense of mission. Tactically, Spartacus put up a superb show, but the overall strategic planning was lacking simply because the range of possible long-term objectives was necessarily limited. The rank and file were hardly united as well. The rebels were a very motley band, and it has been cogently argued that 'national differences played an important, even fatal, part in the failure of their insurrection' (Vogt, 1974: 71). Thirdly, they had no clear support from any outside source – a factor which is seen to be vital in modern self-styled liberation movements. And, fourthly, and most critically, it had no secure base among the free population. It is true that many of the free poor sympathised with them, and some joined in the fight, but the response was patchy, at best. The ambivalence is understandable. Who wants marauding armies wandering over the countryside commandeering and even confiscating food and livestock? The poor were poor enough as it was, without further calls on their all-too-meagre resources. It is fairly obvious that the attitudes of the free poor were mixed, and in general characterised by a nervous ambivalence toward the whole enterprise. They both admired and feared the rebellion. As is so often the case in civil wars, the ordinary people neither win nor lose; they are relatively powerless no matter who is making the demands.

Perhaps, in the end, slaves have to lose simply because they are slaves. They are an underclass, and therefore are a suitable reference point in the status game for rich and poor alike. In the ancient world nobody supported them. Intellectuals often pitied the lot of the slave, but did not seriously question the need for slavery *as an institution*. Slavery was a *sine qua non* of ancient society; a vital factor in the economy and a necessary solution to the prisoner-of-war problem. Even the more radical thinkers, such as, the Greek Plato or the Roman Seneca – whether they were religious or secular – assumed that it would continue in any kind of 'better' society.

It is difficult to see how it all could have been otherwise given the prevailing ideology of slavery where the slave is regarded as both socially and psychologically inferior to free men. Whether this was a convenient rationalisation to accord with socio-economic requirements or whether it was always believed – or came to be believed – must remain a moot question. Perhaps it was something of both. To the modern mind the idea that certain people are inferior if they have been defeated in battle, or have surrendered ignominiously, is at least comprehensible. Or if the level of culture of those enslaved is patently inferior – a common conclusion in colonising situations in both the ancient and the modern world – the overwheening attitudes of the dominant culture become understandable. But where the slaves in question are not markedly different in culture or courage – as in the Roman/Greek situation – and a belief in the *inherent* superiority of one, and the *inherent* inferiority of the other is maintained, one is tempted to conclude that either the whole system was one of power and wealth sustained by the appropriate ideological justifications, or an evolved expedient to disguise their essential commonality.

# CHAPTER EIGHT

# Massacre as a Spectator Sport:
# The Roman games

There is some uncertainty as to how sport in Rome degenerated from exhibitions of prowess into scenes of death for entertainment. In the ancient world most sport had strong ritual connotations, so the idea of death as an aspect of sporting activity may have developed as a feature of the funeral games which were often held to commemorate the death of a leader or hero – a legacy of early Greece. The *Iliad* indicates such a practice during the Trojan War. The death of a combatant served as a votive offering to the gods; it may have acted as a kind of sacrifice either to the shades of the dead leader or to the gods themselves.

As far as the Romans are concerned, the evidence suggests that their gladiatorial games may well derive from their northern neighbours, the Etruscans. In some ways, these are rather a mysterious people. Considering that they were near-contemporaries of the classical Greeks about whom we have a fair knowledge, relatively little is known about the Etruscans who had a small but flourishing civilisation which was at its peak in the sixth century BC. The main problem is that although they have left us a number of artefacts and some most interesting tomb murals, we are still largely in the dark about their language. There is a grave paucity of written material, and what there is is still virtually indecipherable, so many of the questions we would like to ask about them have to go unanswered. They may originally have settled in northern Italy from Asia Minor which we know had well-established centres of horse-breeding and chariot-racing. This may well account for the development of equestrian sports in early Tuscany. Other contests were also arranged with prisoners of war as participants, and there are strong indications that these included forms of ritual sacrifice, possibly in honour of dead Etruscan warriors. The motif of human sacrifice appears frequently on Etruscan vases 'and Classical authors also refer to the sacrifice of . . . many hundreds of prisoners of war' (Olivova, 1984: 158). In time, this custom seems to have been superseded by contests in which prisoners were given a chance of survival by pitting their strength and skills against those of Etruscan warriors. Reliefs and carvings often depict some of the bloodier niceties of these games. Precise interpretation of some of the motifs is difficult, but another feature of Etruscan festivals appears to have been contests between men and beasts. For example, one decoration in what is called the Tomb of the Olympic Games shows what seems to be a blind man being torn apart by a wild animal. And similar themes are also presented elsewhere. In all, the Etruscans had a variety of games which included all sorts of heterogeneous elements from neighbouring cultures. The social composition of Etruscan society was reflected in these contests, with the more aristocratic strata indulging in equestrian sports, particularly chariot-racing, and the inferior strata involved in the more lethal proto-gladiatorial combats – a legacy which they bequeathed to their eventual conquerors, the Romans.

The military ascendancy of Rome took many years to evolve. From modest beginnings in the eighth century BC and a persistent struggle for survival among the other Latin tribes, Rome did not really make any appreciable impression on the Mediterranean world until the third century BC with her victories over the powerful maritime state of Carthage (modern Tunisia). Once established, she adopted a reasonably open-handed policy to former enemies to join her federation, and thus built up a formidable empire which lasted, in one form or another, for over a thousand years.

Rome's expansionist policies necessitated large, well-trained armies to fight her all-too-frequent wars. These developed from the early citizen militia to the famous legions whose military prowess was respected throughout southern Europe and the Near East. Her troops were trained in a wide range of skills which, certainly from the fourth century, were often demonstrated at festivals of games. And it was this highly cultivated professionalism of military expertise and organisation which marked her armies out from those of her potential enemies who often relied largely on mercenaries to fight their wars for them.

War had an important religious dimension, and this is reflected in some features of the festivals of games. It happened that the Etruscan New Year began in March, the beginning of the campaigning season, likewise the Romans held one of their main festivals in March in honour of Mars, the god of war. It may be that from the early days this was celebrated by chariot races as well as by traditional dances. More important was the festival in honour of Jupiter, the supreme Roman deity, which was held in May, and which also involved chariot races. But, more significantly, it also included the hurling of effigies into a river – a rite that may have symbolised the re-enactment of an ancient practice of throwing prisoners of war into the river as a sacrifice to the gods.

As Rome developed during the Republic, these rites became part of regular state procedures, and certain aspects of religion became formalised as state ritual. The gods were identified with state policies and aspirations; festivals became state holidays, and games (*ludi*) became part of the festivals. In some ways, this was very similar to the Greek position. Sport was a religious activity, and this religious dimension can be seen clearly in the rituals relating to war. Appropriate sacrifices were made before a campaign, partly to identify the omens, and partly to enlist the help of the gods to ensure success. More impressive were the rituals – or triumphs – to celebrate victory. In Rome, the conquering general was feted and rewarded publicly by being allowed to display the booty and parade his prisoners in the city before they were led away for execution. These triumphs often ended with public games, which became more secular in tone, and took on the function of entertainment rather than religious ritual.

From about 366 BC, these games became a separate institution. At first they were held exclusively in September when the games usually lasted for just one day, but later more festivals were added, until by c. 200 BC, five sets of games had been inaugurated, each lasting for several days. Early in the second century BC, Greek athletics, including foot races and wrestling, were introduced to the games, but contemporary evidence indicates that neither they nor the Greek theatrical performances were particularly popular with the Roman public. (There was a strange moral inconsistency here in that Greek displays were sometimes criticised for their nudity.) One suspects that the mass of spectators found these rather tame and were more attracted to the more exotic delights of the wild beast hunts (venationes) which were then becoming a permanent feature of the games.

The high point of the games became the gladiatorial contests. These began in 264 BC when a duel between three pairs of gladiators was staged for the first time. In 216 BC there were twenty-two pairs, in 200 BC twenty-five pairs, in 183 BC sixty pairs, and by 65 BC Julius Caesar arranged a contest between 320 pairs of gladiators clad in silver armour. Such contests were not technically part of the public games (ludi), but became extremely popular as spectacles (in Latin, murero; or in Greek, theatron, hence the idea of entertainment). As early as 160 BC, we find the public deserting drama for the more 'exciting' prospect of human slaughter, and by the following century, candidates for office were found seeking to win votes by financing such spectacles – one of the worst culprits being Julius Caesar himself, who ran up enormous debts to secure election to office. In 63 BC the Senate passed a law disqualifying from election any magistrate who financed such shows for the two years prior to voting (Carcopino, 1940: 231–2). But this was all to little avail.

All this coincided with an acute demographic problem. By the time of the late Republic, Rome had a vast population, many of whom had no visible means of support. From 58 BC wheat was distributed free to perhaps 25 per cent of the populace – for each recipient about two-fifths of the minimum subsistence allowance for the average family. This wheat dole cost the state about one-sixth of its revenues, but it was money well spent, not just as an act of charity, but as an innocuous expedient to keep the masses quiet. But the public craved not only bread but circuses (Juvenel's *panem et circenses*). So monumental buildings were erected to cater for this growing craze for sensational amusement. By the mid-first century AD, 159 days of the year were designated as holidays, 93 of them given over to games, largely at the state's expense. These became a necessary soporific for the masses, and it paid those in control to satisfy this demand with greater and more extravagant displays. Besides the Circus Maximus and the Circus Flaminius which were the traditional sports centres, especially for chariot-racing, five amphitheatres were built in Rome alone, quite apart from the numerous architectural clones found throughout the empire. The largest was the Colosseum built by the Emperor Vespasian (69–79 AD) which could accommodate over 50,000 spectators and which existed for little else other than the games. Beneath each amphitheatre were areas which were used for changing rooms, etc., besides providing housing for the various wild animals that were used in the games which by this time had become a major industry.

The economic implications of the games were staggering. First there was the enormous cost of building the amphitheatres themselves. These were complex, sometimes three-tiered structures (for example, the Colosseum), comprising, as we have seen, underground accommodation and commercial areas besides the arena itself. But this was just the beginning. Vast numbers of animals of all kinds had to be imported, involving the cost of capture and transportation, all to provide nauseating scenes of mass killing for amusement. When the Emperor Titus, for instance, inaugurated the Colosseum in 80 AD, 5,000 beasts were killed in one day, and in the *munera* of Trajan (d. 117 AD), generally considered to be one of Rome's more enlightened rulers, about 2,700 were slaughtered – carnage that seems both brutal and unnecessary by modern standards. The scale of the slaughter was so great that eventually it was difficult to find enough animals to kill. The empire was scoured for beasts, and high prices were paid for more exotic creatures, but the games finally succeeded in 'driving the hippopotamus from Nubia, the lion from Mesopotamia, the tiger from Hyrcania, and the elephant from North Africa' (Carcopino, 1940: 239).

Predictably, these operations were handled by special contractors (*lanistae*) who acted as the middlemen for this 'death-for-amusement' industry. They had an unenviable reputation even to those who commissioned them. They were seen as something between a worker in an abattoir and a procurer – people who were prepared to make money from any base transaction. They were almost certainly tied in with syndicates of prostitutes who hung about the amphitheatres. There seems to have been a well-attested correlation between sadistic and sexual excitement. It was the *lanistae*, too, who managed the schools of gladiators. They fed and housed the men, and negotiated with the city's officials (usually the *aediles*) when their services were required. These schools were run with prison-like discipline, and were usually well-served by those who could expect to lose half their number on any one engagement.

The gladiators themselves were frequently slaves or possibly former prisoners of war; sometimes they were members of the very lowest classes who, *in extremis*, had committed themselves to a contract to fight. Less frequently they were down-on-their-luck members of the upper classes who were either heavily in debt or seeking unconventional excitements. Gladiators could enlist from the age of eighteen and could actually be paid a bounty for joining. If they could then survive until they were thirty it was a supreme achievement. In that time, a man could expect to have over twenty combats, and one analysis shows that over a given period those who died between twenty and twenty-five had had only an average of seven combats each. Flamma, a particularly successful gladiator, had thirty-four contests of which he won twenty-one, had nine indecisive (drawn) combats, and was defeated four times but reprieved by the generosity of the crowd (Auguet, 1972: 179). But Flamma was an exception. Normally, accomplished gladiators might survive for as long as three years, and when their contracts expired actually be bought back for higher fees. Training was very harsh and the prospects unenviable, yet on rare occasions the benefits could be considerable, and gladiators enjoyed the kind of adulation which today is given to, say, champion prize-fighters. Nero (54–68 AD) rewarded his favourite with wealth and villas, and Caracalla (211–17 AD), who prided himself on his own prowess, pitted his favourite against three opponents in one day. It didn't work, but the man was given a brilliant funeral.

Gladiators had to be extremely brutal in order to survive. It was part of the gladiatorial ethos – the sub-culture of the *agon* (struggle) – that they knew not only how to kill but how to die. They had to be able to endure all day if necessary in scorching sun, often dripping from their wounds, always conscious of the need to secure the approval of the crowd. If they had to surrender, they were at the mercy of the dignitaries and the spectators. And if the verdict went against them, they knew it was a question of offering the throat to the sword without flinching. Some crowds, and particularly some Emperors, had scant respect for losers. Claudius (41–54 AD) for example, favoured contests in which only one man could survive (*sine missio*), and it is said that before the *coup de grâce* was given he liked the victim's visor to be raised so that he could see the expression on his face as he died. Claudius was not quite the studious eccentric that Robert Graves has depicted in *I Claudius*. In fact, he liked to be at the amphitheatre at dawn to witness the real butchery – that of the unarmed criminals or prisoners, and even went without lunch so as not to miss any of the delights of the arena. It is almost as though this rather elderly, feeble man who had more than enough trouble in his domestic life – and who eventually was almost certainly poisoned by his wife, the mother of the homicidal Nero – derived a strange perverted pleasure from other people's pain. But then he was by no means alone in this. He was just one of the more notable people that urged the contestants not to 'dance around' but to 'kill', 'cut his throat', etc.

The Roman games were practised throughout Roman-held territory. Quite extensive amphitheatres were built – and can still be seen – in places as far apart as Yugoslavia and Mesopotamia. In Tunisia alone, at least twenty are known to have existed, some little more than hollows in the hillsides, such was the enthusiasm for this form of spectacle. Even the high-minded Athenians were accused by Dio Chrysostom of a 'crazy infatuation' with gladiatorial shows when they were staged at the theatre of Dionysus (quoted in Wells, 1984: 274). What appears to modern minds as a kind of collective insanity was obviously common throughout Roman-held or Roman-influenced territories. It is important to stress, therefore, that they were not the function of a particular type of political structure; they were a feature of the Republic as well as the Empire. They should not then be specially associated with autocracy, although it must be said that they reached almost stupifying proportions under the Emperors. What is patently obvious from the evidence is that these often horrifying spectacles were carried on with state support, but largely at *public* demand.

As we have seen, the games took many forms. Chariot-racing, which was popularly associated with the Circus Maximus, may have begun in honour of Consus, the god of the underworld. It required considerable skill and training, and could – like, say, modern car racing – be very dangerous for the participants. Death and maiming were not uncommon, and there is some justification for believing that sometimes this did not occur accidentally. It had a fanatical following: respective teams (the Blues and the Greens) had their own discriminating devotees including the Emperors; successful drivers were feted and fortunes were made and lost on wagers. Ammianus Marcellinus, in the fourth century AD writes of 'this mass of people [who are] unemployed, and therefore with too much time on their hands, for [whom] the Circus Maximus is temple, home, social club and centre of all their hopes . . .' (quoted in Olivova, 1984: 177).

The beast hunts, which normally began at daybreak as an *hors d'oevre* to the main attractions, featured animals which were sometimes pitted against other animals – not unusually in bizarre combinations. The animals were frequently kept half-starved, and once in the arena were goaded and enraged with long lances and burning torches. Exotic scenes were sometimes contrived so that the fighting took place in forest and even marine settings. Presumably this gave an added *frisson* to the crowd. More commonly, animals were set against trained hunters, bowmen and swordsmen. This often took place on a massive scale. Julius Caesar (*c.* 100–44 BC), for example, organised a display involving 500 infantrymen as hunters, and during Nero's reign a spectacle was staged in which 400 boars and 300 lions were killed on just one occasion. For extra excitement, the hunter might be chained to the animal, and as a climax to the proceedings a gladiator might be promised his freedom if he could kill an elephant single-handed.

A variant of the hunt was that of sending in condemned criminals to the beasts. (The term *bestiarii* is used here. It can denote trained hunters, but in the literature usually means those condemned to the beasts.) This practice may have been copied from Carthage and first used for Roman army deserters. Needless to say, the Romans added various refinements. The condemned might face the animals armed or unarmed – or perhaps merely armed with dummy weapons. Sometimes they were tied to stakes to await their attackers; and even if they were only mauled, they were rarely spared because they were condemned to death anyway. The early Christians were often treated this way, as in the persecutions under the refined – almost ascetic – Emperor Marcus Aurelius in 177 AD. Jews too were similarly treated. Titus, who had conducted the sack of Jerusalem after the Jewish revolt in 66–73 AD, had 2,500 Jews killed in this way to celebrate the birthday of his brother Domitian. The execution of the Jews – so we are informed by Josephus (Jewish War vii 5) – was a popular measure and was greeted with 'shouts of universal applause'. One wonders what ever changes.

The high point of the spectacles was the gladiatorial contests which, in their own way, were as popular as chariot-racing. Normally, they were straightforward combats though often between differently trained contestants; for example, Samnites fought with shields and swords against the popular *retiarii* who carried nets and tridents. Again, there were variations, often dependent upon the whim of the autocrat. The unpredictable Caligula, for instance, who was sometimes known to condemn gladiators to death for cowardice, sometimes liked to force ordinary citizens into the arena for a novelty. But then anything like this could be expected from a man who did not hesitate to order the death of a king and his friends because their attire caused a sensation at the games – presumably outdoing that of the Emperor.

Fights did not have to be fair. It was not unusual to set trained men against amateurs. The whole exercise encouraged sadism and perversion, and even some Emperors were not above making a personal contribution to the proceedings although they had, of course, orchestrated things in such a way that they could hardly lose. Commodus (180–93 AD) fancied himself as a gladiator and sometimes pretended he was Heracles (Hercules) and killed cripples personally with a club; he also liked to butcher animals to the plaudits of the crowd. Domitian (81–96 AD) caused hilarity when he had women, dwarfs and cripples pitted against each other.

The scale of these displays was often quite incredible. Augustus produced 625 pairs of gladiators for the average spectacle – many of them actually fighting at once. Even mock sea battles were arranged. Augustus, who must take a great deal of responsibility for escalating the scale of these spectacles, once had an area 598 by 393 yards excavated and filled with water, and over two thousand contestants took part in a 'sea battle'. In another type of marine spectacle, Nero, who perhaps surprisingly was not that keen on gladiatorial contests, had polar bears killing seals. The spectacle was also a convenient way of dealing with unwanted prisoners of war. Trajan, after his successful campaign in Dacia (roughly modern Romania) brought back 50,000 prisoners. Some 10,000 of these, many quite unskilled in armed combat, were made to fight one another and the remainder were sold into slavery.

These carnivals of slaughter provided good vicarious enjoyment for the non-combatant crowd. They generated a kind of mass hysteria. Gladiators were heroes, exemplified in their salutation to the Emperor when entering the arena, 'those who go to the death, greet thee'. They were fervently admired and had their 'groupies' in all classes of the population. The whole system had such public approval that few were prepared to offer any criticisms. Indeed, on one occasion a monk tired to stop a contest by running into the arena and was promptly killed for his pains.

Although the games continued for some years after Rome officially became Christian, it was undoubtedly the teaching of the new faith which gradually undermined its more abhorrent practices. There is some degree of poetic justice here because it was Christians, together with the Jews, who probably suffered disproportionately more than others from the cruelty of the games. Yet this presents us with an interesting anomaly. Normally the Romans were reasonably tolerant about such matters as race and religion. They often recruited some of their best troops from the provinces, and they did not usually worry too much about foreign religions which they sometimes actually imported, such as the worship of Isis from Egypt and Cybele from Asia Minor. Perhaps the key to the problem was that Jews and Christians were intolerant of the Romans.

It is here that we must make some distinction between belief and practice (as opposed to mere ritual). Jews, particularly from the Roman point of view, were troublesome and rebellious, and therefore had to be suppressed. As we have seen, Titus, who was generally regarded as a more tolerant ruler, was merciless to Jews. And the Christians were regarded as a mysterious cult who were thus suspect and misunderstood – something that can be clearly seen in the misperceptions of such eminent Roman writers as Tacitus and Suetonius. Worse still, Christians tended to be anti-state and anti-Emperor, and if they did not recant were often condemned to the arena. Rome could be very easy-going with its subjects, but only so long as they toed the line.

Even distinguished Roman intellectuals were strangely ambivalent about the games. Cicero, writing in the first century BC, before the cruelties and the excesses were at their worst, condemned pointless murder: 'can a cultured man delight in seeing some poor devil torn apart by a beast or transfixed by a lance?' But he also applauded the bravery and self-control of the gladiator, and insisted that 'these barbarians' gave an example to 'others of finer sensibilities [because] no lesson in how to endure in the face of pain and death could be more efficacious' (quoted in Auguet, 1972: 191–2). Pliny the Younger, writing over a century later could still say that the games inspired the highest virtues of courage and the desire for glory. Seneca too, in the early Empire, one of the most respected philosopher-statesmen of his day, and one-time – and possibly disappointed – tutor to Nero, condemned spectacles in which unarmed men were driven into the arena with whips and branding-irons, and then slaughtered. Yet in some respects he was somewhat divided on the matter. He approved of 'true' combats between trained contestants, but deplored the senseless butchery of condemned men. As a stoic and a man very conscious of his class, he seems to have been more intolerant of the 'rabble' baying for blood than the actual killings themselves.

It is this undoubted ambiguity about the horrors of the games which was the crime of the intellectuals. Many clearly saw the evils for what they were but did not speak out against them in a forthright way. But perhaps that was too much to expect at the time. It was left to certain Hellenized philosophers, poets and historians such as Plutarch, Lucian and Dio Chrysostom to speak openly against the spectacles, and Early Church Fathers such as Tertullian to sound the death knell to such practices.

When military conquests are made and prisoners are taken, there are only a few options open to the conqueror. To take the extremes, prisoners can be either magnanimously released or summarily executed, but many conquerors – perhaps most in the ancient world – did not resort to either of these expedients. There were all kinds of intermediate arrangements.

Sometimes important prisoners would be released on payment of a ransom, possibly others would be enslaved. A quite common 'solution' was the execution of the males, particularly those of military age, and the enslavement of the women and children. This effectively neutralised the possibilities of future insurrection, and showed a profit into the bargain.

What we have considered is a somewhat bizarre variant of this. It was the 'logical' no-nonsense Romans who decided not to a make virtue of necessity so much as an entertainment of necessity. They were glutted with slaves; they already had a huge reservoir of unemployed labour with more time than they knew what to do with, so why not keep one group happy at the expense of another? This does not 'explain' the games, or the continuing and horrifying fascination they had for the Roman proletariat, but it does indicate one particular dimension of politico-economic expediency which is singular in both form and extent to the Roman world.

# CHAPTER NINE

# Massacre as a Succession Device: Achaemenid Persia

The eminent economist, J. K. Galbraith has cogently argued that 'modern mass horror now results, if anything, less from international conflict than from internal conflict and massacre. The most elementary requirement of a new world order is the need to stop internal butchery' (Galbraith, 1991). Correct as he obviously is about slaughter on the international scale, it is also obvious that *internal* conflict is no new thing. As we have seen, especially from our studies on classical society, class antagonisms, in the broad sense of that term, have been with us for a very long time, and often gave rise to the most appalling atrocities. But there is another kind of internal conflict which has little to do with class issues, but which merits some attention, namely, that within royal families over the matter of succession. This problem has generated the most awful blood-letting in a number of societies, particularly in the Middle East, of which few have been worse than Achaemenid Persia.

The Persians first became a power in the Middle East with the demise of the great empires of Assyria and then Babylonia. A Persian prince, Kyrash of Ansham, later known to us as Cyrus the Great, united with the Median tribes to overthrow Babylonian control in 539 BC. After an impressive series of conquests, he was succeeded by his son, Cambyses, who, after killing his brother, a rival claimant to the throne, took on the task of extending the empire. He had already inherited the throne of Babylon from his father, and he went on to conquer further territories including Egypt where he was proclaimed Pharaoh. By the time of his death (522 BC) the boundaries of the Persian empire stretched from the Nile to the Caspian Sea.

These extensive and rapid conquests had given little time for consolidation, and the empire went through a period of unrest and the trauma of rebellion which was put down by the nobles who had the conspirators executed. The throne then passed to a distant member of the Achaemenid family, Darayavaush (Dareios or Darius), who acted decisively to secure his position and restore the authority of the monarchy. Provincial governors (satraps) were brought into line, and those that tried to set up independent principalities were given very short shrift. Notable among these was Oroites who not only wanted to establish his own independence but also wanted to take over other satrapies as well. He lured the uncompliant tyrant of the offshore island of Samos, Polycrates, to the mainland and had him impaled, and then turned on a fellow satrap and killed both him and his son. Herodotus tells the colourful story of how Darius decided to employ cunning rather than direct force on Oroites and sent a courier with sealed letters for the guard with instructions to kill him. In this way he tested the loyalty of his scribe and the courier, and the guards themselves, and got rid of a powerful but rebellious satrap who governed much of Asia Minor and had considerable forces at his disposal (Herodotus, 3, 127). Darius didn't believe in taking chances, and in Egypt he went so far as to execute one of his satraps simply because he suspected that given the opportunity he *might* revolt.

Darius was extremely industrious in both extending and reorganising his empire, but although his sovereignty was absolute, he was still under an obligation to respect the customary privileges of the Persian aristocracy. The empire was divided into twenty satrapies (though this figure is disputed and may only represent those with formal tax obligations) and Darius controlled these through a council of nobles from which orders went via the bureaucracy to the satraps in the provinces. The satraps had considerable autonomy, and were sometimes ruled like personal fiefdoms although there were understandably certain restrictions on their military functions. Theoretically, they could only initiate military action if it was sanctioned by the Great King who employed an army of inspectors to monitor their activities. In addition to these, in each province there was an official whose specific task was to ensure the regular collection of the royal taxes. All the provinces had to contribute fixed amounts to the royal treasury, in all some 14,500 silver talents, of which about a third came from the Indian satrapy. In addition, they were expected to make contributions in kind; this could be very demanding as with, say, the satrapy of Babylon which was expected to feed the army for a third of the year (Ghirshman, 1978: 144). In order to link the different parts of this huge, unwieldy empire together and facilitate both tax collection and communications, Darius commissioned a network of roads (the most impressive before the Romans) the most notable of which was the Royal Road which stretched 1,677 miles from Susa in Persia to Ephesus in the west.

Local administration was in the hands of the subject peoples themselves who appear to have had an appreciable degree of liberty providing they were appropriately subservient and paid their dues on time. Dreams of secession were not on the agenda, and any attempts at real freedom were ruthlessly crushed, as happened when a number of Greek cities on the Ionian coast revolted in the early fifth century BC. The tyrant of one of these, the city of Miletus, feared that his standing with the Great King was in doubt and instigated a revolt by calling on the other cities to proclaim their independence from Persia (499). In practice this meant getting them to refuse to contribute any longer to the State's coffers. A number of the coastal towns rallied to the call including some in Persian-dominated Cyprus, and for a while they thought that they might just have succeeded. Darius was slow and ponderous in his response. His empire was rather like a huge, ill-programmed robot that suddenly finds something tapping insistently at its feet. Finally, in 497, he acted by enlisting the help of other subject peoples in the vicinity, especially the maritime Phoenicians, and his task was made that much easier by the disunity among the rebels themselves. Many of the most important rebel cities deserted the cause, and by 494 the only main contender left was Miletus, the city that had started it all. It was besieged by the Persians who deployed a force of 600 ships. Yet, despite defections, Miletus held out for another two years. When it was eventually captured its fate was dire indeed. The city was razed to the ground; most of the men were butchered and the rest of its inhabitants enslaved (492). The fleet continued on to the cities of Chalcedon and Byzantium which were also burnt, and to the neighbouring islands of Chios and Lesbos where youths were made eunuchs and deported to the Persian court, and girls were sent to its harems (Ghirshman, 1978: 150).

The Persian nobility liked neither subjects nor satraps with aspirations, and the records – perhaps exaggerated – indicate the most ruthless treatment of rebels, involving torture, mutilation and death. They also extol the most fanatical loyalty of Darius' intimates. Herodotus relates that when Darius was conducting a very prolonged and unproductive siege of the rebellious city of Babylon, his friend, Zopyrus, approached him with a bizarre plan for its capture. The siege had already lasted many months and looked like going on for many more, the Babylonians having strangled many of their women to conserve what few food supplies they had. Zopyrus deliberately cut off his nose and ears and shaved his head as though he were a criminal, and lashed his body with a whip. He then 'fled' to Babylon posing as a man who had been punished by the Persians and who was now seeking revenge for his mutilation. The Babylonians didn't know whether to believe him but entrusted him with a modest force to engage the Persians, and Darius allowed a thousand of his men to be slain in order to maintain the subterfuge. This same costly stratagem was employed twice more, and then the trap was sprung when Zopyrus, now completely trusted, was put in charge of guarding the wall. At the opportune moment, Darius' troops were let into the city. They destroyed its gate and its defences and impaled three thousand of its leading citizens. The hero, Zopyrus, was then made its governor and exempted from taxes for life (Herodotus, 3, 152–7).

Darius' military campaigns spearheaded by his *corps d'élite*, the Immortals, took him as far as India, and to southern Russia where they spent a frustrating time trying to get to grips with the Scythians in a campaign which reputedly cost 80,000 men. Fearing that his lines of communication were becoming too extended and running short of men and supplies, Darius turned west, passing over the Bosphorus on the famed bridge of boats. He fared well in Thrace (largely modern Bulgaria) until he found himself in more difficulties in his abortive encounter with the Greeks (490) who – whatever he might have thought – did not regard themselves as being within the Persian sphere of influence.

The long reign of Darius really represents the zenith of Achaemenian achievement. This is particularly evident in its art and architecture. The palaces, in scale and grandeur, were some of the most magnificent in the ancient world. These were found at the main capital, Susa, and the former capital at Ecbatana which also served as a summer resort for the court. In a tri-lingual inscription found at Susa we find that workers from all over the empire were recruited for work on these edifices, and materials were often brought to Persia from quite remote areas. Babylonians made the bricks, the stone-cutters were Ionians and Lydians, and the gold-smiths were Egyptians and Medes. Cedar came from Lebanon, special woods from Gandhara; lapis lazuli came from Sogdiana and turquoise from Khwarezin, while gold was brought from Bactria and Sardis (Frye, 1976: 108). The ceremonial capital at Persepolis was legendary for its wealth and splendour. Among its buildings was a vast central terrace where the audience hall (apadana) – the 'hall of a hundred columns' – was approached by monumental stairways flanked by reliefs of tribute bearers. All of this of course, testified to the glory of the Great King himself, and to the favour that he found with the gods to whom, in declaration, at least, he always gave honour and precedence. It was left to Alexander and his friends during a drunken spree, intentionally or unintentionally, to start a fire which virtually destroyed this magnificent complex (330).

The death of an Achaemenian monarch was almost invariably attended by a struggle for the succession, and this usually meant palace *coups* and assassinations. Rivalry and intrigue – and not a little corruption – were commonplace before the succession was a settled issue. In some other societies this problem was largely obviated by one or another of a variety of control mechanisms. After all, there are a number of ways in which societies can make priority-statements which will give legitimate precedence to one claimant rather than another and thus eliminate, or at least reduce, socially divisive disputation (Carlton, 1977: 14–16). There was the practice of royal incest as found most notably in ancient Egypt and pre-conquest Peru. This ensured the continuation of an uncontaminated royal line, and theoretically outlawed the counter-claims of other royal children that were sometimes made by their concubine mothers.

Closely related to this expedient was the claim to cosmic birth. The insistence that the claimants in question were really divine progeny, if believed, could often ensure a successful and relatively trouble-free succession. Of course, these and other variants did not always succeed, but their continued acceptance in many societies testifies to the general effectiveness of such pragmatic fictions.

If all else failed, royal houses could always fall back on rival elimination – the Achmaenenian solution. By custom, the first son born *after* the crowning of the king was regarded as the heir-apparent, but, in practice, this was usually contested by others, especially in the later days of the dynasty. In order to ensure that no one but his children could claim descent from the founder, Darius married Cyrus' surviving daughters and granddaughter, but the son who by tradition should have been heir did not succeed to the throne in 486 when Darius died (Cook, 1983: 74). Instead the title went to a designated successor, Xerxes who had learnt the trade as viceroy at Babylon for twelve years, and was therefore reasonably well equipped to take command of the empire.

Xerxes, however, had inherited a problem from his father that just would not go away – what to do about the European Greeks. Darius had made the mistake of sending a punitive expedition to Greece where its commander, Datis, besieged the small town of Eretria which, although hopelessly divided along class lines – a common situation in classical city-states – determined to resist the aggressor. But there was some sympathy for the stabilising benefits of Persian autocracy among some Greeks; later history would show that there were always those who were either intimidated by Persian power or influenced by its 'golden archers' (the Persian daric coins). Thus Eretria was betrayed by a few 'medizers', and the town was burnt and its inhabitants enslaved. This was a serious error of judgement because it united other Greeks who were now resolved to counter Persian oppression. So when Datis disembarked his troops on the plain at Marathon he was completely outclassed by what was impressionistically a much inferior force (490). Darius was extremely annoyed by the failure of his troops, but the losses were of minor importance to a monarch who felt that his power was such that he could obliterate the Greeks any time he chose. They were just an irritation, and, anyway, he had far bigger problems on his hands with a revolt in Egypt. By the time of his death four years later he had never actually got around to doing anything decisive about the Greeks. It was now left to Xerxes to teach them a lesson.

What happened next is well known. Xerxes placed himself under the protection of the gods, offered the requisite libations – casting a cup, a bow and a sword into the waters – and mounted a huge campaign in the west with an army drawn from 46 'nations' and commanded by 29 generals. Some idea of Xerxes temperament can be gleaned from the story in Herodotus (7, 37–41) of a rich Lydian who, having entertained Xerxes and his troops on their way to Sardis (481–80), had the temerity to ask the king if his son could be excused military service. Xerxes was enraged that a minion should request such a favour and had the boy cut in two and displayed on the gates of Sardis as a warning against presumption. Some Greek cities did not resist and went over to the enemy, especially in Macedonia and, to some extent, Boiotia. Others which did resist were harshly treated; much of Athens itself was destroyed, and the defence of its Acropolis resulted in the burning of its temples and the deaths of its defenders. But in the end the Athenians and the Spartans – normally such uneasy bedfellows – and their respective allies valiantly defeated the Persians both on land and at sea (480–79).

History hasn't been too kind to Xerxes. He has been remembered as a weak and vacillating monarch who was dominated by his eunuchs, and as the person who launched the 'insane attack' on European Greece (Olmstead, 1970: 230). But this was no more than a setback for the man who re-conquered Egypt and Babylon, which were both treated with incredible brutality. After this initial period of military activity, Xerxes settled down to court life and to the completion of the building plans that had been made by his father.

The Persian court was the 'oriental' court, *par excellence*. It was fabled as a centre of opulence; the display of wealth amazed those foreign visitors who feigned to despise its decadence. The tapestries, carpets and furnishings bespoke extreme riches. The cost of maintaining the nobility, the staff and the bureaucracy was enormous – just one meal might cost as much as 400 talents. To add to the expense, Achaemenian kings normally keep harems of 360 concubines – modest by the standards of later times. Many of them travelled with him though always in closed carriages, attended by eunuchs. Their duties were not confined to the mandatory sexual favours, but extended to less exotic entertainments such as music and dancing – not unlike those of a Greek courtesan (*hetaira*). Plutarch, writing much later about the magnificence of court life, says that when the king presented himself, his clothes and jewellery alone were worth about 12,000 talents (quoted in Cook, 1983: 138). It is little wonder that Greeks who were unaccustomed to such wealth either marvelled at what they saw or impugned such extravagance, or that they began to cast envious eyes on the Persian empire.

The court was also characterised by ritual obsequiousness towards the king although the adulation seems to have been more for the office than the person. Courtiers and officials were expected to prostrate themselves before him (*proskynesis*), a practice which the Greeks found degrading, and which disgusted the Macedonian conquerors in the fourth century when Alexander adopted the practice. Technically, all the Great King's subjects were his slaves, and he had power of life and death over them, and all property was also at the king's disposal. But although he was careful never to claim divinity for himself, because he was divinely *endowed* with the reins of justice he was therefore theoretically infallible. In practice, of course, being a mere mortal, he was subject to certain constraints. A powerful monarch was still at liberty to do more or less as he pleased, but he had to watch his back. His greatest enemies were likely to be members of his own family.

The Achaemenids were not quite as murderous as some later ruling houses such as those of the Parthians or the Ottomans, or even the Safarids, the ruling dynasty in Persia in the sixteenth and seventeenth centuries, who had the unpleasant habit of blinding possible rivals for the throne. But family feeling was not always as close as it might have been. The court was racked with intrigue, and Xerxes had one of his brothers and his brother's sons murdered for plotting against him. Hostility built up, and Xerxes, as a precaution against assassination, refused to allow people into his presence who did not keep their hands in their sleeves. Eventually, in 465, a member of his own guard, Artabanus, together with a eunuch servant and one of Xerxes sons-in-law murdered the king is his bedroom. He left three legitimate sons, Darius, Hystaspes and the youngest Artaxerxes, and such was brotherly love that after the murder of Xerxes, Artabanus contrived to pin the crime on Darius, and have him killed by Artaxerxes who then became king. He then tried to go one better by killing Artaxerxes, but in trying to do so was himself killed so leaving Artaxerxes to fight it out successfully with his surviving brother, Hystaspes.

After this rather unsavoury and inauspicious beginning, Artaxerxes enjoyed a long reign punctuated by the customary insurrections and revolts. These were mainly confined to the outer reaches of the empire, where the burden of Persian domination were most keenly felt. The problem was the level of taxation which subject peoples came increasingly to resent. For example, in the time of Xerxes, as we have seen, the Indians paid 360 talents in gold every year, the highest tribute in terms of actual value; Libya and Egypt gave 700 silver talents; and Babylonia – so harshly treated for its recalcitrance – paid a 1,000 talents of silver. This, together with payments in produce, gradually increased so that by the time of Artaxerxes, the situation became intolerable. Despite these difficulties, the king survived until 424 when he apparently died of natural causes. We have to say 'apparently' because tradition has it that his queen died the same day. If this is true, the deaths have to be a little suspicious unless, of course, the poor lady decided voluntarily to accompany her late husband to the grave.

The death of Artaxerxes was followed by a period of quite sickening violence among the nobility. Artaxerxes had three possible successors, all technically illegitimate sons, reputedly of Babylonian concubines. Each made claims, and each appears to have been aided and abetted by palace eunuchs in their efforts to secure the throne. The immediate successor (Xerxes II) was murdered in his bed after a drunken party by another son, Sogdianos, after he had reigned only forty-five days. But the usurper Sogdianos had reckoned without the machinations of the third son, Ochos, who had married his scheming half-sister, Parysatis, who was even more unscrupulous than her husband. Sogdianos had already alienated the palace guard by killing their commander in a personal quarrel, so when Ochos raised an army and was joined by palace troops as well as the powerful satrap of Egypt, Sogdianos was forced to surrender and executed after having reigned just over six months. Ochos seized the throne and took the title Darius II. He began his reign by having a courtier stoned to death for burying Xerxes II without permission, then went on to eliminate others that were regarded as possible threats to his position. The reign was an uneasy one. There were fluctuating relations with the Greeks; it was the time of the Peloponnesian War between Athens and Sparta, and the Persians intervened politically and economically wherever they could see some advantage to themselves. They certainly influenced the outcome of the war by their financial support for Sparta. There were also revolts in Syria, Egypt and elsewhere by some of Darius' own satraps, and in one insurrection he was forced to kill his own son-in-law for treason.

Like his predecessor, Darius did not lead his military expeditions in person, but managed successfully to conduct affairs from the comfort of the palace which was riddled with plotting and dissension. He died in 405/4 having stored up yet more trouble for the state by succumbing to his wife's pleas that the most important satrapies in Asia Minor should be bestowed upon her son Cyrus – an honour which jeopardised the future of the legitimate heir, another Artaxerxes. When the older son succeeded to the throne, Cyrus, always ready to do his mother's bidding, is reported to have tried to murder his brother while he was putting on his coronation finery. He was caught in the act, and would have been executed had it not been for the emotional entreaties of his mother. Artaxerxes pardoned Cyrus and even allowed him to return to his satrapies; but he was to rue the day when he let his treacherous sibling go free.

In less than three years Cyrus, who had already murdered two of his cousins for not paying him due homage, was back with his own troops and a formidable army of Greek mercenaries to challenge Artaxerxes for the throne. In the battle, which was fought at Kounaxa near Babylon in 401, the rebel army nearly won, but Cyrus, carried away by the prospect

of almost certain victory, tried to kill his brother personally and failed
and was slain instead. Artaxerxes was no longer prepared to excuse
youthful impetuosity; he had Cyrus' body mutilated and his head was
paraded before the army. The mercenaries were then allowed to leave
after their leaders had been summarily punished. New leaders were
elected and the subsequent trek of the mercenary army back to Greece
amidst terrible hardships has become one of the great sagas of Greek
history (Xenophon: *The Persian Expedition*).

Although Artaxerxes had managed to get things sorted out with the
mainland Greeks, the internal state of the empire was giving increased
cause for concern. Taxation generated further troubles. Egypt had
revolted and had still not been successfully re-conquered, and now the
western provinces, Cyprus, Phoenicia and Syria all proclaimed their
independence, and these were followed by territories in Asia Minor. This
was met with savage repression, but this only served to increase the
rising tide of discontentment. The situation became so bad that rebel
satraps started to issue their own coinage – the ultimate act of defiance
to the central government. A protracted struggle ensued and the empire
was only saved by the fact that the satraps fell out among themselves;
one was assassinated by his colleagues, and another was betrayed by his
own son and crucified.

The long reign of Artaxerxes was one of almost uninterrupted decline.
Things were bad enough in the empire, but in some ways there was even
more disappointment in his own family. His eldest son, the Crown
Prince, conspired against him and was executed. He then had high hopes
of one of his illegitimate sons, but he too was murdered. Of his other
two legitimate sons, one committed suicide, perhaps 'encouraged' by the
other, Ochos, who then became king as Artaxerxes II (359–8).

From the outset the new king was determined to stop the rot, and he
began by having all possible claimants to the throne killed – in all, this
ran to several dozen half-brothers and sisters. He then set about putting
the empire to rights by suppressing the satrapal revolts and attacking the
rebel strongholds. Typical was his assault on the city of Sidon in modern
Lebanon. He executed the governor and burnt its buildings. Many of its
citizens tragically – perhaps voluntarily – died in the conflagration and
others were deported. Egypt was reconquered, and the Pharaoh fled to
Ethiopia where cities were razed, temples pillaged and priests killed
unless they paid enormous ransoms.

The reign ended somewhat like it began – with a palace *coup* (338).
Artaxerxes was murdered, poisoned by his doctor together with nearly
all his sons on instructions from Bagoas, a eunuch usurper who held
high military office. One son was spared and set up as a puppet king,
but, realising the precariousness of his position, tried to oust Bagoas and

was himself killed, together with his family, having reigned less than two years. A possible successor, Kodomannos, was found who had no illusions about the scheming kingmaker, and before he joined the casualty list, was able to force Bagoas to drink the poison that apparently was meant for himself.

For all his early promise, Kodomannos, who reigned as Darius III, was not up to the task that he had inherited. The empire was over-extended and ripe for dissolution. For a determined enemy, it was there for the taking – and there have been few military dynasts more deter-mined than Alexander the Great. The preliminary plans for the conquest were laid by his father, Philip II of Macedon, and when Philip was assassinated in 336, the young Alexander set out with a relatively small but highly trained army to conquer what was perhaps the greatest empire the world had ever seen. Whether such a campaign was really 'necessary' is disputable. Ostensibly it was an act of revenge for the Persian invasion of Greece 150 years before, but this now appears as a flimsy justification for a war that would bring untold wealth to the conquerors. Alexander fought a series of brilliant and, at times, particularly brutal battles which eventually brought him an empire that was just as unmanageable as it had been for the Achaemenids (Carlton, 1992). After his early death, it broke up into a number of reasonably viable sub-empires ruled by his warring, ambitious subordinates. As for the last of the Achaemenid Great Kings, he was ignominiously, and characteristically, killed by a kinsman, Bessos, and his companions during their frantic attempt to elude the pursuing Macedonians. Alexander had little patience with regicide, so Bessos was harried and caught, condemned by a specially convened Persian council and then mutilated and executed. Alexander set a pattern for the future. Everybody's fate was now in the hands of the new master of the world. It was to be a mercifully temporary interlude, because Alexander, for all his military and organisational genius, was no less a despot than his Persian predecessors.

# CHAPTER TEN

# Massacre and Counter-massacre: Turks, Greeks and Armenians

Massacres are most likely to take place in circumstances where a dominant power is carrying out a policy of repression in relation to a subordinate or subject state. Sometimes, of course, it is the dominated people that commit atrocities either as revenge or as part of a campaign of insurrection and terrorism in the cause of 'liberation' (see Chapters 16 and 17). And occasionally there is a variant of this. For example, the situation in which there is an escalation of emnity over a long period of time between two societies who indulge in massacre and counter-massacre. Such was the case of the Turks and the Greeks, particularly in the last century or so, the repercussions of which are still with us today.

The Turkish Ottoman Empire ruled much of the Middle East as well as territories in Europe from the fourteenth century when it overwhelmed the Serbs and the Bulgars who had both found it quite impossible to pacify the Balkans. The Turks received some setbacks when they came into conflict with the predatory Tartar armies led by the ruthless Timur Lenk, but they extended their power considerably with the conquest of the Byzantine Empire in the mid-fifteenth century. The Empire reached its zenith in the following century with the defeat of both Egypt and Syria, and the accession of its greatest ruler, Suleiman the Magnificent. In its formative years, its army was mainly composed of feudal peasants and a household bodyguard of slaves that was expanded into a standing army (the Janissaries). The Janissaries had a personal allegiance to the Sultan although, technically, as slaves they were always liable to summary execution. This gave the army a strange kind of internal stability, and it developed into a formidable and much-feared fighting force.

Another factor making for stability was the Ottoman 'solution' to the problem of succession. Mehmed I (d. 1421) had fought his brothers for twelve years before he felt safe as Sultan, and his successor, Murad II (d. 1444) had similar problems. So Mehmed II, the conqueror of Constantinople, introduced a new clause into the 'Code of Laws of the House of Osman' which effectively outlawed rival claimants to the throne. Whoever was next in succession had the right to slay all his brothers and their sons. It was impious to shed royal blood, so they were strangled with a silk bowstring – a death reserved for them alone. Mehmed III (d.

1603), for instance, had nineteen princes put to death, but even so his 'grief' had to be assuaged, so he was given 50 virgins and 500 concubines by way of compensation. This practice was regarded as a small price to pay to avoid dynastic wars and civil strife. As one contemporary put it, the death of a prince is less regrettable than the loss of a province (quoted in Lewis 1971: 22).

In the sixteenth century, the Turks conquered the strategically important island of Rhodes, and also took Tunis and Algiers. In 1570, they took Cyprus and displayed the heartlessness for which they became renowned by massacring 20,000 inhabitants and flaying the governor alive. They seemed invincible, but *en route* they had made too many bad friends. Those that were not yet greatly affected decided that enough was enough. The Spanish and the Venetians collaborated to defeat them at sea at Lepanto, and their eastern borders were threatened by the might of Persia. Their incursions to the north were also brought to a halt by the powerful Habsburg Empire which controlled much of central Europe. And so there began a long and painful period of decline punctuated by occasional revivals such as the drive along the Danube basin and the siege of Vienna. Here the Turks were only just held until a huge combined army arrived to save the situation. The defeated Turkish commander was beheaded by order of his superior, and such was Turkish discipline that even the Grand Vizier was probably fortunate not to have been impaled (Bowle, 1979: 430). This was really the turning-point for the Ottomans. Their lines were vastly over-extended, and their structures were unable to sustain an empire of this magnitude.

The Turks were still a powerful force, but their great days were now over. In the eighteenth century, the Empire suffered defeats at the hands of the Russians, and in the early nineteenth century by revengeful Serbs. Again, there was revival, and the Turks launched ferocious attacks on the Serbs. In the orgy of slaughter that followed, their armies were allowed to kill any male Serb over the age of fifteen. Such were their policies in relation to the Balkans.

This brings us to our primary concern, the relationship between the Ottomans and Greece which they had controlled since 1460. Except for a brief interlude when Greece endured a partial Venetian occupation (1686–1715), they retained that control until the Greek War of Independence which lasted from 1821 to 1832. Greek resistance to Turkish rule had begun in 1770 when the Turks were having problems with Russia to whom they had to make a number of territorial concessions. Russia's pressure on Turkey continued in the nineteenth century, and would have increased had it not been for the Russian preoccupation with the Napoleonic invasion (1812).

By the early nineteenth century much of the Turkish Empire was in ferment. The Turks had proved their capacity to conquer, but they were not able to assimilate their subject peoples, especially the Greeks. And by this time, even the capacity to conquer had begun to diminish. Their elite *corps*, the Janissaries, had become disaffected and mutinous, and consequently less effective. Eventually they had to be disbanded. Turkish officials had become even more corrupt, and had little respect in the conquered territories; their administration was often brutal and not particularly efficient. And the once powerful and aggressive sultans had become 'haunters of the harems' (Revill, 1962: 562), seeking solace among the odalisques and accommodating bath attendants of the seraglio.

The situation was now such that despite the modest reforms of the reigning Sultan, Mahmoud II, the Empire was considerably diminished in size. He was fortunate that, within limits, he could take some advantage of the political hustling that was going on in Europe. Elsewhere, however, things were not quite so bright. The Russians were a menace, and the Egyptians were increasingly restive, but the biggest immediate problem was the Greeks. It was these fortuitous diversions that gave the dissident Greek elements the opportunity to revolt. Hostilities started initially in the Peloponnese, and, at first, the insurrection was savagely repressed. There followed a further revolt by an ambitious minion, Ali Pasha, who tried to set up an independent state in Epirus (modern Albania). This sparked off a popular uprising, and led to full-scale war.

Except for the Greeks in Constantinople who, in general, had prospered under Turkish rule, Greek subjects had suffered badly from Turkish oppression. So once the revolt was underway, in some areas peasants murdered almost every Muslim they could find. In one town alone, Tripolitza, 8,000 were slaughtered indiscriminately. And, in all, perhaps some 20,000 were killed – a fact that has been largely overlooked in the light of Turkish oppression.

This was all too much for the Turks. They regarded arbitrary oppression as their particular prerogative; they were certainly not going to allow this kind of treatment to go unpunished. Their retaliation was swift and calculated. They turned first on the more favoured Greeks. The leading Greeks in Constantinople were executed, including the Patriarch who was almost certainly not involved in any subversive activity. Four bishops and thousands of other Greeks were killed, but still the revolt gathered momentum. The blood-letting continued on both sides for four years, and still the Sultan seemed unable to do much about it. The Greeks were successful in forming a fleet and liberating parts of central Greece, yet, at first, these efforts went unrecognised by the world at large. European statesmen took little notice, '. . . feeling much as Metternich did when writing in 1821 "it matters not much if over there beyond our frontiers three or four hundred thousand people get hung, strangled or impaled" ' (Barber, 1972: 132).

Slowly attitudes began to change. There was a growing sympathy with Greek aspirations. Adventurers and romantics such as Byron who were not immune to the spell of a bygone, idealised civilisation, hastened to support the cause. The Turk's situation worsened and they called upon Egypt, a vassal state, for assistance. Egypt at this time was under the undisputed authority of Mehemet Ali, a shrewd but illiterate peasant who was a gifted and ruthless military leader. Mehemet was not to be trifled with. He had already consolidated his control by eliminating a powerful rival faction, the Mamelukes, by inviting 500 of their leaders to a meal in Cairo and butchering all of them, except one. At first, he had considerable success against the Greeks, but world opinion became incensed by the Turkish–Egyptian barbarities. The Europeans decided to intervene, though their intention was undoubtedly tinged with partisan interest. The English and the French, in particular, wanted neither a strong Turkey nor a strong Russia. They were all a little nervous of each other; helping the Greeks was just one move in a deft political game. Nevertheless, at Navarino, the British, Russian and French fleets combined to destroy much of the obsolete Turkish navy (1827). Then the Turks again became increasingly embroiled with the Russians (1828–29), and this further distracted the ailing Ottomans from taking the customary reprisals on the Greeks. Finally, the British sent their fleet to Alexandria to neutralise possible Turkish activity in the Mediterranean; the Russians advanced on Adrianople, and the French occupied Morea. The Turks could not possibly continue, so the British, anxious to forestall further Russian 'appropriations' called a conference to end the war and set up an independent kingdom of Greece.

From now on it was a process of gradual retrenchment and decay for the Ottomans. This was reflected in the state of the monarchy which was sinking into increasing decadence. The current Sultan, Abdul Mejid, built himself a palace on the Bosphorus in an artificial bay carved out years before by 16,000 captive slaves. It contained 300 rooms, sported the largest ballroom – and mirrors – in the world, and cost a fortune in marble, silver and alabaster, including 14 tons of gold-leaf. It reflected not only reckless indulgence, but also a growing indifference to the fate of the Empire.

Turkish difficulties with Russia eventually precipitated the Crimean War in 1854 in which there was a re-alignment of the powers concerned. Britain and France linked up with the Turks against the Russians who were compelled to sue for peace in 1856 – a humiliation which gave their arch rivals, the Ottomans, a new lease of life. Turkey was guaranteed freedom from interference, principally in the Black Sea, on condition that she instituted a number of well-overdue reforms in her subject territories, especially the Balkans. The Turks were very slow to implement these reforms partly out of conviction and, one suspects, partly out of lethargy. Mejid's successor in 1861, Abdul Aziz, was, if anything, even more self-indulgent than his dead brother. He promised improvements and economies that were not forthcoming, but continued to maintain a harem of 900 concubines, guarded by 3,000 black eunuchs. In all, the Dolmabache palace had a staff of 5,000 servants and the Sultan entertained on such a scale that he required 400 musicians to amuse his guests. In fact, his inordinate extravagance finally plunged Turkey into enormous debts to foreign bankers – something which seriously compromised her negotiating ability with both the world outside and her own subjects who were anxiously looking for reforms.

One way and another the Empire was growing restless. There were further outbreaks of violence in the Balkans, and, predictably, the Turkish response was ruthless in the extreme. They employed units of Circassian troops who were not paid but fought only for loot to repress these uprisings. The German and French consuls in Salonika were murdered, and this was followed by widespread mayhem. News of the brutality was, at first, thought to be exaggerated, but authenticated reports came from the American press telling how villages were destroyed and hundreds of inhabitants burned alive. The Sultan, who was soon to commit suicide, personally decorated the officer in charge of these massacres which claimed some 12,000 lives. Outside opinion was horrified, and the rebel states were only saved from virtual destruction by the further intervention of the Great Powers who again stressed the need for institutional change. The Turks, under Aziz's successor, proved to be characteristically intransigent, and this occasioned a further conflict with Russia which resulted in yet another Turkish capitulation (1878).

There followed a complicated re-shuffling operation by the Great Powers in which minor states and parts of states, even down to relatively insignificant strips of territory in the Balkans and Mediterranean, were allocated, re-allocated or, in some cases, actually made independent. The Turks were left with nothing to speak of in Europe except Constantinople – and probably the Russians would have seized this had it not been for the presence of the British fleet.

None of this made for a lasting peace. Most ominously, this arbitrary re-drawing of the map of southern Europe included the division of Armenia, part of which was restored to Turkey by the Russian Tsar. The Armenians were in some ways akin to the Turks in cultural though not in religious terms. They too were seeking long-promised reforms and, much to Turkey's fear, also entertained nationalist aspirations. These were encouraged by Armenians abroad who lived in more democratic environments, and soon the agitation became so vociferous – and so irritating to the Ottomans – that the government decided to deal with the matter once and for all. In 1894, the Sultan sent agents to inform all Muslims living among the Armenians that they were free to confiscate any Armenian goods or property they chose, and to kill the owners if they protested or resisted. It was really a methodical campaign of genocide, but, interestingly, it was not carried out, in general, by paid executioners or by battle-inflamed soldiers, but by poor, acquisitive citizens who sought to gain from the death and dispossession of others. Similar horrors were also experienced in Macedonia, and the Sultan himself demanded details of all these outrages which included frightful tortures and atrocities. In all, at least 100,000 people are believed to have died in these massacres; indeed, many Muslims eventually became so sickened by them that they had virtually ceased by 1896. Later, this particular ruler, dubbed Abdul the Damned, who had masterminded the Armenian atrocities, was deposed by his own subjects, but this did not end Turkey's troubles. There was still unrest and squabbling in the Balkans. The Great Powers were again quick to take advantage of this, and Turkey was deprived of yet further territories (1912–13).

The whole system was now not just corrupt but also out of date. Tax collection had given way to tax farming, the Empire's trade and industry had remained backward in comparison with the industrialisation of the western powers and, in their traditional contempt for the west, her once all-conquering armies had not adopted the mechanisation and weaponry – the 'infidel inventions' – of their rivals (Lewis, 1971: 18). The Ottomans were now living on borrowed time and most of that was squandered.

The lessons of repressive rule still had not been learned. Memories were tragically short. The revulsion generated by the terrible carnage of 1895–6 did not prevent further, and in many ways worse, atrocities against the Armenians. There were more sporadic outbursts of violence early this century, and yet again the Great Powers were insistent that Turkey should introduce reforms which would make life easier for her subject peoples. The outbreak of World War I inhibited the implementation of these reforms; in fact, one suspects that the Turks took advantage of the changed circumstances to deal with the Armenians whilst the world was distracted with more pressing issues. What followed was a full-scale assault on the Armenian people. Their leaders and intellectuals were arrested and deported. Anyone with any wealth or influence, from civil deputies and jurists to merchants and bankers was included. Their removal left the majority of the Armenian community virtually defenceless, and easy prey for further depredations. There was nothing casual or improvised about all this. It was a carefully planned government policy to get rid of the Armenians and, as with the earlier pogroms, the government enlisted the help of regional officials and the people gener-ally; any who resisted were promptly disciplined and, where appropriate, dismissed from office.

The war made the task both easier and more difficult; easier because it could all be made to look like an emergency measure, but more difficult because of the threat posed by the advancing Russians. So the Turks decided to expedite matters by recruiting local 'labour' and they, together with the military, began to carry out mass executions. This policy was then adopted elsewhere, even far from the battlefront; indeed the whole programme began to lose coherence, and the situation became unpredict-able and haphazard. Sometimes women were spared, at other times they were killed along with the men. Sometimes people were spared if they professed conversion to Islam – the old Muslim practice of 'submit or die' – but at other times this made no difference or would be disal-lowed (Toynbee, quoted in Kuper, 1981: 109). There were many regional variations but they all had a concerted genocidal intent.

The privations and the suffering of the Armenians have been graphi-cally described (Toynbee, 1915). Old and young alike endured torture and humiliation; those, including women, who lagged behind in forced deportation marches were frequently bayoneted to death and their babies killed – often with the connivance of the local police and even the peasants themselves – and many died of starvation, exposure and disease. All this, and the destruction occasioned by rival factions at the end of the war had further repercussions on the Armenian community. Even-tually, the belated representations of the victorious powers ensured that Armenian rights were recognised but, by this time, their numbers had been almost incalculably depleted. The population had been reduced from about two million to approximately 30,000, yet incredibly few were ever brought to book for these monstrous crimes. They still await the overdue 'verdict of history'.

Turkey's ultimate defeat in World War I, in which she had unwisely chosen the wrong side, reduced her territories to their modern dimen-sions. The Armenian issue is still remembered, unsurprisingly mainly by Armenians; the Turks today seem quite untroubled by their past. Their problems with the Greeks still remain, and their reputation for human rights still leaves many questions to be answered.

CHAPTER ELEVEN

# Massacre and Economic Efficiency: The Stalin era

The Russian revolution of 1917 was an haphazard, untidy affair in which a small group of intellectuals led a minority party to an uncertain and unexpected victory. When they gained power by a *coup d'état*, the Bolsheviks were only one group among a fractious mêlée of contending revolutionaries and were quite outnumbered by their main rivals, the Mensheviks and Socialists. Furthermore, the revolution had not gone according to the book. There was no breakdown of capitalist society, strangled, as Marx had suggested, by its own inherent contradictions. In Russia conditions were different. Society was not highly differentiated, there were not the subtle gradations of status which one finds in the developed capitalist system. Essentially it was a two-class state. Orthodox Marxist doctrine decreed – or at least, assumed – a revolution from a broad industrial base. This did not really exist in any extensive sense in Russia, but had to be created after the fact, as it were.

The Bolsheviks, led by Lenin, were determined to establish a system of one-party rule based upon the rather vague notion of the dictatorship of the proletariat. With the gradual elimination of the opposition, including some workers and peasants besides distrusted intellectuals and members of the bourgeoisie, 'the dictatorship of the proletariat became successively the dictatorship of the Communist Party, of the central committee of the Party, of the . . . [Politburo] of the central committee, [and finally] of the leader. Bolshevik democracy became totalitarian [and] the Communist state [became] monolithic' (Charques, 1959: 225).

Peace with Germany prior to the ending of World War I was purchased at a terrible price. The treaty of Brest-Litovsk in March 1918 deprived Russia of a quarter of its population and its arable land, half its industrial capacity and something approaching three-quarters of its iron – not an auspicious beginning for the new regime. Added to this were the even more threatening problems posed by various groups of counter-revolutionaries and volunteer armies that challenged the authority of the regime: small bands of Cossacks; considerable armies of renegade deserters and ex-prisoners of war; and, most notably, the White Russian forces led by a one-time Admiral. To complicate matters still further, the Allies who were obviously deeply suspicious of what was taking place, sent small expeditionary forces to intervene in Russian affairs. They were especially distrustful of Russia's premature withdrawal from the war, and the new government's repudiation of all foreign debts. There is little doubt that they felt that what was happening in Russia was likely to affect the precarious stability of post-war Europe.

The civil war became a bitter and protracted struggle. Units of Red Guards were mobilised and they, together with workers' detachments, carried out the will of the new government while the newly-formed Red Army militia was in training. The conflict went on for two terrible years. It was a period of considerable hardship and near famine culminating in an ill-timed invasion from Poland which was also successfully repulsed. During this time, there were also internal threats to the regime. This resulted in the reorganisation of the old security police that became known as the Cheka, which in the interests of 'social order', and no doubt also as a means of paying off old scores and eliminating known and supposed opponents, carried out a series of purges of 'class enemies'. An attempt on Lenin's life provided the opportunity for murder on a massive scale; in Petrograd (Leningrad) alone some 500 were shot, and further appalling atrocities were perpetrated, especially in the Ukraine where massacres of unrepentant savagery took place. The regime had few friends and felt that it had to deal with the opposition on a ruthless, if *ad hoc*, basis if it was going to survive. There was little room for negotiation or compromise. Nevertheless, the brutality with which it treated those who contested its control sometimes beggars description. It certainly began as it meant to continue, and those who suffered most were the peasants themselves – theoretically, the very people the regime was supposed to serve.

These internecine struggles took their toll. Industry and agriculture were at a very low ebb, and the situation necessitated the introduction of drastic social measures. Key enterprises were nationalised including the banks and much of industry, and state monopolies of important commodities were created. Workers' control was established through factory committees which had the right to supervise management in some aspects of administration. Shortages were so acute that rationing became a normal way of life. The economy was so unstable that barter took the place of purchase as money lost its value. Corruption was rife, although where detected was rigorously suppressed. A form of labour conscription was put into operation and state confiscation became a further unwelcome feature of the emergency.

From the beginning there was a fundamental contradiction between the drive towards centralisation and the principle of workers' control. Nowhere can this dichotomy of policy and practice be more clearly seen than in the area of agriculture. There were periodic outbursts of anarchy among the peasantry who were particularly incensed by the forced labour measures taken by the government. There was even a mutiny among naval personnel in 1921 in support of the principle of local (soviet) control. Agricultural production fell to such a low level that Lenin conceded that grain requisitioning would have to be abandoned in favour of a system of taxation which would give the peasants the right to sell their surplus on the open market – a concession to the partial independence of the producer. This new economic policy had far-reaching – and for the government, disturbing – effects. Selling surplus in a free market was really a form of embryonic entrepreneurialism and not at all in keeping with the spirit of Bolshevik socialism.

The government was obviously not ready for incipient capitalism. Its intention was increasing centralisation. It wanted to maintain complete political and economic control and was no more ready to hand over the productive capacities to private enterprise than it was to release its hold on the nominally autonomous republics. Most immediately, it was not prepared to relinquish its monopoly of foreign trade or its far-reaching plans for the revitalisation of industry. Still less did it wish to give up its prerogatives concerning the organisation of agricultural production, especially with agriculture in such a parlous condition. Government plans were further thwarted by the failure of the harvest in 1921, and their inability to cope with the resultant famine meant that huge numbers died. Consequently, a certain amount of private enterprise was allowed as an incentive to both peasants and workers in order to regenerate the economy.

These policies were seriously modified after the death of Lenin, and Stalin's accession to power in 1924. Stalin had been the General Secretary of the Party, but he gradually assumed more and more authority by a succession of deft political *coups* which virtually left him in undisputed control by the mid-1920s. His main rival, Trotsky, was ousted in 1926. One of their principal disagreements was the issue of whether or not Communism – certainly in the short term – should be developed in one country (Stalin) or whether Russia should pursue a policy of permanent revolution and ideological evangelisation (Trotsky). Stalin's view was that world revolution could wait – Russia had enough on her plate already. His triumph heralded the first Five-Year Plan, the purpose of which was to subordinate the entire economy to central control so that Russia might overtake the other great industrialised states. Needless to say, this was not to everybody's liking. In the words of one commentator it took 'all the resources of propaganda ... to stimulate a mood of heroic sacrifice and ... obscure the harsh materialism of this essay in social construction' (Charques, 1959: 242).

This plan began formerly in 1928 and was actually completed in four years. It entailed the rapid expansion of industry and the strict regulation of labour, and differential rationing acted as a strong incentive to greater productivity. The main problem was how to feed this industrial work-force now that so many peasants had been taken from the land to be part of the industrial proletariat. The answer, such as it was, was the reorganisation of agriculture as a modern version of the Roman *latifundia*. The government formulated plans for the virtual abolition of small peasant holdings by a process of collectivisation. Huge numbers of small farms were amalgamated into large communal units, a system which was supposed to bring greater control and appreciable economies of scale. It was also intended to neutralise the tendency towards petty capitalism and individualism, and to inculcate instead some appreciation of socialist principles and practice. Large-scale production was to be achieved by mechanisation for which a state-sponsored tractor hire scheme was available.

At least, this was the theory. In practice, the actual implementation of the scheme presented problems from the outset, not least of all because of the continued resistance of the more prosperous peasants – the Kulaks. Persuasion failed to generate any enthusiasm, so coercion was applied, again, without very much success. Eventually, the government, in effect, declared open war on the obstructive Kulaks. There was an extreme irony here because in November 1917, a decree on land had nationalised the landlords' estates and granted all agricultural land to the peasants for their use in perpetuity. But this was all during the first flush of the revolution. It was an ideal which was not to be realised. Perhaps, in the light of economic realities, it had been somewhat ill-considered and over-zealous in the first place. Even more devastating at that time were the measures of doctrinaire War Communism which had resulted in state control of just about every aspect of national life. All private trade had been banned; all public and private wealth had been conscripted, although wages had been paid in kind. The state had taken powers to direct all labour and the right to requisition all food-stuffs and grain from the peasantry. All this did little for the economy: stocks became even more depleted, and industrial output fell to even lower levels. In fact, it created such problems that Lenin had tried to appease the growing resentment of the peasants who felt that the state had given them land with one hand, and had forcibly confiscated its produce with the other. Ameliorative measures were taken which encouraged the growth and importance of the better-off peasant sector, though making sure that the state still commanded the bulk of labour power. This retention of control was particularly evident in industry. A 1923 census showed that although 88 per cent of enterprises belonged to the private sector, that sector involved only 12.5 per cent of the total number of workers employed (Kochan,

1967: 272). It was not until 1928 that there was any real change in this system of competing economies.

The fundamental problem – as the State Planning Commission soon discovered – was that the Russian agricultural sector was totally unamenable to planning. Yet the state insisted that somehow it had got to be done. After the revolution the government was in a double-bind. It needed foreign capital to finance industrialisation, but this could only be raised by increasing agricultural exports. More money was needed to capitalise the reforms, not least of all to agriculture itself. The situation was not dissimilar in the 1920s. Industrialisation and agricultural mechanisation had to be paid for. Indeed, the achievements were remarkable, but they were only accomplished at the cost of severe social deprivation. Factory wages were increasingly depressed, and industrial workers had to endure acute shortages, but nowhere was hardship more keenly felt than among the peasants. The vast majority of them worked smallholdings that barely kept them at subsistence level. The only answer seemed to be to collectivise these and apply special pressure to the wealthier peasants to ensure their cooperation. In other words, in one way or another, make the peasant pay for industrialisation. Needless to say, the Kulaks were far from being convinced by the new state economics, and they determined to resist a policy that was calculated to destroy their livelihood.

At first, the restrictions on the Kulaks were moderate by contemporary standards, but their unwillingness to cooperate generated more repressive measures. Allegations of grain-hording by Kulaks brought a spate of imprisonments and the inevitable confiscations. The government sought the support of the poorer peasants who formed committees to combat the power of the Kulaks. Obviously, they had an eye to the main chance; the more denunciations that were made, the more chance there was that Kulak-land might accrue to the poor. Initially, collectivisation had some success. The number of amalgamated farms nearly doubled between 1928 and 1929. These were run by peasants who were so poor that they had nothing to lose. But the Kulaks held out, and their recalcitrance virtually ensured their extermination.

Stalin gave the signal in 1929: 'we must break down [their] resistance ... the present policy of our Party [is that] of eliminating the Kulaks as a class ...' (quoted in Kochan, 1967: 288). What followed was almost akin to civil war. The government encouraged the poor peasants to take over the Kulak's property and machinery. The Kulaks retaliated by destroying their crops, killing their livestock, and even burning their own homes. The poor profited by the confiscations, and in the first three months of 1930 the number of collective farms actually doubled. But the situation rapidly got out of control, and the government had to intervene to restrain the rapacity of the poor peasants. They decided to put the brakes on this acquisitive bandwagon. Various reforms were introduced which would curb this social instability but which, at the same time, would give the peasants a little more independence and prosperity. Coercion was eased and people were allowed to withdraw from the collectives if they wished to do so. Furthermore they instituted a system whereby once the farms had fulfilled their quotas, the peasants were allowed to sell surplus stocks on the open market.

Agriculture thus became the servant of industry, and Russian industrial growth in the 1930s was quite phenomenal though rarely as great as the planners envisaged. It was only made possible by a huge investment in the public sector of the economy which entailed forced saving and severe cut-backs in internal consumption, together with an almost total mobilisation of under-utilised labour. The problems in the countryside attracted many peasants to the towns to work in industry and to employment on the many massive constructional projects such as the Dnieper Dam which were a feature of the Five-Year Plan. In short, the impressive increases in production were achieved at the cost of an equally impressive increase in state power. This involved 'the use of force . . . on a scale that beggars the imagination: whole social groups were brutally coerced and individual security undermined' (Acton 1986: 221). The state security police, the OGPU (after 1934, the NKVD) were there to ensure that the state's edicts were strictly observed. Their operatives were to be found at every level in education, in industry, in the military, and certainly in the administration of the ambitious agricultural programme of collectivisation. It was impossible to stand against an organisation where the echelons of power were such that the OGPU was actually able to monitor the conduct and loyalty of the Party members themselves.

The repressive policies of the regime certainly changed the nature of Russian agriculture but there was no way in which they could ensure its success. In fact, on balance, collectivisation was a disaster. With all the 'reforms' and changes of policy, the ordinary peasants were no better off. Theoretically, collectivisation was supposed to bring more social justice, economic efficiency in production, exchange and distribution, but what it really brought was a new phase in the now-familiar Russian imperialism. Its effects on agriculture brought nothing but misery to the peasants. In 1931 and 1932 the harvest failed due to an unfortuitous combination of adverse weather conditions and the dislocation caused by collectivisation. This helped to bring about the catastrophic famine of 1933 in which perhaps two to four million people died of disease and starvation.

The communes were overseen by people who were, effectively, Party appointees, so dissent was virtually stifled from the beginning. Yet they could not guarantee the production levels that were required. There was still little incentive for the peasants. If production increased, they were only too well aware that this would mean higher requisitionings by the state – so why bother? As government procurements rose, so more peasants gravitated towards the industrial centres. It was a common pattern: industrialisation went hand in hand with urbanisation. Those who stayed maintained a meagre living by selling produce from their private plots and those who resisted government directives, whatever these might be, were categorised as 'class enemies' and were either killed or sent to the special camps where they laboured under the most appalling conditions. Some five million peasants were deported to far off regions in the east and north, and had to eke out a precarious living either in forced settlements or labour camps. By the mid-1930s the camp population was probably not far short of three million. They provided a convenient supply of cheap manpower for the exploitation of the rich mineral and forest resources to be found in these remote areas.

This policy of terror and repression served a number of purposes. It broke the power of wealthier peasants both in economic terms and as a 'class'. It both directly and indirectly promoted the cause of industry which, in turn, meant the development of a formidable war machine. Almost certainly, Russian agriculture could have been made more productive without inflicting such human misery, but then Stalin had ulterior motives in initiating this programme of repression. It also contributed towards the 'russianisation' of the Soviet Union in that it increased the dominance of the central authorities over the non-Russian republics by bringing would-be separatists into line. Not least of all, it consolidated the power of the Politburo and particularly that of Stalin himself, by eliminating the untrustworthy ideological elements within the Party by a process of deportation, imprisonment and execution.

In all this, Stalin was acting within a well-established tradition of terror characteristic of the Tsars. Ivan the Terrible had his secret police and Peter the Great carried through his reforms at the expense of wholesale repression (Seth, 1970). Obstensibly, Stalin's measures were enforced to further the ideal of the 'classless society', yet they actually ushered in a system that was as highly stratified as anything experienced in imperial Russia. Communism had its own rigid class divisions ranging from the top leadership of the party, state and military administrations which together constituted the upper stratum, to the party members and party intelligentsia – the new middle class – in the second stratum, and to the working proletariat who constituted a third stratum. On a generous analysis, one might include the slave labourers as a fourth stratum but really these were outside the system of classification, having minimal rights and precious few prospects (Fr Chirkovsky, 1967: 189).

Estimates vary as to the number of deaths that resulted from the direct violence of the Russian revolution, and from the repression and privations that followed. After the carnage of World War I – a war from which Russia was glad to extricate herself – it seems almost inconceivable that her citizens should then embark upon a civil war. Deaths resulting from this war of Red against White (reactionary) Armies and others, and the war against Poland probably numbered about half a million. The public terrorism which accompanied various outbursts of civil violence and guerrilla activity may have accounted for at least another half a million. Lenin, for all his astuteness, favoured violence and proclaimed war against all counter-revolutionaries and class enemies. Consequently, there was an almost indiscriminate proscription of the bourgeoisie. Mass executions were carried out by the secret police (Cheka) and the armed forces. To these figures must be added those which resulted from 'domestic violence', of worker against peasant in the struggles over grain distribution in 1918 when men were hanged, beaten and burned to death for food. Finally, for our purposes there was the death and suffering resulting from the repressive measures attending the policy of collectivisation generally, including, more questionably, the famine that followed. On a rough estimate, perhaps somewhere between eight and ten million deaths, in all (Elliot, 1973: Ch. 3).

These figures must be somewhat conjectural, but who is to quibble about minutiae when the general picture is so compelling. Like China and Cambodia later on, there was the infliction of incalculable human misery in order to further the interests of a questionable social experiment. Massacre is almost mandatory in this kind of social engineering, though it was, of course, also bound up with autocratic ambition and the exercise of despotic power. It was also the ruthless operationalisation of an ideology – an attempt to realise the ideal of the collective state.

It is instructive to look at the immediate aftermath of all this. Contrary to expectations, productivity during the first Five-Year Plan fell dramatically. In order to boost industrial output, the regime found itself obliged to initiate policies that were an uneasy combination of both stick and carrot which included bonus schemes, extended working hours and shorter holidays. Infringements of the new codes were met with such sanctions as the withdrawal of ration cards and factory housing, or even harsher penalties such as imprisonment. Strikes were out of the question, and unions were emasculated to the extent that they became mere adjuncts of the management structure. But there were also incentives – a system of wage differentials and honorary awards which smacked of the kind of quasi-capitalism that the regime would once have eschewed.

All this was sustained by a barrage of propaganda aimed at keeping the workforce – be they workers or peasants – both acquiescent and productive. They were encouraged to join the Party and thereby to further its aims and policies and, in time, many responded to these blandishments, and identified with the ideals of the 'true' socialist state. This undoubtedly occurred because there were genuine improvements as well as impoverishment. Progress demanded a new kind of elite, so with the expansion of industry came also an expansion of white-collar occupations and a burgeoning bureaucracy. Education was the key. During the first Five-Year Plan enrolments in higher education trebled, and there was a marked shift from arts to technical education. Furthermore, more and more students who aspired to specialist qualifications and consequent promotion were drawn from the manual working classes. Between 1928 and 1941, the number of graduate engineers, for example, rose remarkably from 47,000 to 289,000 (Acton, 1986: 234). But this was all very much the lot of the minority; the vast majority were not so fortunate. Their disappointment over the delayed socialist millenium and the near-squalor of their living conditions was often reinterpreted in terms of short-term expediencies which would one day give way to a new and better order. Any discrepancy between the ideal and the real, between the declared aims of the system and the disillusioning reality, was said to be the result of foreign hostility without and class enemies within. There were recriminations against the more liberal intelligentsia – for a long time a term of undifferentiated abuse – and denunciations of those who were felt to be less than enthusiastic about the new socialism.

In the later 1930s, the focus of repression switched from the proletariat, who by now were sufficiently persuaded, coerced or otherwise dragooned into compliance, to other recalcitrant or suspect members of the state. No one was excluded, but it particularly affected the rulers themselves and those in power in the provinces. It now became the turn of the military and political elites. No one who was anyone was safe any more. The charges were usually trumped up affairs, 'rightism', 'leftism', spying, conspiring against the regime – almost anything that would bring a conviction. Those who had once repressed others were themselves proscribed. This even extended to members of the security police, some 3,000 of whom were executed in 1937/8. Those who had rejoiced at the fall of their political rivals found themselves either in prison or marked for execution. About 300–400,000 political arrests were reported in the spring of 1937, and in the two years 1937 and 1938 some 44,000 names of those listed for execution were submitted to Stalin for his approval (Conquest, 1985: 28, 30). The military elite was almost obliterated – a disaster which almost certainly inhibited Russia's response to the German invasion in 1941.

Today we might well ask what it was all for. Merely, it seems, to reinforce the fear and authority of the autocrat. Each wave of terror did not foment rebellion, but simply generated more fraticidal suspicion and with it an almost cringing subservience to Stalin. So much for the unity of the 'comrades'. Even Hitler had more feeling for most of his accomplices than this. Stalin virtually eliminated all the older generation of leading Communists, including Lenin's closest collaborators, and effectively destroyed about three-quarters of his central committee. But he did ensure the unswerving loyalty of those that remained (Schapiro, 1967: 51). Ruthlessness was no longer just about stabilising social order or facilitating economic efficiency – it was massacre for the consolidation of power.

# CHAPTER TWELVE

# Massacre as Fratricide: The Spanish Civil War

The Civil War was really a form of revolution. It is therefore necessary to begin our discussion by thinking about revolution in general. How do we define the term? Not unusually views differ as to what exactly constitutes a revolution. In the 'trade', two main approaches are taken. Some maintain that the term should be reserved for 'true' or 'great' revolutions such as the Russian revolution or the post-war Chinese revolution in which there is a fundamental reconstitution of the state. It follows from this rather exclusivist view that 'true' revolutions are relatively rare as they result in radical transformations in society (Cohan, 1975: 1–2). Others argue that the term can be used about seizures of power such as, say, an army *coup*. Here the emphasis is not so much with the underlying rationale of the revolution as with the violent and/or extra-legal ways in which it is achieved.

The distinction, then, is a fairly simple one. The first classification concentrates on causes and effects, and asks: What are the *reasons* for the revolution? What are its immediate goals and long-term objectives? The second concentrates on the *means*. What mechanisms are employed to effect these transfers of power?

Implicit in both these classifications is the problem of *why* revolutions take place. How are we to account for them as socio-political phenomena? Perhaps the most commonly accepted theory is that suggested by Marx, namely, that revolutions occur in order to resolve the structural contradictions of society. By this, of course, he was thinking of class conflicts which must eventually result in revolutions of some kind. It is really a 'last resort' theory. Marx is postulating that in given social contexts the situation between the dominant classes and the subordinate classes – crudely, the rich and the poor – will become so bad that revolution becomes the only answer. In fact, Marx is really saying that in certain structural situations, revolution is not only desirable, it is actually inevitable. A variant – indeed, a refinement – of this theory is that revolutions are most likely to happen when a prolonged period of economic and social development is followed by a short period in which these trends are reversed. People then begin to fear that what has been achieved at great cost is going to be lost, and their mood becomes revolutionary (Davies, 1962). In other words, it is not when people have reached truly desperate straits that revolutions occur, but when things are actually improving. The increased prosperity generates rising expectations, and disaffection sets in when this is suddenly threatened. In this form, the theory would help us to appreciate, say, the Nazi takeover in Germany in the 1930s.

This type of analysis is countered by those who maintain that over time societies have produced the institutions they need in the forms they require. These theorists argue that the trend in society is towards stability and persistence rather than conflict and change, the implications being that revolution, rather than being desirable, is disruptive and dysfunctional. Revolution comes about when societies' traditional arrangements are jeopardised by some economic or political upheaval such as war. In the wake of the conflict, the normal restraints go, and in the aftermath conditions are such that a revolutionary ethos prevails.

These theories are really quite unexceptional, and in these highly generalised forms are not much more than intellectualised commonsense. But they can be fruitful when applied to certain kinds of question. For example, in dealing with civil conflict, we must ask what *kind* of revolutionary ethos is generated – is it radical or reactionary? Or is it both? And what determines the nature of the outcome? These are all interesting issues, and it now remains to be seen if such ideas help us in our understanding of the Spanish Civil War.

Impressionistically, one feels that civil war, being 'confined' in territorial and cultural terms, should be amenable to some kind of reasonably constructive analysis. The domestic nature of the situation should give it a 'simplicity' which is normally lacking in inter-state conflicts. But this is not so. In the Spanish Civil War, the immediate causes are not difficult to fathom, but the underlying bases of the conflict are not that easy to disentangle. This is further exacerbated by the actual divisions within the two sides characterised, as they are, by a maze of ideological factors.

The period we are concerned with is that known as the Second Republic which lasted from 1931 to 1939. The early left-wing governments of this period attempted to bring about radical changes in Spain's social structure. These measures, modest by current standards, were considered radical by many at the time. They ranged from simple reforms such as those governing working conditions, to more extreme institutional changes such as the abolition of the nobility. The early Socialists had been pragmatic reformers, determined to introduce, by non-violent means, innovations that would improve the material conditions of the workers. The Republic tried to follow this example, and it was its proud boast that whereas only 505 schools a year had been built between 1908 and 1930, the Republic had built 7,000 in its first year alone. As much as anything the Socialists introduced legislation that would reduce the great disparity between the wealthy and the mass of landless peasants, but for a whole series of reasons this could not be successfully implemented. Such radicalism was opposed by a formidable combination of the church, the army and the rich landlords who all saw their various interests threatened. No one seemed completely happy about these reforms – not even those they were supposed to help. They 'failed to benefit Spain's lower orders and succeeded only in terrifying the privileged' (Lee, 1988: 232). The government fell in 1933, and the political pendulum swung to the centre-right. This ushered in a period of considerable instability and by 1936 – the year of the outbreak of the Civil War – there had been many crises and ministerial changes.

It was at this point that a critical election was held in which the battle lines were drawn between the Republicans (Popular Front) which consisted of a montage of Communists, more moderate Socialists, Liberals and even Anarchists, and the Nationalists (National Front) including the powerful CEDA party (the Spanish Confederation of the Autonomous Right), really a Catholic alliance organisation, and the monarchists, especially the Carlists. Not strictly aligned with either of these blocs were the Basques and the Fascist-orientated group known as the Falange. The election was very close. The Republicans won with a narrow majority, leaving the large Nationalist minority simply waiting its chance to reverse the situation.

There is some evidence – much of it anecdotal – that once in power, many of the more militant Socialists dispensed with the conventional niceties of political behaviour. Politically-orientated street gangs displayed unruly and intimidating behaviour, and the newly-formed Marxist Revolutionary Party (POUM) and the Syndicos Libres movement capitalised on the sporadic violence, all of which inflamed the Right still further. In May 1936, anarchists and Marxists took over factories, and some peasants attempted forcible land-reform in parts of the south-west, and finally – among the burnings and assaults – were added murder and counter-murder. Civil war became virtually inevitable.

Formal hostilities began with an army plan to overthrow the government. The scheme was largely the brainchild of Francisco Franco who, as a disaffected and influential general, had been originally exiled by the Popular Front government to the Canary Islands. Having returned he now decided to lead veteran contingents of troops from Spanish Morocco to southern Spain – something that would have been practically impossible without the indispensable help of Italian and German transports. The plan was that these troops were to meet up with other units from the north under the command of fellow-conspirator, General Mola.

At first, no one made very much progress. The Republican strongholds were mainly in the east – Madrid, Barcelona and Valencia – and these key centres were besieged and bombed in the hope of an early submission. This too was done with the aid of the Germans and Italians for whom it was what Paul Johnson has described as an 'ideological proxy-war' – a 'cynical ritual' with Stalin as the main adversary (Johnson, 1983: 321). The Italian contributions began in quite a modest way, but as time went on the Italians found themselves embroiled in what seemed an interminable conflict. They sent hundreds of planes, tanks, artillery and machine-guns in addition to a vast amount of small arms ammunition. Eventually, too, troops were sent. Not that they were that effective. Italians did not have the best reputation as fighting soldiers, but they did make a difference to Nationalist fortunes. They were certainly not as proficient as the much more professional Germans. Their Condor Legion – which became a byword in Spain for ruthlessness – was commanded by an independent German officer, and had levels of equipment and training which far exceeded those of their fellow participants. They undoubtedly found this a profitable dress rehearsal for what was to come a few years later. The Italians pressed, not very successfully, for some economic return for their assistance, whereas the Germans made their terms clear from the beginning, demanding special concessions in the Spanish iron ore mines. They were disappointed in 1940 when Hitler tried to enlist Spanish help against Britain; Franco was cagey and displayed what the Germans felt was a singular lack of gratitude for all their assistance in the past.

The Soviets also joined the fray in 1936, but on the Republican side. Again, the shipments of material, particularly aircraft, were impressive, although these diminished after the spring of 1937, and ended altogether in 1938. The Soviets did not supply many fighting men, although they did provide officers for many of the Spanish military units. Stalin was suspicious of his officer *corps*, so these men were watched by the NKVD (the Soviet secret police) whose express purpose was to weed out any dissident elements among both the Spanish as well as the Russians. Probably the whole Spanish affair was rather marginal for Stalin who was much more pre-occupied with initiating the purges which decimated the higher echelons of the officer class in the Soviet Union. However, he was not slow to exact payment for Russian services. In 1936 he had secured most of the Spanish gold reserves estimated at about 500 million US dollars.

The Republicans were also helped by the various International Brigades that were recruited among sympathisers from all over Europe and America. Their numbers were relatively small and included doctors and nurses besides the rank and file but their presence had a real propaganda value, though it hardly made a significant difference to the outcome of the war. Their training was often brief and inadequate, and this is reflected in the high proportion of casualties they sustained. One estimate of the British contingent, for example, is that of the 2,762 volunteers, 543 were killed and 1,762 were wounded (Johnson, 1983: 330). The Nationalist forces were also supplemented by voluntary personnel, mainly from Portugal and the USA, presumably because they identified the National Front with the Catholic cause. Technically, none of the states that supplied volunteer units was officially involved, and whilst the war was in full swing, 'a macabre piece of play-acting' was taking place in which these interested parties were holding regularly convened meetings to ensure commitment to a policy of non-intervention despite some degree of provocation (Bell, 1986: 215).

These broad coalitions of Right and Left were therefore divided among themselves. The Nationalists included those who wished to restore the monarchy, others (the Falange) who desired a corporatist state along the lines of Italian fascism, and those – like Franco himself – who were bent on a particular form of dictatorship. Franco was able to unite these aspirations by a broad appeal to national pride, historic traditions and conservative values. In such a quest, he understandably had the support of the church which was keen to combat the threat of atheistic communism. The Republicans, on the other hand, aspired to a state based on general socialist principles but also had somehow to harness the reasonably disciplined but extreme policies of the Left, and the non-coherent, often non-rational equally extreme intentions of the anarchists. Broadly speaking, these groups were prepared to subordinate their respective aims to those of the general socialist cause. In fact, the Communists were positively instructed by Moscow to curb their own specific enthusiasms until the war was won. They were to give absolute priority to defeating Franco, otherwise they were in danger of alienating other members of the Popular Front (Lee, 1988: 238).

Although in one sense the Civil War was a class war, with the landlords versus the peasants, the wealthy versus the poor, it was also an ideological conflict at another level. The problems were not just political and economic in the broader sense, but philosophical in that it was a conflict between Catholicism and anti-Catholicism. Much of the anger of the Republicans was directed against the clerical establishment because the institutional church was identified with unheeding conservatism. Critics simply saw religion as an ideological apparatus to justify and support an unyielding *status quo*. It is therefore understandable – though not excusable – that many of the atrocities on the Republican side concerned defenceless nuns and priests who represented such a system.

At the outset of the campaigning it looked as though the Republicans had most of the advantages. They held the largest cities with their reserves of industry and manpower. They also commanded most of the navy and

the merchant shipping which gave them control over the money-earning
export trade. And they also held the gold reserves until they were effectively sequestrated by the Soviets. By contrast, the Nationalists had
colonial help and about 60 per cent of the various para-military organisations, including the civil guard. Both sides, as we have seen, also received
outside military and technical aid which was only continued for a bare
two years by the Russians, but for the duration by the Nationalist's
'allies', Italy and Germany, with Britain and the USA supplying oil and
other vital credits. It follows, therefore, that a short war favoured the
Republican side, but when this became impossible, the growing strength
of the Nationalists was bound to tell. In the end, it was – like so many
wars – determined by the availability of resources.

In the early stages, the Nationalists made most of the running. There
were periods of attrition, and there were some notable Republican successes particularly at Guadalajara in 1937, but, in general, it was a story of
gradual Nationalist conquest. When the Soviets backed out, a Nationalist
victory was merely a matter of time. In fact, by April 1939, it was all
such a foregone conclusion that most European states – democracies
and dictatorships alike – recognised Franco's regime as the legitimate
government of Spain.

It had been a horrible war. All war is terrible, particularly – and sadly
– fratricidal war, but this one was marked by unspeakable atrocities.
They were perpetrated by both sides: the Republicans took their revenge
early, the butchery and the destruction being largely an expression of
fear and suppressed hatred, whereas the Nationalist atrocities were more
calculated and protracted – mass executions rather than hasty killings.
But in neither case were there extenuating circumstances. Of course,
there were the usual media exaggerations and misrepresentations. For
example, one account of some Barcelona workers said to be covered in
blood after carrying out a particular massacre, turned out to be men
from an abattoir who had rushed out to resist a military rising (Beevor,
1982: 70). But misunderstandings and sensationalist rumours like this
should not blind us as to what actually took place.

The atrocities which caused the greatest consternation were those
involving the clergy. In general, the church was a bastion of conservatism;
it did support the wealthy landowners, and its promises of spiritual
rewards for the poor were regarded as hypocritical and specious. But
this was not true of all clergy, especially the minor clergy. Critics tended
to confuse the teachings of primitive Christianity with that of the institutionalised church; to overlook the poverty and sincerity of many
priests, and see only the rich display of the higher clergy. During the
war the Nationalists claimed that 20,000 priests had been killed, but
afterwards admitted a figure of 7,937 'religious persons' (presumably this

would also include nuns) out of a community of about 115,000. Whether this earlier figure was a genuine mistake or deliberate propaganda is now difficult to determine. Another estimate gives figures of 20 per cent of the bishops, 12 per cent of the monks and 13 per cent of the priests plus 283 nuns (Johnson, 1983: 327). Some were killed in haste, others with malicious deliberation such as the Bishop of Jaen and his sister who were executed publicly on the orders of a militia woman known as La Pecosa. The onslaught against the clergy was far from systematic. Villagers rarely killed their own priests, but might join others in killing priests elsewhere. Only 16 Basque clergy were murdered including the Bishop of Mondragon. Not altogether surprisingly, many areas were completely untouched, yet in others the killings were meticulous and sadistic. Some were mutilated, some were burned, and a number were made to savour the prospect of their own deaths by being forced to dig their own graves.

These horrors and humiliations were all carried out in the name of reform. The clergy, especially the higher clergy, were, in general, anti-liberal and some were intensely nationalistic, but most were not fascist in the usually understood sense of the term. They were almost certainly more concerned with what they saw as an encroaching atheism than with the finer points of fascist doctrine, of which most were probably unaware. Interestingly, some of the few small Protestant communities were also affected, but, in this case, they are said to have been attacked at the instigation of their old enemies – the Catholic clergy.

The Republicans also murdered nationalist, especially fascist, sympathisers. These killings were often done by murder-gangs which patrolled the towns in the early hours of the morning, sometimes taking people 'for a ride' movie-style. They were particularly evident in Barcelona, and in Madrid those people denounced for having known or suspected anti-Republican tendencies were hauled before revolutionary tribunals and then executed. Some were just shot out of hand, especially by the anarchists, some of whom were freed convicts who became impatient with these quasi-legal charades. It just didn't pay to have the wrong political complexion.

It is now believed that a number of the victims were falsely accused; where there is a general proscription, it has long been a practice to settle old scores – one or two more on the list doesn't seem to matter to the accusers. Mercifully this rarely extended to the wives and daughters of the condemned; they were usually only harmed if they offered any resistance to the militias. Some people who realised they were in danger fled to embassies that they knew were sympathetic to the Nationalist cause. One revolutionary group, aware of this, set up a false embassy, and then some time later shot those that had come there for refuge.

Some of the worst atrocities were straightforward revenge killings against police officials and industrialists who had themselves employed gunmen against union leaders; 'blacklegs' too were prime targets for the militias. Such killings were planned and deliberate. But there were also unorganised, *ad hoc* atrocities such as the popular rising in Ronda where 512 were thrown to their deaths into a gorge which bisects the town. These popular revenge massacres were often occasioned by particular incidents. For example, after a Nationalist air-raid on Malaga, anti-Republicans were dragged out of prison and shot against the nearest wall, and a similar incident happened in Bilbao. Perhaps the worst of these impromptu massacres took place after a bombing raid on Madrid, and when – coincidentally – reports were coming through of the whole-sale slaughter of Republicans in an area in Badajoz. Enraged militiamen and civilians marched on the local prison and shot 70 of the inmates (Beevor, 1982: 72–3). Altogether, the Left probably murdered about 55,000 people including some women and children.

In many ways the Nationalist atrocities took a different form. Anyone suspected of sympathising let alone supporting the Popular Front was in danger. As soon as an area was taken over by Nationalist forces there was often an initial period of reprisals, sometimes even against those who had been promised their lives. After this there was often a second wave of killings. Undesirables of all kinds were rooted out; intellectuals, politicians, teachers, doctors and certainly anyone involved with the revolutionary tribunals. Left-wing and Liberal intellectuals were particularly suspect. Perhaps the best known victim of Falangist distrust was the poet Federico Lorca who did not belong to any party but, so it was alleged, did more damage to the Nationalist cause by his writing than by military involvement. His execution, following that of the mayor and five university professors in his home town of Granada was a taboo subject in Spain until the death of Franco in 1975.

The Nationalists had their counterparts of tribunals in their own purge committees. These were composed of more eminent right-wing citizens such as land-owners, industrialists and civil guards. The figures of those done to death by Nationalist militia and soldiery are very difficult to assess, but certainly exceed those of the Republicans. One Nationalist leader boasted of ten to every one Nationalist killed. This seems to be somewhat exaggerated, but if the killings that took place *after* the war are added to the wartime atrocities, this ratio may not be that wide of the mark.

Particular incidents have now become part of the memory of the Civil War. Particularly remembered are the horrors committed by the Moroccan troops who had a sadistic predilection for knives and bayonets. In Alcazar, some 200 wounded militiamen in hospital were finished off with bayonets and grenades. But this was nothing compared with their activities at Badajoz and Seville where some women had to endure the ordeal of repeated rape before they were killed. It should be noted that women also participated in the atrocities, especially in the mutilation of victims. Death had a macabre attraction for the public. Some women actually took their children to witness the executions which were sometimes celebrated as festive occasions with vendors, coffee stalls, and so on – in fact, all the fun of a very grisly fair.

The slaughter eventually became so sickening, especially after the Nationalist retributions exacted at Malaga, that even the Italian ambassador – not renowned for his social sensitivity – felt that he had to protest. He apparently did not want Italian troops to be thought guilty by association. In all, perhaps about 50,000 people were killed gratuitously by the Nationalists during the war – about the same score as the Republicans. But it may be that this figure can be increased to a quarter of a million if we take the methodical programme of extermination that continued after hostilities had officially ceased.

None of the theories or models of revolution that we began with quite applies to the Spanish Civil War. Much depends on how we date the revolution in Spain. Are we content with 1936 and the onset of formal hostilities? Or are we to see the Civil War as a culmination of a class struggle that had been going on for years? If so, the Marxian model clearly has some relevance. On the other hand, it could be argued that, in its cruder forms, this model is only marginally appropriate because although the class dimension was very pronounced the people were not reduced to economic desperation. What is more of a problem is that this was a revolution of the Right not of the Left; the groundswell of *initial* discontentment took reactionary rather than radical forms, although, admittedly, once the Nationalists had precipitated the conflict, the class issue was very important and determined much of the subsequent activity – not least the atrocities themselves.

The entire phenomenon of revolution is permeated by the question of values, and values are expressed as belief, and belief is often intellectualised as ideology (Carlton, 1990). In any consideration of the Spanish Civil War, or any other war for that matter, it would be extremely unwise to discount, or even under-rate, the question of ideology. Of course war is about power, and the wresting of advantage. But even where these are most evident, as with Franco's unambiguous intention of setting himself up as dictator, the implicit values underlying the revolution were hardly obscure. Spanish fascism was a heady amalgam of nationalistic fervour and religious crusade and made a direct appeal to those who wished to maintain tradition and establish a stable social order. With powerful ideological and material support in Western Europe at the time, it was a combination that was almost certain to succeed. But it was countered by an equally potent socialist ideology which had a great deal of popular support. This clash of values between factions that were equally convinced of the rightness of their respective causes was the formula for the worst kind of fratricidal strife.

# CHAPTER THIRTEEN

# Massacre as a Tactical Exigency: The choice-of-evils-problem

This chapter presents us with one of the most intractable moral problems in this whole discussion. It can take various forms, but essentially it involves not so much a clear choice between good and evil (assuming we know exactly what these are in any given set of circumstances) but the invidious necessity of choosing between equally persuasive evils. The decision is difficult because the solution is not obvious. It is not even easy to know upon which criteria to base the judgements.

Perhaps the scene could be set by a personal reminiscence. As a young soldier in the Parachute Regiment, I met a number of the still youthful victims of the Arnhem campaign. Arnhem was, of course, a noble lost cause – an imaginative but futile exercise that was ill-thought through yet bravely executed. At various points on the periphery of the action, small units of paratroopers were winning in the skirmishes although, overall, the battle was being lost. In these minor engagements tiny groups of prisoners were being taken – but what could be done with them? Is it possible to take, let alone keep, prisoners in this situation? One of my informants recalled one occasion when he and others brought back some prisoners. Their sergeant told them meaningfully to 'take them down the road and get rid of them'. They all knew exactly what he meant. I didn't ask what they did. I don't think I really wanted to know, though I have often wondered what I would have done in the circumstances.

The case studies we are going to consider both concern World War II, and both reflect unfavourably – or, at least, uncertainly – on the Allies as well as the enemy. We rightly regard the atrocities committed by the Germans and the Japanese and their Axis partners as particularly heinous, but the Allies too were not entirely blameless. Both cases involve different aspects on the same moral dilemma: in the first case, what to do about prisoners that one is not in a position to keep, and in the second case, what does one do about material that cannot be allowed to exist even though its destruction means the loss of innocent lives?

The war in the jungles of the Far East was fought with a terrible ferocity which often meant that little or no quarter was given on either side, although nothing that was done by the Allies to their prisoners compares with the brutality of the Japanese. This can be illustrated from just one set of incidents that took place in the early days of the fighting in Burma. In an engagement in which an Indian unit was trying to dislodge a Japanese force from a small town, the battle was so fiercely contested that quite soon the insubstantial houses caught fire and there was a general conflagration. Civilians and soldiers tried to get out, and we are told that 'several hundred Japanese and rebel Burmese were caught and killed while trying to escape from the burning town' (Slim, 1956: 46) – an unambiguous statement which means that there was some unnecessary butchery. The Indian forces also had to make good their escape too, and their columns were attacked by Japanese aircraft. Trucks and ambulances loaded with wounded were either damaged or set on fire by the attack and had to be abandoned. Neither side was going to err on the side of chivalry. While this was all going on, a small Allied detachment approached a village on the west bank of the Irrawaddy and was welcomed by the inhabitants who assured them the area was free of Japanese. The troops carried out a perfunctory reconnaisance, and took the villagers on trust. They should have known better (the Burmese were often not to be trusted; there were considerable numbers in the Burma National Army, a puppet set-up officered by Japanese). The trap was sprung. Some troops managed to get away, many were killed there and then by both the Japanese and the villagers, and the few wounded that remained were kept until the next day, then tied to trees and used to demonstrate bayonet practice to the admiring villagers.

The fortunes of a prisoner of the Japanese depended very largely on the caprice of the officer in charge. He might be summarily shot or otherwise executed, or he might be 'merely' beaten, starved and tortured. He would almost certainly not escape ill-treatment of some kind. This was not conditioned by the degree of innate brutality of the Japanese which, as far as we can tell, is no more and no less than that of other people, but it does seem to be directly linked with the Japanese military culture's whole attitude to courage and cowardice. The defeated, especially those who simply surrendered, were regarded as being beneath contempt (Carlton, 1992).

It must be said, however, that the Japanese did seem to have a taste for gratuitous cruelty. There are a number of accounts of their treatment of prisoners, even of the wounded and incapacitated, which almost defy description. There were occasions, for example, when ambulances, in emergency situations, had – rightly or wrongly – to be abandoned, and were later found with every occupant bayoneted or knifed to death. In 1943, when the Japanese were intent on capturing Chittagong, presumably as a first stage in the projected invasion of India, they made a successful attack on the administrative centre of the Allies' 7th Division. They overran the dressing station which was crowded with wounded while the surgeons were still operating. The helpless men were murdered on their stretchers and the doctors taken out and shot. Even the Indian orderlies, who were sometimes treated rather better than the British, were made to carry the Japanese wounded, and then murdered when the task was done. At least one account of this incident (Slim, 1956: 240–1) makes it clear that the British later took what was regarded as justified revenge – but we are politely spared the details.

The Japanese treatment of prisoners is now well-known. Their camps were run on such frugal rations, scarce medical supplies, and harsh discipline that many men were physical wrecks by the time they were liberated. Statistics just numb the mind; it is not possible to conceive – let alone understand – the awful equation of human misery and human depravity. This can be exemplified by the situation in northern Borneo: when Singapore fell in 1942 thousands of prisoners were captured, and about 4,000 were incarcerated in northern Borneo where they worked on airfield construction. They were largely men from support regiments, engineers, electricians and the like. By the early summer of 1945 hundreds had already died, and those that remained were physical wrecks suffering from ulcers and sores – some of them even had flesh rotting on the bone. With the war now irretrievably lost, the Japanese commander, an ex-student of the University of Washington, decided to march these poor wretches from the coast to the interior. The jungle terrain would have been tortuous even for fit men; it was almost impossible for these who were all sick in one way or another. When men fell from exhaustion, they were either bayoneted or clubbed to death, or simply left to die where they were. Just 353 arrived at their new camp at Ranau, and those that then did not die quickly enough were executed. Out of the original 536, a mere six prisoners ultimately survived, Australians who had escaped *en route*. For the Japanese, the irony was that they had unknowingly driven their captives towards the invading Allies, not away from them as they intended (reported in Smith, 1990).

There are really very few things one can do about prisoners. They can be killed or ransomed – the common practices of the ancient world – or they can be incarcerated and then perhaps repatriated. The Japanese did not quite resort to any one of these as a policy: instead they 'kept' their prisoners – if this is the appropriate term – in conditions that were often tantamount to a living death. They worked until they dropped. It was an achievement just to survive in these circumstances. The Japanese do not seem to have had any compunction about the execution of the vanquished or moral qualms about ill-treatment in general. Their view was that good food and medical services were not to be wasted on their military inferiors, and what they got – little as this was – they had to work for. In fact, the Japanese often seemed reluctant to take prisoners in the first place, and, to be fair to them, had no wish to be taken prisoners themselves, as is evidenced by their suicidal defence of imposs- ible positions in the latter part of the war. So when they did take prisoners, they took the view that they merited only minimal con- sideration.

The issue here then is about *treatment*, and is only indirectly related to our main problem in the present discussion, namely, that of whether to take prisoners at all – especially in particular military situations. This is where we turn the coin over, as it were, and look at another side of the issue, this time concerning the behaviour of the Allies. Documentary evidence is obviously sparse on this matter. People do not freely admit to atrocities even so long after the events in question, though certain things can be inferred from accounts that are available. It must be stressed, however, that such reports do not provide us with *proof*, but they do constitute grounds for circumstantial probability.

If we take again, the war in the Far East, we encounter what might be termed the 'Chindit problem'. The Chindits, named after the mytho- logical Burmese temple guardian, were originally the 77th Indian Brigade who acquired a considerable reputation as a guerrilla force led by General Orde Wingate. He was apparently a respected but somewhat enigmatic commander who had learnt his trade in Palestine, where he had helped in clandestine Jewish raids against the Arabs, and in East Africa where he had led units of Abyssinian partisans against the Italians. His inspir- ation was T. E. Lawrence, and he felt that what Lawrence had done in the Middle East in World War I, he could do in the Far East with Burma as an ideal site for guerrilla operations.

Wingate led his first 'raid' across the Chindwin river in February 1943. The Brigade was then divided into several columns all of which were supplied by air, and some penetrated as much as two hundred miles into Japanese-held territory. In two months they destroyed bridges and cut railway lines, and generally wrought havoc, but did not seriously hamper the Japanese. The Brigade lost about a third of its 3,000 men and, on balance, the whole venture was judged to be a military failure although its dramatic nature gave it a considerable and much-needed propaganda value. The damage it did was little more than a nuisance to the Japanese, and it certainly had no serious effect on their plans or their troop dispositions. In all, it probably did not justify the expense in men and material, but it was a brave and imaginative undertaking nonetheless.

As the Chindits moved into enemy territory, the main thing that mattered was that their movements were undetected, and we find that there were angry complaints about the lack of security on the march. From the beginning almost everything went wrong. In fact by the end of the first week, Wingate had lost over 25 per cent of his men. Early on they had intended to attack a Japanese base, but some platoons ran into a Japanese patrol some of whom escaped and alerted their HQ. This was exactly what was *not* supposed to happen. Some Japanese were killed in this engagement, but we are not told what happened to the prisoners.

This exemplifies the essential dilemma. In circumstances such as these where secrecy is all important, can the enemy be allowed to live? When troops are far from their base and, indeed, may have the most serious difficulties in getting back to base, is it possible to take prisoners? We find that when the Chindits came to the primary objective of their mission, the cutting of the railway in Upper Burma, they 'mercilessly ambushed' the Japanese who then launched a counter attack only to be 'shot down to the last man'. Meanwhile, another Chindit platoon had surprised and killed all but one of a lorry load of Japanese (Sykes, 1959: 401–2).

This sort of thing happened time and time again. It was regarded as being necessary and resourceful. Such expedients were seen as legitimate military exercises. They were not massacres, as such, any more than were the attempts of the Japanese to ensure that none of them returned to base. For the Chindits, to search and destroy was the whole purpose of the exercise. They were there to ambush and kill and destroy communications. If Japanese escaped – and they often did – it was a misfortune which could not be helped. But prisoners were a liability; there is no word of Chindits taking them into captivity.

The second Chindit expedition in March 1944 across the Irrawaddy was also doomed from the outset because the troops were seen early on from a Japanese observation plane. Their task, therefore, became extremely hazardous, and they could take no chances. Their policies regarding their own troops became as harsh as those governing the treatment of the enemy. So the sick and wounded had to be left because they could not be allowed to jeopardise the progress of the expedition or increase its vulnerability. There have even been rumours that some were mercifully despatched to save them from the predictable 'niceties' of the Japanese.

War is a dirty game. There is no way of playing it according to some well-defined and generally accepted values. Regardless of the Geneva Convention or any other high-minded code, circumstances and wartime exigencies will usually determine military behaviour. Guerrilla warfare, in particular, has to make its own rules: partisans and commandos do not normally make provision for captives except when they are needed to supply information. After that they are dispensable. For most it probably all becomes a matter of routine – few give it a second thought. It is all part of the job. But the routine does disguise a serious moral dilemma. What does one do when the normal conventions of warfare have to be ignored?

Even if there is a desire to preserve human life and retain prisoners, is it really possible in the context of certain tactical situations?

All massacres are tragic, and massacres of one's allies – no matter what the reasons – have a particular poignancy. But desperate situations, so it is argued, require desperate measures, and few situations have been as desperate as that of the British in 1940. France, which some had thought to possess the finest army in Europe, had been overrun in a mere six weeks, and no one was left actively to prevent Germany's complete mastery of Western Europe except Britain.

It looked to be a very one-sided contest. The British army had been hopelessly outclassed in France, but then, to be fair, it had not received much help from the dispirited and demoralised French forces. The breakdown of resistance to the German forces was such that within only ten days of the offensive which began on 10 May 1940, the British were left with very few choices. It was decided to fall back on the Channel ports and hold a defensive perimeter long enough for the British Expeditionary Force to embark. But whether this could be done in concert with the French and the Belgians was very uncertain. Understandably, the suspicion arose among the French that the British were playing a double game, encouraging the idea of a French attack while at the same time, withdrawing to the Channel coast. These suspicions were exacerbated – indeed, for some, confirmed – by the British government's reluctance to release fighter squadrons to bolster the rather weak French Air Force. By 28 May, the Belgians had capitulated and the French War Committee was already discussing the possibility of an armistice. The French had come to distrust British promises. While their army was being crippled by German *blitzkrieg* tactics, they felt that all the British could do was to save their own skins. *Their* choices too were limited, but the High Command knew that there was always the possibility of continuing the war from the colonies, especially with their fleet intact.

The British really had only three options: capitulation, an almost certainly fruitless last-ditch stand, or, the most realistic, evacuation. They chose to cut their losses and run, and hope to fight another day. All troops were away by 3 June. They had lost most of their equipment but saved the bulk of the army – more than was thought possible at the time. In fact, as is now so well known, the escape was so successful that it came to be regarded as a kind of miracle. Certainly there was a fortuitous (strange?) combination of factors that facilitated the escape: the weather, the German High Command's blunder of halting the panzers when victory was in sight (a pause which saved the British), and not least, the hubris of Hermann Goering in thinking that the Luftwaffe could do the work of annihilation instead. Whatever the reasons, Dunkirk subsequently entered into British military mythology.

Behind their 'moat', the British felt far from secure. Throughout the summer of 1940, they were expecting the invasion which never actually materialised. They had enjoyed three centuries of immunity from war on their own soil, and some comforted themselves with the thought that the British traditionally lose every battle except the last. But for the majority there was considerable apprehension combined with a pride in their own determination to survive. They were insistent that they would go it alone against all the odds. As George VI wrote to his mother at the time, 'Personally, I feel happier now that we have no allies to be polite to . . .' (Thompson, 1966: 132). It is perhaps significant that in May 1940, according to a Gallup Poll, only 3 per cent believed, or admitted, that they would lose the war, and by the end of the year when the danger of invasion had obviously receded, the proportion was less than 1 per cent.

This confidence was not based upon a very firm foundation. The British had rather an inglorious record in relation to their friends and allies. There was Czechoslovakia which had been shamefully sold out at Munich; Poland, which they were too late to help; Norway, from which there had been an ignominious retreat after a botched campaign; and now retreat from France. Little wonder that the Germans and many neutral observers thought that surrender was only a matter of time. Such views also extended to some of Britain's friends, and even to British nationals. The British Ambassador to Spain, Sir Samuel Hoare, effectively demoted by Prime Minister Churchill because of his association with the appeasement policies of the pre-war years, was reported to be pessimistic about Britain's prospects. R. A. Butler, Under Secretary of State for Foreign Affairs, admitted at the time that he would favour a compromise peace if it could be on reasonable terms. It was even rumoured that the Duke of Windsor was also disposed to the idea of an acceptable settlement – perhaps that is why he was shipped off out of harm's way to the Bahamas for a sinecure as Governor General.

In this unenviable situation, Britain's main hope was that the United States would join in the war, but American public opinion, insofar as it could be assessed, was firmly against intervention. In May, Gallup Polls showed that only 7 per cent were in favour of entry, and after the fall of France only 32 per cent thought that Britain could still win. German propaganda was aimed at increasing this uncertainty. Extreme isolationist views not only advocated keeping America out of the war, but also insinuated that aid to Britain was simply a waste of time. None of this was helped by certain prominent Americans. The celebrated flyer and Germanophile, Colonel Lindberg, was a positive hindrance, as was also the American Ambassador, Joseph Kennedy, whose pessimistic pronouncements did little to encourage hope in Britain's future. Fortunately,

there was a good deal of sympathy from the American President, Theodore Roosevelt, who bravely courted unpopularity during his election
campaign in order to secure some kind of economic help for Britain.
He influenced opinion with his famous 'America as the "arsenal of
democracy" ' speech, and an arrangement was made to let Britain have a
number of aged, though still serviceable, destroyers. But what would
have happened had America herself not been attacked by Japan in
December 1941, and especially if Hitler had not gratuitously declared
war on her – perhaps a bigger mistake than attacking Russia – is now
anybody's guess.

The French signed their armistice with Germany on 22 June, and one
of the most urgent questions this posed for the British was what was
going to happen to the French fleet? Britain braced herself for immediate
bombing attacks now that Germany had air bases near the Channel coast.
She also prepared for the anticipated invasion, and the keys to this, as
far as the Germans were concerned, were total air supremacy and enough
naval firepower to ensure that her troop transports made it safely to the
English coast. The British believed that this could only be achieved if
the relatively weak German navy was supplemented by units from the
comparatively powerful French fleet which was based largely in North
Africa. So the problem was to ensure that the Germans did not get
control of the French navy, and, if possible, to activate the French navy
to declare for the Allied cause and thus neutralise the effectiveness of
Germany's Axis running-mate, Italy, (not an inappropriate term in view
of Italy's subsequent military record) who also had a powerful fleet in
the Mediterranean. It was a threat the British could not afford to ignore.
With very few friends to help, she could not take any risks.

The original armistice terms between France and Germany stipulated
that all French ships should return to French metropolitan ports and be
demobilised under Axis supervision. However, after further negotiations,
the Germans relented and agreed that the French could demobilise their
own ships, if necessary in colonial ports, and further agreed that they
would not use such ships for aggressive military purposes. The British
became aware of this, and by this time no right-thinking Briton trusted
the Germans to abide by such a treaty – surely a just anticipation in the
light of Germany's later violation of the armistice conditions after
the Allied invasion of French Africa in 1942.

Only ten days after the armistice was signed, the British – despite
their reputation for indecisiveness – took very decisive action against
the French fleet. The Minister of Marine, Admiral Darlan, had already
promised that he would not let his ships be taken over by the Germans,
and had instructed his officers that their vessels and their crews would
remain French, under French command, and would stay in their respect-

ive ports. If, however, the Armistice Commission were to revoke their previous undertakings, then the ships were to leave their ports and sail for the United States. If this was not possible, he instructed that preparations should be made in case an enemy or an ex-ally should attempt to seize the ships. If this happened, they should be scuttled. Darlan was therefore emphatic that the fleet should not fall into foreign hands – certainly not unfriendly hands – but he also did a little bet-hedging by insisting that it must also not be used against the conquerors who had now arrived at a negotiated settlement with the French government.

The British decided that despite all these assurances, they must put the French warships beyond even the possibility of Axis control. Some of these vessels were in foreign ports, some at Toulon, but many were in colonial ports including those at Mers-el-Kebir near Oran. This French Atlantic squadron comprised about a fifth of the entire fleet, and included the battleships *Bretagne* and *Provence*, two battle-cruisers, the *Dunkerque* and the *Strasbourg*, besides thirteen destroyers, four submarines and a sea-plane carrier. On 3 July, this squadron was confronted by an equally formidable British force consisting of three battleships, two cruisers, eleven destroyers and an aircraft carrier. Its commander, Vice-Admiral Sir James Somerville, was under orders to present the French with four possible options: (i) join the British in the war against the Axis; (ii) sail to a British port from which the crews, if they wished, could be repatriated; (iii) sail to a French port in the West Indies, from whence the ships could perhaps be handed over to the Americans; or failing all these (iv) scuttle the ships within six hours. If none of these was complied with, Somerville had instructions to destroy the French ships.

Darlan's orders prevented the French commander, Admiral Gensoul from obeying British orders, and certainly ruled out the first two options. He sought anxiously to get some guidance from the French Admiralty, but there seems now to be some suspicion that they did not receive the full text of the British proposals. It appears that Gensoul gave them the impression that it was a straightforward ultimatum, either scuttle your ships or be destroyed. The negotiations continued throughout the day, with the French Admiralty far from the scene counselling resistance, and Gensoul desperately playing for time. He said that he would not be intimidated by threats but promised that if the Germans or Italians reneged on the armistice terms he would ensure that his ships would be taken either to another colonial port or to the United States.

It is here that things get a little hazy. Some accounts suggest that Somerville was under pressure from London to settle matters as promptly as possible, preferably *that* day. Perhaps, too, he felt that the French were just prevaricating, although actually they had already started to demobilise. The French crews seem to have been confused by this, as some had the impression that they were actually going to join the British to carry on the war against Germany. British patience was exhausted by the time the ultimatum expired in the early evening, and the command was given to attack the French ships which were anchored in such a way that any retaliation was difficult, if not impossible. They were effectively unprepared for the assault; and could hardly believe that an ally – albeit, technically an ex-ally – could even contemplate such a thing. The *Strasbourg* and five destroyers did manage to get away, but the *Bretagne* was blown up, and the *Dunkerque* and the *Provence* were seriously damaged. It was later estimated that 1,648 French seamen were killed, wounded or reported missing, presumed dead.

The whole tragic affair had a very mixed reception. The British press hailed it as a great victory, and this was echoed by the Americans. But it didn't do much for Anglo–French relations, especially in the aftermath of Dunkirk. Germany rejoiced because they felt that it finally set the old allies, Britain and France, on opposite sides, and there were unsuccessful calls for France to join the Axis in the war against Britain. Perhaps the last word should be that of the man who carried out the operation, Admiral Somerville, who said that 'It [is] the biggest political blunder of modern times [and] will rouse the whole world against us . . . We all feel thoroughly . . . ashamed' (quoted in Thompson, 1966: 182–3). It was a massacre that the French would not easily forget. To them it was incomprehensible. They understood tactical exigencies, but this was between friends. They felt that there had to be another solution short of wanton slaughter.

# CHAPTER FOURTEEN

# Massacre as a Matter of Policy:
# The SS at Lidice and Oradour

Nazi Germany has to be one of the best examples of the modern police state. From its early years the Nazi party developed its own forces to support and protect the regime. Pre-eminent among these was the SS (*Schutzstaffel*), a para-military unit whose members were bound by personal oaths to the Führer-dictator himself. It began as the leader's personal bodyguard, and developed into an extensive organisation with its own cadres of police, espionage and counter-espionage agencies, including the sinister Reich Security Services (SD). Its early protection squads also developed into a powerful military force (Waffen SS) which existed in tandem with, and sometimes in competition with, the Army (*Wehrmacht*) itself. In effect, the Party established a state-within-a-state consisting of picked, loyal supporters who could be completely relied upon in times of special emergency and, when the occasion arose, to carry out those onerous 'special tasks' (a euphemism for executions) that might be required. Thus when in 1938, the Germans moved into Austria – already very much a kindred state – and particularly Czechoslovakia, the SS was the apparatus that automatically assumed responsibility for the internal order of those countries.

By a none-too-subtle combination of bluff and intimidation, Hitler succeeded in getting Britain and France (which had special treaty obligations) to agree to the dismemberment of Czechoslovakia in September 1938. It was a fruitless and shabby climb-down on the part of the Western Powers, because in the following March, Hitler reneged on the settlement agreed at Munich, and swallowed the whole of the country. In this he attained complete control of the sixth industrial power in Europe including a flourishing and extensive armaments industry, the weaponry and material of the well-organised Czech army, and about 1,500 aircraft of which, admittedly, only a minority were front-line planes. There was also a plan to dispossess Czech landowners, and settle Germans on the vacant farms but this was not a particularly successful operation. There were obviously limits to the changes that could be made in the short term because the German armaments industry was too dependent on its Czech counterpart to cause any unnecessary disruption to German preparations for the anticipated conflict ahead. Plans were made, however, for the deportation of 'undesirable' elements in Czech society, namely, selected members of the intelligentsia, Communists and other 'trouble-makers', especially the Jews.

There had been a certain artificiality about the creation of the Czech state after the break-up of the old Austro–Hungarian Empire at the end of World War I. It comprised different racial elements, and this generated tensions which the Nazis were only too willing to exploit. Those parts of the country which bordered Germany were absorbed into the Greater German Reich, but the bulk became a special Protectorate. The take-over was supposed to bring 'autonomy and self-government' to this re-fashioned 'Protectorate of Bohemia and Moravia', but in reality Czecho-slovakia became a German province – part of what Hitler insisted was the legitimate *Lebensraum* of the German people. A moderate Reich Protector, Baron von Neurath, was appointed, but to make sure that he was not too moderate the SS saw to it that one of their own minions, Karl Frank, was made Secretary of State. Frank carried out his work so well that he was duly hanged by the Czechs once the country had been liberated at the end of World War II.

The outbreak of the war did nothing to improve conditions in Czecho-slovakia and in September 1941 the Reichsfuhrer SS, Heinrich Himmler, appointed his assistant and Head of the Security Services (SD), Reinhard Heydrich, as Deputy Director of the province. This was done in order to tighten security and ensure complete control of the subject population, and possibly, at the same time, to remove Heydrich, a possible rival, from the power base of the SS in Berlin. Although technically, Heydrich was there to help von Neurath, he actually assumed the reins of govern-ment. This had obviously been the intention of the SS hierarchy in the first place.

Heydrich took to his new task with enthusiasm and ran the Protector-ate like a personal fiefdom. In some ways his approach was like that of a well-placed mafioso; he dispensed or withheld favours at will, and could be absolutely ruthless if he was thwarted in any way. It is interesting that there is some dispute among specialists of this period as to whether his methods were really effective or not. All seem to be generally agreed that he began with a wave of terror so as to instill the right kind of respect in the Czech population. In fact, he opened his account with the show trial of one General Elias, head of the Protectorate's puppet government in Prague who was suspected, or so it was said, of covert contracts with the Czech resistance movement. The Security Service abrogated to itself the right not only to carry out summary executions where necessary, but also actually to overturn legal court decisions, especially if they felt them to be too lenient. Elias was duly tried – if this is the correct term for what even then was regarded as a travesty of justice – and hustled away for execution within a matter of hours. Thus

Heydrich began as he apparently meant to continue. Other arrests followed. The Gestapo broke up resistance groups, and Heydrich earned himself the sobriquet, 'Butcher of Prague'.

What follows is a matter of serious controversy and this has indirect implications for the awful massacre which took place the following year. Once his immediate purposes were accomplished, and the population and its Czech leaders suitably cowed, Heydrich dispensed with the summary courts and settled down like a minor potentate and tried to woo the people with more relaxed policies and appropriate handouts of largesse. This more liberal regime seems to have paid off, at least in part, in terms of increased production and cooperation. Czech industrial workers were given more generous rations and better holidays, especially those in the armaments industry, and the people seemed to settle down to Nazi domination. He cunningly exploited the divide-and-rule game by playing off the workers against the bourgeoisie. It was a 'stick and carrot' approach that was obviously effective. Resistance continued to exist but much hostility was temporarily neutralised. Things were not quite as bad as many had thought they were going to be. So much so, in fact, that the Czech government in exile in London became disturbed by reports and felt that they must do something about Czech complacency. At least this is the impression given by some authorities (e.g. Hohne, 1969: 455–7), and this also seems to have been the verdict of certain contemporaries (e.g. Goebbels, 1948: 51) – but then perhaps they wanted to see things this way. A more neutral authority, Gerald Reitlinger, says that 'in Prague Heydrich had an assignment which he could carry out with all the limelight directed on him. After a few months ... everyone [except the Czechs] agreed that [he] had made himself popular ... with the honest working population of Bohemia and Moravia' (Reitlinger, 1981: 214). Other writers take a much more sceptical view and emphasise the growing resistance movements in the Protectorate and the increasing incidence of sabotage and terrorist acts generally (e.g. Infield, 1981: 98).

A plot was eventually hatched in London by the Czech government in exile to assassinate Heydrich which was to have momentous repercussions. And the point at issue is whether this was done because conditions in Czechoslovakia were becoming more and more intolerable or whether it was because Heydrich was being too successful, and Nazi policies were actually working.

In England, two members of the free Czech army, Joseph Gabchick and Jan Kubis were groomed for the task of assassinating Heydrich at a number of special training establishments in England and Scotland. They were primed on the basis of underground reports although plans could only be finalised when they saw the situation for themselves. In late December 1941, they were parachuted into Czechoslovakia and made their way to Prague where they contacted members of the resistance with whom they planned just how to get at the Protector. Heydrich had made his headquarters at Hradcany Castle but his residence was some fifteen miles outside the city, so it was decided to ambush him on his way to his HQ. The spot chosen was on the Prague–Dresden road where Heydrich's open convertible Mercedes would have to slow down to negotiate a hair-pin bend. The Protector was so confident of his standing with the Czechs that he was driven unescorted to his offices, perhaps out of sheer bravado. Given the conditions, therefore, it was assumed that the assassination would not present too many difficulties. The plotters spent several months perfecting the plan which they decided to put into operation on 27 May 1942. They were joined by two other resistance personnel, and were armed with a combination of sten guns (small machine guns), revolvers and grenades.

What followed was a mixture of tragedy and farce. The weaponry was faulty, the sten gun jammed, and as the Mercedes slowed right down, Heydrich, who by this time realised what was happening, drew his own pistol and fired equally vainly at his attackers. Kubis then lobbed a grenade into the car; there was an explosion but neither of the occupants seemed to be affected. Heydrich began to chase his attackers, still firing until he exhausted his ammunition. But all to no avail; the assailants made a successful getaway.

Pain is a strange phenomenon, and as can so often happen in the heat of the moment, the wounded may have no immediate experience of pain. This happened to Heydrich, but he was, in fact, mortally wounded. The explosion had forced particles of leather and bits of steel springs into his stomach, and some had actually punctured the spleen. He was rushed to hospital and given first-class emergency treatment, in fact some of Germany's best doctors were brought in to treat Heydrich, but he died on 4 June.

It was an unexpected but not undeserved end for the architect of the 'final solution' (the programme for the extermination of European Jewry). Presumably, like his murderous assistant, Eichmann, he departed this life unrepentant of the monstrous crimes of which he was guilty. Perhaps he found some repose in death; one investigator, Dr Bernard Weiner, of the criminal police, actually described Heydrich's death mask as having 'deceptive features of uncanny spirituality and entirely perverted beauty . . .' (Hohne, 1969: 457).

A state funeral was held in Berlin attended by 600 German officials and members of the Czech puppet government. Some 50,000 Czech workers, angry at the assassination, are said to have conducted a protest march, perhaps because they realised that things were bound to change from now on. Hitler ordered Karl Frank to take over temporarily from

Heydrich and, at all costs, to find those responsible for this outrage. The Nazi response was extreme and was met with mixed feelings in London. Some 10,000 people were arrested, and executions took place daily in Prague. In one way, it was something of a victory – a significant gesture from those Czechs who wanted to fight back but were impotent to do so at that time. In another, it had precipitated a programme of revenge that shocked the Allies. The question is, was this their intention in the first place? The most cynical view of the assassination is that it was deliberately planned so as to unleash a spate of atrocities which would stir the Czech people out of their lethargy and make them more active in their resistance. If it was reprisals and counter-reprisals that were intended, then the planners got all they hoped for.

Executions were carried out by military courts in Prague and else-where. Kurt Daluege, who succeeded Heydrich as Reich Protector reported that 1,331 people were killed, including 201 women. Predictably, most of the victims were Jews. In Berlin, on the day Heydrich died, 52 were killed by the Gestapo in a 'special action' and their property for-feited to the state. Within a week of his death, 3,000 Jews had been transported from the ghetto of Theresienstadt in the Protectorate for 'special treatment' in the East, and the special unit that had carried out recent exterminations of Jews in Poland on Heydrich's instructions were 'dedicated to the hero's shade under the name of "Einsatz Reinhard"' (Reitlinger, 1981: 217). Hitler's zeal for revenge was such that he warned Emil Hacha, the head of the puppet government, that if he had any more trouble he would deport the entire population.

The most terrible and inexcusable of the measures taken against the Czechs for the killing of Heydrich was the massacre of the people of Lidice, a small, inconsequential village near Prague. People have asked since, why Lidice? The SS attitude was, why not Lidice? The Reichsfuhrer SS was avid for vengeance, and Lidice was chosen with characteristic irrationality. It had been discovered, almost incidentally, that the Mayor of Lidice had a son in the Free Czech forces in Britain; furthermore, he also owned an illegal radio. So Lidice was targeted as the killing ground in Czechoslovakia for which the SS would be remembered. On 9 June 1942 units of the security police surrounded the village, and having 'contained' the population, the Germans took their time about the executions. Men and boys were led out in batches and shot. There were no explanations – perhaps few, if any, knew why they had to die – and there was certainly no mercy. The SS were deaf to the pleas of the grieving women and children. In all 199 men and boys were shot and the women and girls were deported to concentration camps; 195 women were taken to Ravensbruck camp where 52 of them died before the liberation, and 90 children to Gneisenau. The village was then razed to the ground – but it could never be erased from memory.

Kubis and Gabchick were successfully hidden by members of the underground, but were eventually betrayed by a fellow agent who wanted to take advantage of a German offer to protect those and their families who were prepared to give information to the authorities. The two assassins were finally cornered; Kubis was killed, and later in a furious shoot-out with the SS, Gabchick and some other resistance fighters killed themselves rather than fall into the torturing hands of the Gestapo. But even this wasn't the end. Those who were believed to have aided and abetted the assassins were rounded up and it is estimated that within two months of Heydrich's death an additional 1,600 people had been executed.

After the war most of those involved in these atrocities escaped punishment. Karel Gruda, the traitor, was hanged as was Karl Frank who had overseen the whole operation. The courts dropped the charges concerning the abduction of the children because technically they were orphans. But the commander of the unit that carried out the massacre, Colonel Max Rostock, was captured by the Russians and extradited to Prague where he was hanged in August 1951.

There is a postscript to this tragedy which has its own particular kind of irony. There is now evidence to suggest that Himmler, who was undoubtedly jealous of Heydrich and was pleased to get rid of him by posting him to Prague, actually fed information about Heydrich's movements to the Czech underground in the hope that they would do the rest. Himmler gave every appearance of being concerned, and dutifully ordered executions to convince his colleagues. But, given that Heydrich was one of Hitler's rising stars, Himmler almost certainly took the view that this was another potential rival out of the way.

Terrible as the massacre at Lidice was, it was no more than routine for the SS. Indeed, it is almost insignificant compared with the systematic programme of executions that were taking place throughout Europe. The Nazis introduced a tariff system especially for reprisal operations. In Western Europe it was significantly 'better' than in the East. In France, for instance, 50 executions for the death of one German officer seems to have been the going rate, whereas in the East it was twice that. What was considered appropriate was often quite arbitrary. In Italy, for example, in September 1943, when 32 German soldiers had been killed by a bomb, 330 Italian hostages were executed. Perhaps convention demanded less expiation when the victims were other ranks and not officers. At other times, as we have seen, whole areas would be devastated in retaliation for perhaps just one or two deaths of members of the occupying power. In all, the French toll of hostages killed was probably about 27,000; this can be compared with the East where the figure is quite literally incalculable. And all this is, of course, in addition to the thousands of houses destroyed and the massive numbers of internments – all calculated to intimidate would-be resisters.

Things were bad enough for dissidents generally, but those actually caught *in flagrante delicto* were given very short shrift. Under the conditions of the infamous Commando Order of 1942, Allied commandos were all to be executed, whether they surrendered or not. This was often preceded by interrogation, but any cooperation that might be given in these circumstances rarely saved the prisoner's life. Similarly, captured saboteurs – in instructions given in 1944 – were to be slaughtered on the spot. No mercy was going to be extended to those who raised their hands against the Reich, especially in the critical days following the Allied invasion. This gave rise to a number of notorious incidents in the later days of the war. One of the best documented of these cases of massacre as reprisal (but reprisal carried out within the general context of institutionalised repression), is that of the brutal killing of the people of Oradour-sur-Glane in July 1944.

The attack on Oradour was not entirely isolated; in fact it was preceded by a number of 'actions' against the French resistance. This was all part of normal German occupation policy and practice, yet these particular actions had rather more significance because they were carried out in the prevailing anticipation of the Allied Second Front, which would rely heavily on effective disruption by resistants behind the German lines, and because of the heightened level of actual resistance activity as a precursor to the Allied invasion. In March, for instance, some 500 maquisards, who had held out for some time against the Milice, the French collaborationist force at Glieres, were attacked by an overwhelming force of German mountain troops. They lost about 150 men; some escaped, but the Germans killed all the wounded they could find (Mountfield, 1979: 120). In May also, immediately prior to the invasion, the SS carried out a 'blood and ashes' action against the French partisans in the mountains of the Auvergne. In particular areas, France was seething with guerrilla activity, and this increased enormously after the invasion in the hope that final liberation would come – at most – in just a few weeks. Often this was as fruitless as it was courageous. Partisan groups sometimes pitted themselves against impossible odds such as at Vercors where some 2,000 members of the maquis died in July 1944. But these were localised victories only for the occupation forces. The Germans tried to cope as best they could, but they were seriously disadvantaged in terms of men and equipment; they only had 59 divisions to counter the combined might of the Allies, and many of these were woefully under strength. Replacements were always being promised, but the Germans had just too much to do elsewhere. There was resistance activity just about everywhere: the 'side-show' in Italy, the battle for Normandy, and, most of all, the Eastern front. Germany was haemorrhaging badly in the West, but in the East where she had 156 divisions, she was slowly bleeding to death. Between July 1943 and May 1944, Germany had lost 41 divisions in Russia alone and even after the Allied invasion, losses on the Eastern front were still four times as high as those in the West.

It is against this background that one must see the incident at Oradour. There was a desperation about the increasingly hopeless situation of the German armies that in certain ways dictated events. This is not to suggest some kind of determinist explanation which divests those involved of any sort of moral culpability. What is implied is that the circumstances existing at the time were key factors, both in the overall situation and in helping to determine what eventually took place at Oradour.

The Waffen SS were not squeamish at the best of times, and were certainly responsible for atrocities in circumstances which were not as critical as those of 1944. It was very common for detachments of the military SS to accompany the Security Service (SD) units in their 'actions' against the Jewish populations in the East. Such operations were mere routine for these ideologically motivated champions of the New Order. In fact, the Das Reich division of the SS which carried out the massacre at Oradour, had been involved in similar incidents before. For example, in the heady days of August 1941 after the battle of Yalmya near Smolensk where the division achieved some distinction, a rear-guard company was delegated to join the SD extermination squads at Lachoisk near Minsk where, according to their own reports, they massacred 920 Jews.

The Das Reich was one of the four 'classical' Waffen SS divisions (Das Reich, Viking, Adolf Hitler and Totenkopf) which were all converted into armoured divisions. At the outset of the Russian campaign they were made up of predominantly German personnel. During the first season of the campaign (1941–42), in which they had taken the brunt of much of the fighting, they had been so badly mauled that they were temporarily withdrawn from the front. The Das Reich division, in particular, had taken a terrible beating in the winter battles outside Moscow, and was due for some kind of rest. In 1942, divisional numbers were made up by contingents of both German and non-German recruits, and in this way – according to some authorities (e.g. Reitlinger, 1981: 168) – lost some of their original character. The Das Reich division, for instance, which was reformed in March 1942 in south-west France, was supplemented by Hungarians, Romanians, and a large contingent of Alsatians. After fighting again in Russia in 1943, it returned to France in readiness for the Allied invasion which was expected in the north or the south – or both.

Shortly after the Second Front began in June 1944, Das Reich, now redesignated as a panzer division with twice as many men as a normal *Wehrmacht* panzer division, was ordered north to join the units already engaged in the battle for Normandy. Although many of its most recent recruits were largely untrained youths – some as young as seventeen – the Das Reich was still a force to be reckoned with. Despite the inadequacy of some of the rank and file, its NCOs and officers were, in the main, battle-trained, dedicated professionals who were not prepared to question the will or wisdom of the Führer; 'they possessed neither charity nor mercy', they had a high code of chivalry to those they deemed worthy of respect, but 'those whom [they] did not deem worthy of ... respect – above all enemy civilians – [they] treated with unflinching ruthlessness' (Hastings, 1981: 20).

In 1944, Das Reich was commanded by Heinz Lammerding, an engineer by training, who had risen rapidly in the ranks from an engineer-captain at the outbreak of the war to general of this prestigious unit, possibly – if rumour is to be believed – more by his 'connections' than by his competence. What we do know is that by this time he had already picked up a reputation for unfeeling brutality in his dealings with partisan groups in Russia where he had once served as chief staff officer with the Totenkopf (Death's Head) Division. There is documentary evidence that he ordered the destruction of entire villages and towns which were believed guilty of aiding anti-German forces. So he had obviously served a suitable apprenticeship for what was to come.

On their way north from Montauban to Normandy, the Das Reich was persistently hampered by attacks from the maquis. Once the Allies had landed resistance movements were active throughout much of the country, particularly where there was a chance of delaying the movement of German troop formations to the battlefront. Anything that could halt the traffic of men and supplies was of enormous help to the Allies as they strove to maintain their precarious foothold in Normandy. The whole enterprise was going to be either won or lost at this point.

It was, of course, an equally critical time for the Germans. Hitler had ordered his armies to contain the invasion at the beachhead. For a while it was really a matter of touch and go. The only hope was the early arrival of the panzers, but the Das Reich was having awful difficulties in getting there. They had hardly got going when some of their units had to make something of a detour to Tulle where the maquis were having considerable success. As we have seen, the resistants were no match even for half-trained formations once they attacked in strength. The Das Reich took over the town, and some 3,000 civilians were rounded up and concentrated in the yard of the local arms factory. The officer in charge assured the Prefect that there would be no reprisals – after all, the citizens had not been involved in the actions of the maquisards, and they had shown considerable concern for the German wounded who were being cared for in the town hospital. But then a new order went out – presumably from Lammerding himself as the General in command – to the effect that three Frenchmen would pay for each one of the forty Germans killed by 'communist gangs'. The proclamation made it clear that 'for the maquis, and those that help them, there is only one penalty, the hangman's noose ... [therefore in future] for every German soldier wounded, three maquis ... will be hanged [and] for every German soldier killed ten maquisards, or an equal number of their accomplices will be hanged' (quoted in Hastings, 1981: 118).

There was a rumour at the time that the bodies of the dead Germans had been horribly mutilated, and it may have been this as much as their deaths which precipitated the reprisals which followed. In fact, there is some evidence to suggest that a number of German prisoners may have been shot out of hand, and that when the tables were turned, some Germans wanted more extensive reprisals than actually took place. In all, 99 hostages were hanged from lamposts and from balconies, and their bodies then ignominiously flung on to the town rubbish dump. Even as all this was happening, signals were arriving urging the formation to hurry to the battlefront. It was still only 9 June, just three days after the Allied landings, and every man was needed to prevent the enemy from breaking out of the beachhead; they must not be diverted from their main task. At the later 'war crimes' trials, the defendants looked back on this incident as a duty, and quite in keeping with divisional orders. The executions had simply been a diversion. A necessary, if painful, distraction before the main operations began. On balance, something that was best forgotten.

The maquis continued to harass the SS on their way north. The Germans, according to their tactical reports, were still inflicting considerable losses on the maquisards for relatively few men killed and wounded themselves. However, they did have to put up with appreciable damage to their equipment, particularly their transport. In their pursuit of the maquis one SS detachment became convinced that a small town near Limoges, Oradour-sur-Glane, was a centre of resistance activity. There was actually no compelling evidence to support such an assumption, but the Germans were in no mood to quibble. The suspicion was enough, the maquisards and their supporters must be taught a painful lesson. So on 10 June, the SS descended on this rather undistinguished little town which had seen nothing of the ravages of war, and which was now quietly awaiting the liberation. On this sunny afternoon people – young and old

– were rousted from their houses, children were turned out of their school, and all of them, together with a host of casual shoppers, were herded into the town square while the SS troopers set up their machine guns. The women and young children were separated from the others and made to wait in the church. The men and boys were forced in batches into barns and garages from which there was no escape. The troopers were heard laughing and joking while they checked their guns, and then in these faintly incongruous surroundings, the men and boys were shot to death. No one was intended to escape. Troopers wandered among the wounded, dispatching any who groaned or moved after which the barns and garages were set alight. Isolated individuals who had escaped the round-up were shot independently, and – perhaps most poignantly of all – the church was set on fire, and the women and children were either shot or burned to death. In all 652 people – mainly women and children – had been killed; ten survived by simulating death, and it is their evidence that led to the eventual arrest of some of those responsible for the killings.

Posterity had quite arbitrary ways of 'seeing' the nature of such crimes as these. Unspeakable as they were, it has proved all too easy to justify them in terms of wartime exigencies. The actual perpetrators were, by and large, not seasoned veterans but, as we have seen, largely inexperienced youths, Volksdeutsche and Alsatians who were relatively new to the SS. Yet they seem to have entered into the spirit of the regiment with remarkable ease judging by their performance at Oradour. Only twenty of the original detachment have ever been brought to trial; two were executed and the other eighteen had their life sentences commuted from between five to twelve years. The detachment commander, Otto Dickmann, was killed in Normandy only a few days after the outrage at Oradour, and Lammerding himself escaped and was later condemned to death *in absentia*. As usual, the public memory is short. Most governments put an unspoken limit on just how long they are prepared to go on looking for war criminals. Administrations have other things to do, and people have to get on with rebuilding their lives. The general, having made his way to the Allied zone, found that in time, no one was looking for him that intently any more. The British took no action to extradite him because there was no incontravertible evidence of murder. Presumably that means that no one could find suitable witnesses or a written order, or had ever seen him personally pull a trigger. He made his way quietly back to Dusseldorf where he built up a prosperous engineering concern, and died there in 1971 (Hastings, 1981: 228).

These accounts point up a number of features about atrocities. Firstly, that they are not committed by any particular racial stock or cultural groups. What was done at Lidice and Oradour was not 'typically German'. As we have noted there were other racial and cultural groups involved; this certainly applies to the mass murders that were perpetrated in the East where Ukrainians and Lithuanians were known to be implicated. It follows, too, that atrocities were not 'typically Nazi'. People were involved who were not necessarily *that* imbued with the Nazi 'spirit' and were certainly not members of the Party. They carried out orders simply because they were orders, and not for any strong ideological motives. Furthermore, these particular incidents reinforce the conviction that the Waffen SS may not have been significantly different from the SD – the Security Services responsible for the 'action commandos' who carried out mass exterminations. In fact, we know that it was not unusual for Waffen SS personnel to be seconded or posted to SD detachments – sometimes as a punishment. Indeed, if these incidents teach us anything it is that given the necessary conditions, anyone is potentially capable of perpetrating such atrocities.

# CHAPTER FIFTEEN

# Massacre by Proxy: Vichy and the Jews

June 1940 has to be the most humiliating month in France's experience. The German attack had begun on 10 May, and in just about four weeks the French and British had been sent reeling towards the Channel coast by the ferocious onslaught of the German panzers. The rout had begun with the Dutch and the Belgians in the last week of May, and by early June many French roads were clogged with streams of unprepared yet desperate refugees. Everywhere the story was the same. German planes bombed virtually every bridge over the Loire and machine-gunned the roads choked with refugees, especially when they were also crowded with fleeing soldiers. On 11 June, the government hurriedly left Paris, and three days later the Germans arrived at the city which was now inhabited by a fifth of its normal population.

At this fateful moment the proposal was made that the governments of the United Kingdom and the Republic of France make a declaration of indissoluble union whereby they would become one nation. The constitution would provide for joint organs of defence, and have common financial policies. This idea – almost certainly inspired by Churchill – was an attempt to bolster French morale and ensure that her colonies, and especially her fleet, would not go over to the Germans. Of course, it all came to nothing – and probably never would have done so even if the war had taken a turn for the better.

By noon on the 17 June, it was effectively all over; the Marshal of France, the aged General Petain, announced the surrender. The war was lost. The British felt that a military commander might have sued for a peace without dishonour, but it was a very different matter for a country to ask for an armistice while she still controlled the world's second largest colonial empire. It was now the beginning of a very chequered period of French history: a time of frenetic gaity and public apathy, of courageous resistance and squalid collaboration; a period, indeed, which is still remembered, and which still occasions recrimination and debate.

The fall of France was – and to some extent, still is – extremely baffling. Her weakness has been ascribed to a combination of military incompetence and political impotence. Pre-war, France had one of the largest armies in Europe, but her annual call-up had reduced dramatically since the 1920s. War reparations had given her quite a healthy bank balance, but the pattern of her expenditure – especially on the ill-fated Maginot Line – was often ill-conceived. There was also a deeply-entrenched social malaise – a pessimism about the future which was perhaps reflected in the declining marriage- and birth-rates. The country was governed by an uncertain and, in many ways, unfortunate series of coalitions which inspired little confidence in the electorate. And the intellectual mood – especially after the crippling losses of the First World War – was one of disillusionment and disenchantment. The war fostered antipathy to things military, particularly among the young and idealistic. There was a pervasive air of pacifism in France. The First World War was an experience they did not want to repeat.

At first, the terms of the armistice did not appear to be too harsh. Certainly they could have been worse. German documents now show that Hitler's greatest desire was to reach a quick agreement with Britain so that he could have a free hand in the East. He then hit upon what he thought was a stroke of genius, he would occupy only part of France to prevent a united France from rebelling or cooperating with Britain. Instead he would create two Frances, hopefully in conflict with each other (Barber, 1979: 294). So with the capitulation, France was divided into the Occupied Zone under direct German rule, and the Unoccupied Zone which had a notional independence.

Under the armistice terms, Germany would occupy French territory north of Tours from the west coast to the east, and part of the western coast to the Spanish border, thus controlling the Atlantic seaboard. France would have to pay the prohibitive costs of the occupation; the fleet was to be disarmed; French prisoners of war would remain in Germany temporarily – one suspects as hostages against possible future hitches in the occupation arrangements – but German prisoners of war in France would have to be returned immediately. The French were to hand over all German subjects who had fled to France. These were mainly Jews whose names were to be supplied by the Gestapo. The colonies were virtually untouched, but if the French had refused to sign the armistice and had tried to carry on the war from North Africa – part of 'Churchill's ghostly speculation' – it is highly disputable whether the Allies in their weakened state could have done anything to prevent the occupation of these territories as well (Fortune, 1943).

To be fair to the French, at the time of the armistice the Germans held some two million French prisoners of war, so they had to be humoured to ensure their safe return. Naturally, the Germans exploited the situation in subtle, though sometimes intimidating, ways. They used the prisoner issue to get what they wanted. And such was the cooperation of the French that by the end of 1942 they had managed to get nearly half of them back. But this statistic tends to disguise the fact that only one was returned for every three workers sent to Germany. It also overlooks other negative factors, in particular that the German occupation eventually resulted in the execution of nearly 27,000 French hostages.

The new government was set up at Vichy in the Unoccupied Zone and effectively controlled about a third of France. It drew up a constitution which was at the same time extremely conservative *and* revolutionary. The Leftist tendencies of the pre-war governments were abandoned, as the new regime was determined to return to the authoritarianism of the nineteenth century. The ten-man Vichy cabinet was headed by Petain himself who was old yet still vigorous, a one-time national hero of highly conservative views, and his second-in-command, Pierre Laval, who had enjoyed high office in previous governments and who, as a political realist, was much in favour of close collaboration with the Germans. It also included Admiral Darlan who was able and anti-British, a careful man who obviously wanted to keep his options open. These were aided and abetted by a motley assembly of senior officials including Charles Maurras, an avowed monarchist and equally dedicated anti-Nazi who sat alongside Joseph Darnand, head of the Milice, a French Nazi force which eventually merged with the Waffen SS, and Jacques Doriot, an ex-Communist demagogue who had long been working for a Franco–German *rapprochement*. Sadly too, in July 1941, only days after the formation of the LVF (Légion des Volontaires Français) which sent French volunteers to fight in Russia, many French cardinals and bishops, perhaps out of anti-Communist fervour, declared their loyalty to the Vichy government, though it should be pointed out that many priests maintained a determined resistance to the regime.

Vichy's standing was gratuitously reinforced by American diplomatic recognition. This appeared to be no mere formality as their Ambassador to Vichy was Admiral William Leahy, a confidant of the American President himself. It's true that Leahy was withdrawn in May 1942 when the Americans went to war, but they remained somewhat hostile to the leader of the Free French in exile, Charles de Gaulle, whom they regarded as little more than a British puppet (Grigg, 1980: 41). Indeed, when it came to Operation Torch, the Allied invasion of North Africa in November 1942, the Americans fully anticipated the willing cooperation of France's colonial troops, but they did not quite receive the welcome they expected. The French did not send their fleet to help, as the Allies had hoped, although they did scuttle it at Toulon to prevent it from being used by the Germans. When the Allies landed in Tunisia, the French were equivocal and irresolute about coming to their assistance. Similarly, when the Germans occupied previously unoccupied France in retaliation, we find that General von Runstedt noted in his diary that the French army was 'loyal' and 'aided our troops', and that the French police were equally helpful (Bower, 1985: 40). Such was the 'independence' – one might almost say, distrust – of the Vichy regime.

The Vichy government operated through a series of committees. It still had a Senate and a Chamber of Deputies, but the authority to convene meetings was within the gift of Petain himself, and he was not keen to share power with others. This near-autocratic rule resulted in the virtual abolition of civil liberties as the French had come to understand them. Democracy was no longer *à la mode*, and this shift in political orientation seems to have been accepted by the people as a necessary expedient in their present situation. They saw that drastic measures were needed. In the aftermath of defeat there were the seemingly insurmountable problems of unemployment, the repatriation of prisoners of war, refugees and rationing, not to mention the reorganisation of the educational system. But, in calling for a government that could rule by decree, Vichy was effectively introducing the manners of the conqueror. There was probably no other German-controlled territory – and for all its much-vaunted autonomy, that's what it really was – that had such an obvious taint of Nazism as that of Vichy France.

Political parties were abolished, and local councils, a key institution of decentralised democratic systems, were appointed rather than elected (unless they were very small). Public officials, including the military, were very much at the mercy of the State, and some 2,000 were arbitrarily dismissed in the first six months of the regime. The remainder had to take a personal oath of loyalty to Petain – a practice reminiscent of Hitler and his generals. It is difficult to know to what extent the National Assembly, in giving Petain these powers, really intended to do away with the Republic. Some obviously felt that the seemingly genial figure of the old General could bind the nation together, and he did become something of a cult image for the public in the early days of the regime.

But it was not so much the personalities as the policies and practices that really told the tale. Trade unions were disbanded and freedom of association severely curtailed. Those believed to be endangering the security of the State could be arrested without charge, and the law was retroactive on certain 'crimes'. The government even created a High Court which could try ministers and ex-ministers of the Third Republic who had 'betrayed their responsibilities'. The prisons were soon congested and concentration camps were established. It is estimated that by 1942 some 80,000 were incarcerated in this way.

Under the terms of the armistice with Germany, Vichy France was obliged to pay the conquerors 'occupation costs' for the northern (occupied) zone of 300 million francs per day. This was increased to 500 million francs when Germany took over the whole of France in November 1942, and to 700 million after the Allied invasion in 1944. The Germans also requisitioned food and other goods and materials besides recruiting French labour for military projects both in France and later, as forced labour, in Germany itself. Such exactions were thought preferable to actually entering the war as a member of the Axis.

All these demands generated a culture of repressiveness. Any hints of dissidence were suppressed and all those institutions and activities which actually or potentially threatened the regime were ruthlessly extirpated. Certain categories of people were not given the normal protection of the law: foreigners and those with foreign fathers, for instance, were ineligible for public service. Nowhere is this more in evidence than in the case of the Jews: '[the] Vichy [regime] was profoundly anti-semitic and defined a Jew more strictly even than the Nuremberg decrees of the Third Reich' (Calvocoressi and Wint, 1972: 303). But Vichy had a more religious and nationalistic basis for its edicts than the Nazis who were more firmly wedded to spurious historical and physiological doctrines of race, though it should be added that for the French, economic interests were not far behind.

The first anti-semitic laws were promulgated as early as October 1940, and previous laws prohibiting the libelling of racial and religious minorities were repealed. Jews were excluded from public service, from teaching, and from positions of authority in industry and the media. Furthermore, the numbers of those given admission to the universities were kept down to a minimum. Later, in 1941, more laws were introduced which allowed for the confiscation of Jewish commercial enterprises with little or no compensation. The one exception seems to have been those Jews who fought alongside Gentiles in World War I, although there was even some uncertainty about these. With the purging of the administration, one prominent Jewish lawyer wrote to Petain asking about the current social status of several of his relatives who had died in either the First or the Second War, and requesting that his brother be allowed to keep his military decoration for bravery. He got no reply (Dank, 1978: 86–7).

French Jews just could not believe that these stringent laws really applied to them – to foreign Jews or East European Jews perhaps, but not to them. In the immediate aftermath of the legislation they could not quite accept that it was fellow Frenchmen that were making such rigid distinctions. They thought that it must all be surely due to the malign influence of the conquerors. But they were soon to learn better. In February 1941 an SS official, SS Colonel Knochen, probably got somewhere near the truth when he wrote to the German military administration that, 'It seems almost impossible to develop in the French an ideological anti-Jewish feeling, whereas the offer of economic advantage would more easily produce sympathy for the anti-Jewish struggle (the internment of nearly 100,000 foreign Jews living in Paris would give many Frenchmen the chance to lift themselves into the middle classes)' (quoted in Dank, 1978: 225). The Nazis thus played upon the more venial instincts of the French by hinting that armistice conditions might be modified, occupation costs reduced and some arrangements made about the repatriation of French prisoners of war if the French were willing to cooperate on the Jewish question – a matter on which a painstaking report was being prepared for the SS. However, Vichy needed little encouragement.

After the armistice, the Germans, despite the protests of Vichy, annexed Alsace-Lorraine, which they regarded as being rightly theirs, and soon ensured that it was *judenrein*. In the Occupied Zone they set up a General Union of French Israelites which, in effect, represented the Jews to the German military administration. This really meant that Jewish citizens were listed and classified, and their identity known to the SS – a precursor to the inevitable deportations. The first round-up took place in May 1941, and consisted mainly of foreign Jews who thought it was for census purposes and little suspected that they were going to be interned. Significantly, a collaborationist newspaper applauded the action because it would mean that 5,000 less 'parasites' would be spending their time in Greater Paris. Later, in October, six Paris synagogues were dynamited by French fascists with the help of the Gestapo and in November the Jewish deputies to the National Assembly were dismissed.

Before long the Germans were also pressing for deportations from Vichy, which, true to form, had established its own General Commission for Jewish Questions. This was headed by a fanatical pro-Nazi, Louis Danquier, who was commissioned to put Vichy's anti-semitic policies into effect. Initially, the persecutions mainly affected foreign Jews, but eventually French Jews were included as well. In this there were awful, yet inexplicable, inconsistencies. On the one hand, it was not unknown for Vichy officials to intervene to save Jewish friends, especially if they had aristocratic connections. On the other, we find Laval proposing the inclusion of children under sixteen for deportation for the unconvincing reason that families could not be separated. By February 1943, Colonel Knochen was able to report that Laval would agree to virtually any measures against the Jews providing there was some amelioration of the armistice conditions. Certainly Vichy had no compunction about foreign Jews, and any Jews who fled south from the Occupied Zone were liable to arrest and deportation. One of the most sickening and disillusioning aspects of this was the virulent anti-semitism of much of the population; thousands of letters were sent to the military headquarters denouncing Jews who had false papers or who were known to be in hiding. Paradoxically, many Jews found refuge in Italy which at this time, refused to recognise either German or Vichy anti-Jewish laws, although this was to change with the German occupation of Italy in 1943.

Along with the deportation went the confiscations. The Nazis were quick to appropriate the goods of Jews that were designated for 're-settlement' – a convenient euphemism for extermination. The cache from these confiscations was considerable, from the art collections and silver-ware of the prosperous chateaux to the furniture and clothing and other minutiae of those of modest incomes.

In July 1942, there took place one of the most notorious round-ups of Jews in Paris. It was planned with great care by both the Germans and the French authorities. The methodical card index that had been compiled since the occupation was brought into play, and 9,000 French police, including cadets and special anti-Jewish units, were employed in the oper-ation. Certain exemptions were recognised but these were very few. Again, although there was genuine sympathy for the victims among some sections of the population, one of the most disturbing features of this tragic affair was the apparent willingness of so many French people to betray others. Some of the proscribed tried to escape though usually to little avail; some went into hiding with varying degrees of success; and others, totally resigned to the situation, took refuge in suicide.

Altogether some 13,000 people were taken, mostly women and children, and consigned to the death camps. Only about 400 survived their ordeal. It is interesting to note that on the plaque which now com-memorates the incident it simply states that these people were arrested by 'German occupation troops'; the shame of French participation in the massacres has been judiciously overlooked. To add to their disgrace, in the following month (August 1942) the Vichy government had 4,000 stateless Jews arrested in the Unoccupied Zone and turned over to the Germans. And so the carnage went on.

Active opposition to these policies should not be ignored. From the beginning of the occupation, there had been something of an unspoken civil war between the Resistance groups and those who favoured collab-oration. Most French people were not exactly indifferent but took a compromise position of simply doing what they had to do in the circum-stances. In practice, it was a policy of strategic non-involvement. The actions of Pierre Laval and police chief, Rene Bousquet, who ordered round-ups, betray Vichy's sympathy with the Nazi camps. Bousquet, according to German and French archives, eagerly agreed to German demands for 40,000 Jews, and insisted that *his* men were 'capable of rendering [this] great service' (Wavell, 1990). The zeal of his *gendarmes* sent about 76,000 people to their deaths, mostly to Auschwitz where they were gassed. In all, only about 3 per cent of them survived. Yet he and many like him have remained relatively immune from the law to this day.

Bousquet was tried in 1949 but given only a five-year sentence which was lifted in view of his other services to the State.

Admittedly there were objections to the deportations, particularly by Petain, but it is still a matter of debate whether this was out of sensitivity to the plight of the victims or whether it was because some Vichy officials saw these German demands as an unwarranted extension of the armistice terms. German demands violated the ostensible autonomy of the French government. Vichy wanted the right to make its own arrangements with its own Jews. Therefore much of their collaboration concerned stateless Jews – those unfortunates who had fled to France for refuge.

There seems to have been no way of satisfying the SS on the Jewish question. The number of deportations was never enough. Hundreds of Germans, the military, civil servants, as well as the SS, were involved in the persecutions, yet only 196 were named after the war. Of these, a mere thirty were convicted in their absence, and only two actually served prison sentences. Three further men were tried in Germany in 1980 and although patently aware at the time what the destination of the deported Jews would be, successfully protested their ignorance, and were convicted only of being 'accomplices' to murder (Bower, 1983: 56–7).

As far as the Vichy regime was concerned, the High Court tried the leaders of the government; eight were given death sentences, but only three were carried out, those of Joseph Darnand, Fernand de Brinon and Pierre Laval. The vast majority of those accused of collaboration were tried in other courts, and of the 125,000 or so men and women concerned, 2,853 were sentenced to death, and, of these, 767 were executed. France sent more of its traitorous citizens to their deaths than any other occupied country in Western Europe, although the actual ratio was smaller than that of others. General de Gaulle, who ultimately deliberated on these matters, commuted the death sentences of all women (even those who had been auxiliaries of the Gestapo) and all minors. Amnesties began as early as 1947, and in 1954 all those who had been condemned *in absentia* were allowed to return to France and were either acquitted or had their sentences suspended (Dank, 1978: 322–3). The public memory was tragically short.

As a nation, the French had very ambivalent attitudes towards the Jews. The Vichy government, quite apart from German influence or pressure, was noted for its anti-semitic legislation. Its insistence on making its own decisions did help some potential victims, but these were largely saved by default. In other ways, it was assiduous in making sure that certain quotas were met. One is left wondering if there was something implicit in their complicity. Whether this was, in fact, a matter of elective affinity – of doing for the Germans what they wanted done anyway. Indeed, a kind of massacre by proxy.

# CHAPTER SIXTEEN

# Massacre as a Strategic Extremity: The Allied bombing offensive 1942–45

The controversy over the Allied bombing offensive, especially against Germany, has been very ably rehearsed in a number of excellent texts, but no book on military atrocity can afford to ignore the issue or neglect its moral implications. The discussion, therefore, centres upon a number of related questions:

i)   How *necessary* was the bombing offensive? This question involves the still unresolved debate about area/saturation bombing versus precision bombing – and just how precise precision bombing could actually be.

ii)  How *effective* was the bombing offensive? This includes some queries about the choice of appropriate targets, and whether or not these raids had any significant effect on enemy industrial output, etc.

iii) How *justified* was the bombing offensive in moral terms? And who, if discoverable, was responsible for making these critical decisions?

During World War I, aircraft had been too insubstantial, bombers too few and the bombs too small to have any significant effect either on battlefield operations or on the enemy's civilian centres. But then the industry was in its infancy. In fact, by the end of the war only three of the large planes intended for raids on Berlin had actually been delivered. In the 1920s, the tremendous potential of air power came to be appreciated and even exaggerated by its devotees. One of these pioneers, Hugh Trenchard, became Chief of the Air Staff, and a firm advocate of the strategic air offensive which, in his view, would deprive an enemy not only of his productive capacity but also his will to continue the war. The pro-bomber 'school' became unashamedly doctrinaire in their approach to aerial warfare to the point where the bomber was seen as virtually invincible – an instrument of incalculable destruction – which, in Stanley Baldwin's 1930s phrase, would 'always get through'. The bomber, then, was something to be both admired and feared. Its potential for winning wars was beyond doubt. So all that was needed was for *your* bomber force to be superior to the others. It is rather surprising to find, therefore, that at the outbreak of World War II in 1939 neither Britain nor Germany was equipped with an effective heavy bomber force. Both had concentrated on light and medium bombers, partly out of conviction but also because of the production costs involved. It was felt that they had a general all-round functionality. Consequently, Britain had some moderately efficient Wellingtons, and some squadrons of Blenheims, an extremely slow and vulnerable aircraft whose brave crews knew the plane's weaknesses but who were nevertheless prepared to risk the hazards of the early bombing operations. The Germans had the much more effective Heinkel IIIs, Dornier 17s which were 'seasoned' in the Spanish Civil War, and, the later, versatile, Junker 88s. As hostilities developed, however, Britain and the USA quickly remedied the situation, but Germany never produced a really effective four-engined bomber for the whole of the war.

The quite understandable fear of the bomber was such that in 1939 the cabinet seriously felt that it might be wiser not to initiate a bomber offensive in the hope that the Germans would do likewise. It was an unstated policy. They trusted that each might be able to refrain from bombing, especially as far as civilian targets were concerned. Needless to say, they should have learnt from the Spanish experience; the *Luftwaffe* had simply used Spain as a proving ground. Even the ferocity of Germany's Polish campaign did not immediately disabuse them. Perhaps they persuaded themselves that Britain might just escape the worst, especially when the anticipated onslaught on London, which was more or less expected as soon as war broke out, failed to materialise. The 'phoney war' period, too, hardly helped. The relatively little military activity until the spring of 1940 encouraged a certain ambivalence of attitude. It seemed to confirm the hope that some settlement might yet be possible. Meanwhile, the tentative raids that were made in daylight on German naval targets met with such heavy losses that the whole strategy was called into question.

When the war in the West began in earnest in May 1940, the air war intensified. The fall of France only a few weeks later heralded the beginning of what is now clearly seen as the Battle of Britain. The entire situation now changed dramatically. The *Luftwaffe* High Command believed that it could neutralise Britain's military capacity firstly by destroying the RAF – a shrewd policy which almost worked – and then by switching the attack to civilian and industrial targets – a fatal mistake which never really looked like succeeding. During this period, manufacturing capacity was, of necessity, concentrated on producing fighters to combat the German bombers which now attacked Britain in force. It was touch and go for several weeks. The balance shifted from one to the other – the Germans never quite realising just how near they came to victory. Their bomber losses in daylight were high mainly because their escort fighters could not sustain lengthy dog-fights for lack of fuel. By

September the German attack had become devoted almost exclusively to less expensive night raids which probably reached their peak in December, but continued on until the spring of 1941 when Britain became something of a side-show in relation to Hitler's Balkan and Russian campaigns.

Except for the fluctuating fortunes of the British in the western desert at this time, there was no way in which they could effectively carry the war to the Axis powers other than by air attacks. They needed to get to grips with the enemy, both to make some token dent in his very formidable armour, and in order to boost flagging morale on the home front. This became even more imperative after December 1941 and the devastating losses resulting from the Japanese invasions in the Far East. So the bombing offensive began. Until this time there had only been one notably heavy air strike against the Ruhr after the apparently indiscriminate German bombing of Rotterdam in 1940. One suspects that this was retaliatory rather than strategic as it was launched the very next day. The connection between the two raids was hardly coincidental.

In the early raids the intention was to be selective. The concentration was on pinpointed industrial and military targets. At least, this was the policy, the *practice* was rather different – not by design but by default. Regardless of the inflated accounts given in the popular press, the suspicion was rife within certain sectors of the service that the raids were achieving very limited success. It was known that about a third of all bomber crews admitted that they had not been able to find their assigned targets. An enquiry was begun, and it established that only two-thirds of the crews found their way to within five miles of the target, and that on the Ruhr raids this figure was reduced to a mere tenth (the Butt Report of August 1941 was based upon an analysis of pre- and post-raid reconnaisance photographs). Daylight raids had proved costly and not that efficient, and night raids, increasingly the standard operation of Bomber Command, had now been shown to be little short of a farce. It was now quite conclusive that with current navigational aids precision bombing, even in moonlight, was just not possible, and, in fact, would not become anything like possible until 1943–44. When the Americans eventually entered the fray, they insisted that bombing in daylight was much more effective, although until the development of the long-range Mustang escort fighter this policy proved enormously costly in men and machines despite the extensive armament on their bombers.

Largely as a result of the Butt Report, British bombing policy underwent an understated but quite momentous change and turned to the highly controversial practice of area bombing. This was never quite admitted, certainly not in Parliament where a concerned but vociferous minority began to ask questions. Targets were 'extended' to whole towns, not least of all the urban housing areas where it was hoped that death and destruction would not only lower civilian morale but also create significant disruption to the enemy's industrial potential. Killing workers could be as valuable as destroying factories. It all amounted to the same thing. It was nothing more-nor-less than a lightly disguised policy of indiscriminate slaughter, a policy fully supported by the Prime Minister, Winston Churchill, who earlier had written that the only way Britain could bring the enemy to grief was by 'an absolutely devastating extermi-nating attack by very heavy bombers... upon the Nazi homeland' (quoted in Hastings, 1980: 116). He envisaged the creation of a 4,000 bomber force which would literally batter the Germans into surrender.

When Arthur Harris was appointed Commander-in-Chief of Bomber Command in February 1942 the policy was confirmed. He began as he meant to continue. He frantically scoured the system for just about every serviceable aircraft he could find and sent out the first of the 1,000 bomber raids, in this case on Cologne, which devastated some 600 acres of the city. Other similar raids followed on other targets, but the overall effect on the German war machine was still negligible. Ostensibly the targets had some military significance but it became an open secret within the service that the targets were the *towns*. Precision bombing at night was a near impossibility despite improved navigational aids and innov-ative Pathfinder techniques, so any damage to Germany's production capacity was always something of a bonus.

The choice of target was sometimes rather arbitrary, and greatly depen-dent on weather conditions, although there were certain favourite areas: the Ruhr, Hamburg, and especially Berlin – Harris's *bête noire*. The damage to people and property was horrific. Hamburg is a case in point: there were 33 major raids between July and November 1943, and in one concentrated period in which the British bombed by night and the Americans by day, it is estimated that at least 50,000 people were killed, and still the expert German repair teams managed to keep things going.

In 1942, the inexperienced Americans, not yet blooded in Tunisia, agitated for an invasion of Europe to take the war straight to the enemy. Such a venture was shown to be impulsive and premature by the explora-tory and disastrous Dieppe raid in August, in which a largely Canadian force was decimated. As hostilities continued into 1943 there was increas-ing pressure from the Russians to mount a Second Front to divert German forces from the East. The British prevaricated and temporised – perhaps rightly – until they felt that the Allies were fully prepared. The interim measure, the temporary substitute, was the bomber offensive which was joined enthusiastically by the Americans once they had their bomber force in place at British bases. They did not always agree with the British on bombing policy, but eventually they and their 'hosts' gradually assumed complementary roles in practice.

The Allied raids increased in momentum and severity into 1944, but the cost in crews and machines was growing. Losses of between 2 and 3 per cent were regarded as acceptable, but these began to grow significantly as German defence systems became increasingly sophisticated, especially in their deployment of their fighter force. For Bomber Command, the presence or otherwise of night fighters was crucial. Their toll of British planes mounted ominously prior to the Second Front, and losses began to exceed 5 per cent. This culminated in the near-catastrophic raid on Nuremberg in March where losses actually exceeded 12 per cent. Out of a force of 795 planes, 94 were lost and 71 were damaged. The American experience was not dissimilar; their losses, too, became unacceptably severe. Daylight raids – the American speciality – were hazardous affairs. Sometimes the losses were as high as 20 and 30 per cent, and in one terrible week alone they lost 148 planes. Things changed with the development of the Mustang. This was originally a rather indifferent machine, but was revolutionised when fitted with a Rolls-Royce engine and long-range tanks which enabled it to be used very effectively as an escort fighter. Bomber losses were still not good, but they were checked by the employment of these much improved fighter detachments. After D-Day, the Americans attacked with what can only be described as air armadas. In just one raid on 16 June, they dispatched over 1,000 bombers escorted by 800 fighters. The *Luftwaffe* still inflicted grievous losses but they had no real answer to such overwhelming superiority.

How effective was all this? In 1943, for example, 200,000 tons of bombs fell on Germany – five times as much as 1942 – but production levels of German industry in planes, tanks, guns, etc., doubled by the middle of the year and, by the use of conscripted and slave labour and the clever diversification and re-location of industry, had trebled by the middle of 1944. Even the famous Dambusters raid in May 1943, which was carried out with extreme heroism by very highly trained crews, did not really succeed in its intention of impeding industrial production in the Ruhr – and lost eight of the nineteen aircraft into the bargain. It was obviously believed by some that bombing could actually win the war so Bomber Command took a high proportion of all British military expenditure. One estimate puts it at one-third, and another that it cost one pound sterling to deliver every pound of high explosive. But was it good value for money?

The Americans decided that oil was the key to victory – a fact corroborated afterwards by the Germans – and they began to concentrate their effort on synthetic oil installations with considerable success. So much so, in fact, that although German aircraft production was still rising, there was precious little aviation fuel to get the planes airborne. However, Bomber Command's efforts were still principally directed against the cities – and still to little avail. They caused enormous damage to life and limb; the body count rose but, as far as we can assess, these attacks did little to shorten the war. It was only towards the very end that the cumulative effect of the bombing, especially precision bombing of the transport system, really came to be felt. By cutting off its vital resources, the Reich was gradually being choked to death.

It has been argued that not only was the bombing offensive often ineffective, it was also positively unimaginative and counter-productive (Downing, 1977: 211–12). An infamous, but little publicised, example of this was the operation known as 'Charnwood' which was launched in July 1944. The Allies, having invaded Normandy, were struggling to make some headway in the face of desperate German opposition. They wanted to take the key town of Caen, but having failed to envelop it, they planned to attack it frontally. For this they needed an intensive preliminary air strike. It was stipulated that this was to be not less than six miles from the Allied lines, lest they bomb their own men. But the German front lines were also less than six miles from the Allied lines. This error was then compounded by the fact that the strike was timed six hours in advance of the ground attack, so the German defences were both forewarned and virtually untouched by the bombing offensive. In the meantime, the inhabitants of Caen bore the brunt of the attack, and several thousands died in the raid. One commentator has suggested that this was the greatest single atrocity, albeit unintended, of the Normandy campaign (McKee, 1966).

It was also towards the end of the war that some of the most devastating and, so it could be argued, most unnecessary raids took place. The classic, but not the only, case is that of Dresden. The city was congested with refugees and foreign workers: it had little military significance except that it was strategically located, and it was thought that a suitably heavy raid would increase chaos and hamper the Germans in their now headlong retreat from the Russians. Germany was really beaten by this time, but it was decided to hit the city really hard on the 13/14 February 1945 with the usual tactical mixture of incendiaries and explosives. These created a firestorm which eventually killed an estimated 135,000 people – but probably did not shorten the war by one hour.

Even after the destruction of Dresden the policy continued. On 23 February for instance, one formation was given the small town of Pforzheim in the Black Forest as a target. It had a population of about 100,000 and was, and still is, the centre of the jewellery industry. The crews were told that it was a centre for making precision instruments, but that the factories were small and interspersed among the houses. This information was almost certainly correct because the crews found that it was well defended by fighters and anti-aircraft fire. A large area of the town was totally destroyed and 17,800 people were killed in twenty-two minutes. It was seemingly needless destruction so late in the war. As one German fighter pilot put it after the war, 'If you know a tailor in the town is making uniforms for soldiers, do you have to burn the whole town to stop him making them?' (Hunt, 1989).

These operations can be compared with the bombing offensive against Japan. Early in 1945 the Americans decided on a policy of area bombing as opposed to not very accurate, high-altitude 'precision' bombing. The war was in its last stages; the Japanese were on the retreat everywhere except in central China, and it was decided to deal a series of mortal blows to the mainland. On 9 March a force of heavy B29 bombers set out with instructions to burn the city of Tokyo. There was virtually no opposition, and they lost very few aircraft. The firestorm they created was such that they could not take aerial photographs for a week afterwards because of the pall of smoke lingering over the smouldering city. When they saw what they had done the commander, General LeMay, was apparently well-pleased. American estimates give 83,000 civilians killed that night; the Japanese assessment is about 200,000, many more than were killed directly at Hiroshima. Other principal cities were similarly devastated, and one is left wondering just how necessary the gratuitous nuclear destruction of Hiroshima and Nagasaki really was. Indeed, it may be one of the great myths of the war that the atomic bombs brought about the Japanese surrender. It has been argued that for the Japanese militarists, these new weapons were just the 'icing on the cake' and that the firestorms which killed about a million people – quite apart from the inestimable damage to property – had already brought Japan to her knees (Hoyt, 1986: 420).

The cost to Japan may be compared to that of Germany. Again, the damage to people and property is difficult to assess, but probably about half a million civilians were killed by the combined British and American raids on Germany. The cost in aircrew personnel was also abnormally high – about a seventh of all British deaths for the whole period of the war (Hastings, 1980: 11). It may not therefore, on reflection, have been *that* cost effective. It did divert a great deal of labour to repair and reconstruction work, but it certainly did not win the war, and whether it even shortened it is anybody's guess.

The arguments about the effectiveness of the bombing offensive have now become overshadowed by the moral issues involved. It is doubtful if these were given due consideration at the time. Churchill, who ultimately sanctioned the British bombing offensive, was primarily concerned with what was strategically desirable and tactically feasible. He wrote after

the war that we should never allow ourselves to apologise for what was
done to Germany. Indeed, 'There is no reason to suppose that [he] ever
suffered a moment's private misgiving about the course and consequences
of the strategic air offensive' (Hastings, 1980: 107). The programme was
also strongly advocated by Churchill's scientific advisor, the later Lord
Cherwell, and heavily endorsed by Harris who, even after the war, was
prepared to defend what came to be seen as an extremely doubtful policy.
It is interesting that towards the end of hostilities, Harris's truculence
and obduracy about area bombing was increasingly regarded by others
as an obsession. He became impatient and disillusioned by these criticisms, and very embittered when he did not receive the honours that he
felt were due to him.

But Harris was not alone. His emphasis on the destruction of enemy
morale as well as enemy industrial capacity was firmly supported by
most of his colleagues and defended in Parliament by the government.
Only a small minority had the perception and temerity to question it,
and when they did, they were either castigated or ignored. Quite early
in the 1940s, eminent scientists such as Sir Henry Tizard and Professor
Blackett, had pointed out the uncertainties of such a policy. Their arguments were, perhaps diplomatically, advanced at the pragmatic level, but
they appear also to have had moral overtones. As early as 1942, Liddle-
Hart took the government to task after the bombing of Cologne and
unashamedly referred to such practices as barbaric, contending that these
actions were no better than those of our enemies. Criticisms of this
kind either went unheeded or were regarded as the near-treasonable
idiosyncracies of cranks and pacifists. Public concern grew to the point
where Parliament was compelled to debate the issue in February 1944,
but again the sympathies were very largely with the government (Irving,
1985: 225). It is only with the benefit of hindsight in an attitudinal climate
of non-aggression that these issues have come to be seen in a different
light.

It is probably true to say that nobody ever does anything out of a
pure, that is to say, unadulterated, motive. This was certainly true of the
bombing offensive. The motives were broadly Utilitarian. It seemed self-
evident that the prospect of shortening the war was to everyone's benefit,
including that of the enemy. But even for Utilitarians it presented a
dilemma. Was it for the greatest happiness of the greatest number in the
*short* term or the *long* term? The bombing offensive was really a 'pain-
now-pleasure-later' policy. And the complex of motives was not without
an understandable element of revenge, a deliberate and calculated attempt
to ensure that those who had sown the wind should reap the whirlwind.
In the circumstances, this was perhaps pardonable. The clamour for
retaliation was certainly most strident in the aftermath of the Blitz

(Walzer, 1980: 256), but tended to subside later in the war. The reprisal motive can be seen particularly clearly in the different instructions given to aircrews who had to bomb installations, factories and other targets in German-occupied territories, and those that applied to Germany itself. In the occupied zones, a great deal more care had to be taken: crews had to restrict themselves to military targets, and intentional bombing of civilian populations was strictly forbidden. As we have seen, this hardly applied to Germany proper.

It is taken for granted that a bombing programme is essential to the prosecution of a war, but the questions such a policy begs are *how* precisely is it to be conducted, and what are its limits? Even the architect, Churchill, admitted that Dresden, for which he tended to blame the bomber commander, raised a 'serious query' against Allied bombing policy. Terror bombing – bombing as sheer intimidation – is not that simple to justify, although it does lend itself to justification in terms of situational relativism. Realist arguments would concede that all war is, in some sense, immoral, and that all attempts to humanise or civilise it are doomed to failure. Realists would maintain that if we can't outlaw war, what we can do is to rely on a balance of terror to keep the peace – a policy that is particularly applicable in a nuclear age. But such a policy has to rely on the *threat*, not the actuality of violence, otherwise we all lose. Quite apart from the incalculable consequences of the actuality, perhaps the very preparedness to employ gratuitous violence says something rather frightening and cautionary about the human condition.

# CHAPTER SEVENTEEN

# Massacre and Liberation I: The colonial situation

Revolutionary wars are nothing new. We tend to associate them with modern liberation movements, but they have been a feature of restless societies certainly since the days of the Ancient Greeks. Generally speaking, revolutionary wars have been attempts to overthrow tyrannies, to contest ruling elites or, at very least, to ameliorate current living conditions. The principal characteristic of modern wars of liberation, however, is that they are usually more concerned with bringing about basic changes in society. They are often, though not always, Marxist-inspired, and aim at a fundamental restructuring of the social order. Almost invariably they are 'people's movements' and, although ostensibly proletarian in nature, they are characteristically led by radical intellectuals who may not always live up to their early promises. The original inspiration is sometimes muted by success, and the reformative intentions barely materialise; such systems may even degenerate into oligarchies and autocracies – despotism masquerading as altruism. Few improvements may actually take place, and ordinary people are often little better off than they were before. Some critics may argue that this is a caricature of what really happens, a composite that barely corresponds to reality, but is it so very far from the truth? The reasons why oppressed people form liberation/nationalistic movements are often very compelling: dictators such as Idi Amin, for example, have to be banished; oppressive oligarchies have to be ousted; and weak, ineffective governments have to be brought down. But it only needs a cursory glance at what has happened to such movements, both radical and reactionary, in the present century to see how so many have turned sour and have not fulfilled their proclaimed intentions.

The moral issues here are critical. Under what circumstances is it right to revolt or to assassinate? Is it right if its for a 'good cause', or is it permissible only in the interests of sheer survival? How are we to define a 'good cause'? Isn't it possible to do the wrong things for the right reasons? Conversely, isn't it equally possible to do the right things for the wrong reasons? And how are right and wrong to be interpreted in these contexts? Or is it not a question of context – the relativist argument – but more a matter of trying to discern and implement 'absolute values' – whatever these may mean? Definitions are very important. For example, we tend to distinguish between the guerrilla and the partisan. Guerrilla warfare has certain suspicious overtones; it suggests that which is subversive and vaguely ignoble. Partisan warfare, on the other hand, conjures up visions of brave loyalists defending their territory against the unwelcome and often brutal incursions of an invader. Both forms of warfare are irregular, but one has a legitimacy that the other lacks. Yet this, too, has to be qualified. During World War II, the majority of the active resistance leaders in Europe were concerned not just with the defeat of the occupying Axis forces, but with long-term political objectives. Their eyes were set on the future, and the acquisition of political power. Thus, as in Greece and Yugoslavia, for instance, there was interminable squabbling and eventually open warfare between the resistance groups themselves. This seems to have been endemic to the situation (Carlton, 1992). We see much the same sort of thing today in the Arab world which is hopelessly divided in its aims and methods for 'liberation' from the Western 'imperialists'.

All war is terrible, but it has been argued that irregular warfare is the most horrifying of all. It is here that 'the most contemptible behaviour becomes normal, even commendable' (Mountfield, 1979: 9). The line between right and wrong, between legitimate and illegitimate becomes blurred, if not actually indistinct. Criminal acts come to be regarded as necessary and desirable. The observed norms of society may actually be reversed, and lying and hatred, suspicion and betrayal, torture and massacre may become part of everyday life.

The problems may be exemplified and possibly clarified if in this chapter and the next we look at some instances of irregular warfare in colonial and post-colonial situations. We will examine not only the nature of that warfare but also some of the possible reasons for its attendant cruelties. We won't actually solve anything by this, but we may just detect a few useful clues as to why humans are often so inhumane to each other, and to what extent this is conditioned by the circumstances in which it takes place.

Colonialism, as a system, has been variously interpreted. Not uncommonly it is seen as a kind of capitalist conspiracy, and even *decolonialism* is sometimes regarded as *neo*-colonialism, a new form of economic bondage which is little more than an insidious method of securing cheap raw materials and ready markets for capitalist exploitation. These species of conspiracy theory would have some cogency if it could be demonstrated that the imperialist powers actually did get together to fix markets, etc. Instead, the evidence shows that far from conspiring together, they have spent much of their energy conspiring *against* each other (Johnson, 1983: 506), often to their common detriment. That said, those peoples that have been colonised generally resent it, and when the opportunity occurs, have themselves conspired to overthrow it or, at very least, tried to ameliorate its effects. This has often been done by appealing to indigenous tradition, perhaps to nationhood, or, more broadly, to racial identity.

In this chapter, we are going to look at three post-World War II crises, two of them briefly, Kenya and Aden, and another, Algeria, in some detail.

## The Mau Mau emergency

The long-standing occupation of Kenya by the British inevitably entailed privileged living conditions for the white settlers. Nowhere was this more in evidence than in the apportionment of land which was organised on a racial basis – a system common to other colonies as well. In the inter-war years, the British settled largely in the White Highlands, and this generated increasing hostility among the Kikuyu, the dominant tribe in the region. In the ancient world, the incursive culture solved this kind of occupation problem by some form of slavery or enforced serfdom. But modern colonialism settled for privilege based on low-cost labour and depressed native living standards.

In order to redress the perceived injustices brought about by white administration, the Kikuyu formed the Kenya Central Association. It was this organisation that later constituted the basis of the Mau Mau movement. The Kikuyu undoubtedly had genuine grievances, and these appear to have been intensified by the propaganda of the Central Association. But mere talk was not enough, so a more active military strategy was decided upon.

The state of emergency began in 1952, and, for a while, the troubles threatened to spread to neighbouring territories. The Mau Mau had its own 'courts' which had the power to exact 'fines' from wealthier members of the community. Yet, despite all this, it seems that, like the IRA situation in Ireland, the movement did not command general support. The majority of the people were not that sympathetic – not so much with the cause as with its methods. Cadres of young tribesmen went into training in the forests in the Aberdare range where military instruction was given and hide-outs prepared. This volatile situation was further exacerbated by the arrest of Jomo Kenyatta and other officials of the Central Association. Their trials lasted many months, and eventually most were convicted of complicity in the Mau Mau conspiracy and were imprisoned.

Meanwhile, the active service units began the second phase of their campaign which involved raids on farms, the burning of homesteads and slashing of livestock and the killing of civilians. Although the primary aim was that of securing political independence, one of the immediate intentions was to intimidate loyalist Kikuyu and dissuade others from supporting the white cause. Some were persuaded to take the Mau Mau oath which is said to have involved such bizarre practices as drinking the blood of the movement's victims – all in preparation for a campaign of violence. Many educated tribespeople, especially teachers, were mutilated and murdered. Schools were closed and community life disrupted. Tribespeople were cajoled into contributing to Mau Mau funds with the promise of future rewards, principally of white-owned lands, and the money was used to finance the families of those who were members of the military units or who had been detained by the authorities.

The other immediate aim was to defeat the British by making life so uncomfortable for the settlers that they would leave rather than face disruption and the end of their livelihood, and perhaps even the loss of life itself. The Mau Mau obviously could not face the British forces in open battle, but the policy of subversion and terrorism had its effects. Settlers' fears were not unfounded. Sometimes whole European households were put to death, usually in small isolated communities without any military protection. Mau Mau activists, like so many 'freedom fighters', were not averse to the torture and slaughter of the defenceless. This was their stock in trade. Probably the worst atrocities were committed against their own kind. They had no time at all for those who aided the white administration or just wanted to remain neutral. There was no place for a quiet life as far as Mau Mau was concerned. This is exemplified by one particularly awful massacre which took place among the Lavi, a group of anti-Mau Mau Kikuyu who had refused to participate in the movements initiation ceremonies and take the oath. Many were knifed to death or burned alive in their homes; others were fearfully maimed for life. Children were slashed to death and pregnant women sliced open. The savagery was almost beyond description. Yet it was a complete failure. No one was coerced into joining the cause; the massacre merely strengthened the determination of the Lavi people to resist this kind of intimidation.

Atrocities are rarely anything but counter-productive. Sometimes they are little known to the outside world. It is a necessary feature of atrocities that they are covert and secret where possible. But among those who know and are concerned, they create a reservoir of resentment that inevitably has repercussions for years to come. Even where some kind of accommodation is reached, as it was in Kenya, between the authorities and the factions which supported the insurrection, the legacy of five years of conflict does little to create a healthy and stable society.

## The Aden crisis

The resurgence of Arab nationalism both during and since World War II has been one of the most notable features of the modern world. Its most vociferous advocate in the early days was the Grand Mufti who spent much of his life pursuing a policy of rabid anti-semitism, and was quite prepared to order the murder of Arab moderates to further his cause. The mantle of leadership was then temporarily and misguidedly taken on by King Farouk of Egypt, then under British suzeraignty. In 1952 he initiated a campaign against the British in the Canal Zone where they had a vast military base. It was murderous but ineffectual. Farouk had neither the ability nor determination to see it through, and in an officers' *coup d'état* the same year was 'sent . . . packing . . . loaded with a lifetime collection of trinkets and pornography' (Johnson, 1983: 499).

A heretofore relatively minor figure then stepped into centre stage, Colonel Abdul Nasser. His popularity rested on a heady mixture of Marxist-informed socialism and the cause of Arab nationalism. Like so many other would-be autocrats, he combined ideological fervour with shrewd political opportunism. He stressed non-alignment – a new vote-catching orientation at the United Nations – playing East and West off to the advantage of the Third World. Once in power, Nasser consolidated his position by proscriptions of actual and assumed opponents of the regime. He set up People's Courts, and before long some 3,000 political prisoners were languishing in Egyptian gaols. It paid him, too, to try to divert attention from urgent domestic issues to threats from abroad, his pet hates being the British, who still had bases on his doorstep, and the then new state of Israel which was seen as an affront to the Muslim world. Moreover, Israel was supported by the Western capitalist states, Britain and the USA, which had effectively acquiesced to the displacement of the Palestinian Arabs so that the new state could be created (not that Egypt – or any other Arab state for that matter – which had vast areas of uncultivated land, did much to accommodate their Palestinian brethren). Instead, they were content to let the problem fester as the running sore of Middle Eastern politics – a convenient *casus belli* should the moment arise when the anathema state of Israel could be taken off the map. It is reliably rumoured that Nasser imported a number of ex-Nazis to help plan for that very day.

The relative poverty of Egypt meant that Nasser had to secure financial aid where he could, even to the point of going cap-in-hand to the Americans. He had plans for the construction of a high dam on the Nile at Aswan which, it was believed, would bring greater prosperity to the land. A request was therefore made for a huge loan from the World Bank which would effectively have to be underwritten by the Americans who decided to turn it down. The project had many superficial attractions, but they took the view that it was non-viable for both economic and environmental reasons. Indirectly, this may have precipitated the Suez crisis of 1956–57. The British and the French were determined that Nasser's confiscation of the Canal should be resisted by force but, ironically, they were not supported by the Americans who may have inadvertently initiated the crisis in the first place. The Anglo–French effort to counter Nasser floundered more from irresolution than anything else, although if they had left the whole thing to their allies, the Israelis, they would almost certainly have won the day.

So, almost by default, Nasser was allowed to keep the spoils. He then bided his time and prepared for another *coup*, this time in Aden. Aden had been taken by the British in 1839 and became an important coaling station for ships *en route* to India through the Suez Canal which was opened thirty years later. It became part of the Federation of Saudi Arabia in 1963, and subsequently the scene of a bitter and complex struggle between rival nationalist groups and the British.

The terrorist campaign against the British was largely initiated and orchestrated by Nasser who was determined that they should no longer have any control – or even influence – in the Arabian peninsula and the Persian Gulf. The National Front for the Liberation of the occupied South had its HQ in Cairo and its main operational base in the Yemen. It was organised on a cell system, and recruits were given a very thorough training by Egyptian instructors in espionage and terrorism, and equipped with arms and explosives which originated mainly in the Soviet bloc (Greig, 1973: 67). A vociferous barrage of anti-British propaganda poured out from Cairo Radio. Threats were directed against British families, and sometimes specific personalities were named as potential targets. It wasn't all just wild accusation and intimidation. Alarmingly, grenade attacks took place in crowded streets, where other Arabs were mutilated along with the rest, but much as the nationalists hated the British, some of the worst atrocities were committed against Arabs who worked for the British administration, and the whole operation was encouraged and endorsed by the Egyptian media. Perhaps the most systematic outrages were reserved for the Police Special Branch which, within a comparatively short time, had its membership almost reduced to zero. The number of assassinations was such that those who were left felt compelled to offer their resignations. In fact, the situation became so intolerable that the British decided that the vestigial gains of remaining in the Gulf were just not worth the expense. They left in 1966 and Aden became part of the Republic of South Yemen in 1968. The British, however, continued to exert some influence in the area through a series of friendly states such as Jordan and Saudi Arabia in order to secure their vital oil supplies.

Insurrection had paid off for two main reasons: it had the support of the indigenous population, and the active help and encouragement of a relatively powerful neighbouring state.


## The Algerian War

In the aftermath of World War II, the French began to have problems in a number of their colonial territories. In Indo-China (Vietnam) a guerrilla war from 1946 to 1954 eroded French determination to stay in the Far East. After a series of humiliating defeats, the French decided that it was just not worth the trouble. They could probably have won if they had been prepared to invest enough of their military resources, but in the end they came to the conclusion that the whole tide of colonial emancipation was against them; it was no longer sensible to continue the slow haemorrhage of men and materials.

No sooner had the Indo-China issue been brought to an unsatisfactory conclusion, than a rebellion broke out in French Morocco. This took the form of a holy war (*jihad*) by the People's Party (the *Istiglal*) against 'lax' Muslims and the French government. The pattern was familiar: bombs, assassination of collaborators, sabotage, etc.; in short, the well-tried programme of terror and intimidation. In 1955, the rebellion spread from Casablanca to other key cities in the province, and the French, at a loss to know how to combat such a popular rising, retaliated with thoughtless *ad hoc* killings which did nothing to calm the situation. The Bedouin tribes of the interior were mobilised by the rebels, and murder became the order of the day. Two Europeans were massacred at Dued Zem, eight foreign correspondents were also killed, and general rioting broke out in a number of cities, especially Casablanca. The French brought more military muscle to bear on the rebels; their strongholds were bombed and strafed, and the Foreign Legion in particular took a fearful toll of rebels and rebel sympathisers. The whole situation rapidly became intolerable and, again, very expensive in men and material. So the French initiated a series of ineffective compromises, and eventually decided that the province was ungovernable. The territory became an independent sultanate in 1956, and a kingdom the following year. Once more, liberationist terrorism had paid off.

At the same time as the turmoil in Morocco and Tunisia, even more serious problems arose in France's last great overseas possession, Algeria. The territory had had a chequered history: infiltrated first by Phoenicians and then settled by the Romans, it was overrun by Arabs in the seventh century and by Turks in the sixteenth century. When it wasn't under the control of one or another of the great powers. its principal cities came under the authority of local, often despotic, rulers, and its coastal areas became notorious as havens of marauding pirates who preyed on Mediterranean shipping. In the nineteenth century it was taken by the French (Algiers in 1830) and its northern area 'incorporated' as part of metropolitan France. Emigration was encouraged by the home country and there was a steady influx of French settlers (*colons*) into the one-time colony. Gradually Algeria assumed the *de facto* status of a semi-autonomous state.

The settlers lived well – some very well. Conditions were not that dissimilar to Morocco where it is said that, on average, real incomes were a third higher than those in France proper. What was more significant was the disparity in status and living standards between the settlers and the indigenes, and it was obviously to the settlers' advantage that these differences were maintained. But it was not all one-sided. The French did wonders in the medical field, virtually eliminating typhus and malaria, and reducing the infant mortality rate beyond recognition. Welcome as these improvements were, they can be seen to have worked indirectly against the settlers' interests in that they facilitated a rapid increase in the native population. The settlers were simply being out-bred. Furthermore, the prospects were such that immigrants began to arrive in appreciable numbers from a variety of sources. Between 1830 and 1906, the Muslim population trebled, and in the next 50 years it had doubled again.

There was no attempt to give even the impression of equality. The settlers – if, indeed, they could now be called settlers – were better educated, better housed and better fed than their Muslim 'neighbours'. And the electoral system was such that the Muslims were in no position to change their own status or improve their own prospects. There was even some evidence of fraud and ballot-rigging by the *colons* which did nothing to enhance the confidence of the Muslim population that things would actually improve. Add to this the carefully graded racial hierarchy and we have all the ingredients of an extremely explosive situation.

In 1945 there were the first ominous signs of what was to come. Arabs massacred 103 Europeans, and the French retaliated by bombing and shelling villages, killing several thousand people (the figures are greatly disputed). The revolutionaries bided their time. They slowly recruited into their organisation, the FLN, ex-soldiers and Palestinians as well as native stock. Led by a trained guerrilla, Ben Bella, they prepared themselves carefully for the task ahead, acquainting themselves with all the well-tried tools of terrorism. Ideology was paramount. They concentrated on political education as well as military training. Cells were set up in the villages, and every man in the area was required to contribute a tenth of his income to the movement's funds. There was some degree of apathy among the general populace, and at first, much of the FLN's energy was directed against indifferent or unsympathetic fellow Muslims. The customary method of initiation into the rebel fraternity was to require a recruit to kill someone whom the organisation had designated as a traitor. There was then no turning back. Realism dictated strategy. The intention was never to defeat the French army – they knew that was quite impossible – but by the familiar war of attrition combined with extreme savagery, they hoped to wear down the will and resistance of their enemies.

The campaign began in earnest at the end of October 1954 with a cleverly concerted series of attacks on 70 different targets throughout the territory. The methods employed were some of the most frightful experienced in any revolutionary war. Bodies were mutilated, sometimes almost beyond recognition; a special refinement reserved for hostile Muslims was to cut out their tongues, presumably as a punishment for their active cooperation with the authorities – the cardinal sin. Indifference, too, could not be tolerated. So, as in so many revolutionary situations, the worst excesses were reserved for non-compliant Muslims, especially those who sought a peaceful solution to the problems. Ben Bella's written instructions were to liquidate all collaborationists. The rebels were ordered to kill any person attempting to obstruct the militants. This extended to their children, and any who merely paid or collected taxes. Any Muslims serving with the government forces were to have their houses burned while they were away. In the initial period of the war the FLN killed about 1,000 Europeans but at least six times as many fellow Muslims (although unofficial estimates put the figure much higher). But this *was* only the first phase. Things were to get much worse.

In a genuine attempt to conciliate Arab opinion and help to realise Arab aspirations, the French government appointed Jacques Soustelle as Governor-General to the province. Soustelle was a professor of anthropology at the Musée de L'Homme, an expert in pre-Colombian MesoAmerican civilisations, who had once fought as a member of the resistance against the Germans and so had some appreciation of the ideology and methods of liberation movements. He initiated a number of far-sighted measures to try to remedy the situation and foster a policy of integration. Muslims were brought into the administration, police were instructed to adopt more lenient measures against the populace, and orders went out that reprisals were to cease. In general it was an enlightened attempt to generate a whole new ethos in the administration of the country. However, Soustelle wanted no truck with the FLN whose members he regarded as outlaws. He formed special, SAS-type detachments to protect loyalist areas, though at this point he did not take any strong military initiative against the rebels.

All this was to change. The FLN was not going to be defeated by democracy. There was a renewed onslaught on moderate Arabs and liberal Frenchmen alike. In 1955, the FLN implemented a genocidal policy as far as the French were concerned, making no distinctions about either age or sex. The most horrific atrocities were committed against their enemies; dismemberments, disembowelings, indeed a whole catalogue of unspeakable acts, were all part of their extensive repertoire. They knew that if their activities were terrible enough, the French were bound to retaliate and that, hopefully, this would alienate moderate Arab opinion. To a considerable extent it succeeded.

The French were duly provoked. Paratroops were sent to deal with the insurgents, and *les Paras* were not noted for their delicate susceptibilities. They were not inclined to discriminate either, and some 1,300 Arabs were killed. This sounded the death knell for the Soustelle initiative and the disillusioned liberal was replaced by a hard-headed successor, Robert Lacoste. It was now a matter of terror and counter-terror. The FLN issued orders that 100 French civilians were to be killed for every execution of an FLN activist. Lacoste removed the former restraints from the army which was given *carte blanche* to take whatever measures it thought fit to bring the war to a satisfactory conclusion. Torture was introduced to elicit information from suspects and, in all, a ruthless campaign was waged by the French, especially in Algiers itself which, when it became generally known in France, alienated much liberal opinion, but succeeded in ridding the city of terrorism.

The Algerian situation undoubtedly facilitated the return to power of General Charles de Gaulle who had been 'waiting in the wings' for just this opportunity. Only a few months after taking office in 1958, he was elected President, and in 1960 he was voted special powers to deal with the continuing crisis. He temporised with the *colons*, assuring them that they would never be abandoned by the metropolitan government, but, at much the same time, opened up secret talks with the rebels. By this time the general public were growing tired. They wanted an end to the whole affair. At one point an open letter of protest was signed by 121 French intellectuals justifying the evasion of military service by potential conscripts (Behr, 1962: 239). A referendum was held in 1961 which gave overwhelming support to the idea of an independent Algeria. But the French public obviously could not envisage just what this could mean in practice for the *colons* and especially for the loyalist Muslim population. They and the army in Algeria felt that they had been deceived and formed their own terrorist organisation, the OAS (Organisation de l'Armée Secrète) which created havoc over the next twelve months or so killing thousands of civilians and hundreds of police and security men. The state, too, had its own 'special service' units which added greater confusion to the fluctuating balance of terror.

What should have been the end came in March 1962, when a cease-fire was called, and Algeria effectively became an autonomous state. Theoretically, France and Algeria were to face the future hand in hand, but this was one of those political daydreams which no one took very seriously. There was a mass exodus of Europeans from Algeria, and much of the evidence of French culture and enterprise was either destroyed or allowed to fall into disuse. More tragically, those Muslims who had supported and worked for the old administration, and who could not afford to emigrate were now at the mercy of their enemies. Some thousands suffered in the purges; perhaps as many as 100,000 were killed, often with terrible brutality, as retribution for their services to their French overlords.

A clear-cut military decision had been impossible for the French. The drain on their manpower and their Exchequer had become totally unacceptable, so they wisely decided to quit while they could still salvage a little of their reputation. But they left a country in chaos, with only some areas pacified, and some revolutionary groups still fighting among themselves. True to form, the ex-terrorist Ben Bella, became Algeria's first President, and in the 1980s, after some twenty years of independence, he admitted that the country was a ruin, and completely corrupt. But then he was an embittered man; he had spent much of his post-1962 years languishing in gaol at the instigation of his erstwhile comrades. It was but one of the war's unsurprising ironies.

It is little wonder that terrorism still flourishes in the modern world because although it can be counter-productive, it is often, as we have seen, quite successful, especially in the short term, as Idi Amin discovered in Uganda, and Pol Pot confirmed in Cambodia. If terror is competently and thoroughly applied, it can, as our examples have shown, pay quite high dividends in terms of the acquisition of power. But then it often fails because those who have seized power have neither the experience nor the expertise to maintain it. In their frenzy for revenge and their obsession with radical social planning, the successful insurgents, as in Algeria, often destroy so much that is worthwhile in the former culture. Hospitals, schools, etc., are closed or run down, and even public services and utilities are allowed to lapse so that the country gradually grinds to something close to a halt. It often becomes necessary for the old colonial power or some other willing patron to subsidise the regime so that it can achieve some measure of viability.

# CHAPTER EIGHTEEN

# Massacre and Liberation II:
# The colonial aftermath

Mass killing was sometimes part of colonial policy, though, more commonly, merely incidental to its applications. This could often be seen in the treatment of dissidents. Complementarily, massacre and atrocities were common features of the revolts themselves. However, in this present section of the discussion, we are going to look at such incidents as part of the colonial legacy. This is not to suggest that there is any direct *causal* relationship between colonial situations and the civil wars that have taken place in one-time colonial territories, but that there is some *correlation* between civil conflict in post-colonial states and the dislocations caused by the presence – and the recent departure – of European administrations. The relationship is indirect and unclear. Sometimes greater access to education by one tribal or ethnic group as opposed to another, or differences in regional development under colonial rule may have laid the groundwork for future antagonisms (see Kuper, 1981: 68–9).

There is a current tendency to think that everything about white colonial administration was, *ipso facto*, bad, but this is certainly not the case. In fact, it was sometimes because the indigenous peoples admired it that they were anxious to inherit it – if necessary, by force. But very frequently the would-be legatees were not united. Factions developed, all anxious to take over when the Europeans went, hence the fratricidal strife that has characterised so many of these successor-states. Some observers are inclined to dismiss these conflicts simply as the birth-pangs of newly formed – or, more usually, *re*formed – societies, but this is merely to trivialise the lethal power struggles that have taken place, and to minimise the terrible suffering and devastation experienced by the people themselves.

As in the previous chapter, each 'case' of liberation we are going to look at took place after World War II. In many instances, one suspects that the troubles are not really over. The reverberations continue, and have sometimes reached highly destructive proportions. In the Sudan, for example, massacre, famine and disease have claimed innumerable victims since 1955.

Our first case is that of Nigeria. Here we have a classic instance of a situation in which colonisation had interrupted earlier movements of tribal conquest. Decolonisation simply provided the opportunity for this to be resumed as civil war. Prior to independence in 1960, the various regional groups together with the British administration had formulated a reasonably workable federal constitution. In fact, it was considered by some to be the most progressive of all colonial schemes; a *modus vivendi* which tried to give representation to all interested parties. In general, it provided an acceptable basis for a future distribution of power in the territory. But there were certain impediments to the system. Northern Nigeria was more highly populated than the other areas, and its Hausa/ Fulani peoples – once the elite of Nigerian society – were Muslims, and therefore different in religion, language and culture from the other dominant groups, the Ibos in the East, and the Yoruba in the West. The Hausa were organised in a system of highly centralised emirates – a legacy of traditional Islam. The Ibo, on the other hand, were much more egalitarian and had a more loosely-knit structural organisation, whilst the Yoruba combined features of both. If anything, the Yoruba were more inclined to adopt Western culture and particularly take advantage of Western-style education. It was this situation, in which there was a considerable disparity in demographic and cultural (including religious) factors, which conspired to make conflict virtually inevitable.

The rivalry between these tribal groups had long antedated British colonial rule. Indeed, if a system was to be devised to cater for all the different sectional interests, it is estimated that Nigeria would have had to be divided into some 200 separate states – a quite impossible solution if the country was going to retain any sort of corporate identity. Attempts were made to maintain a federal arrangement which gave some degree of parity to all concerned, but the necessary unity of intention was just not there. The system began to creak ominously in 1964, and in 1966 it finally broke down completely when the Federal Prime Minister and some senior political officials and army officers were killed in the North by mutineers (Gutteridge, 1969). This led to large-scale demonstrations against the migrant Ibo community, and several thousand were killed. Most of those who survived fled back to their homelands in the East. Military rule was introduced to try to contain the situation, but this only exacerbated matters, and in 1967 the East seceded and proclaimed its 'independence' as the new state of Biafra. There followed two years of civil war in which only a few weak African states supported the secession- ists; most, including the outside world, backed the legitimate government, although there was a great deal of non-military aid forthcoming for the Biafran people.

One observer, writing just after the civil war, said that Biafra was 'born in massacre and bled in starvation' (Perham, 1970). Possibly as many as a million Ibos died as a direct result of the war, or indirectly through famine and disease. This appears to have been the result of deliberate government policy decisions which were taken with a fair idea as to their eventual repercussions. It was a policy of calculated repression which effectively amounted to genocide. To be fair, there were reprisals against Northerners living in the East; and although these cannot be mitigated, they were largely unorganised and sporadic, the outcome of Ibo anger and frustration about what was happening to their people generally.

In some ways, the formation of the Nigerian state was an artificial affair, a conglomerate conceived by colonial officials as a neat administrative entity. Indeed, it could be argued that those who died were really sacrificed in the interests of a bureaucratic dream – a Utopian vision of a state that never was. But perhaps this is not entirely just. The British had to leave a state that was operationally intact, a functioning entity that was likely to continue. They had planned for a decolonised Nigeria for many years, and had eventually produced what was generally regarded as an enlightened and workable system. There is certainly no evidence, despite all the shortcomings of colonialism, that the conflicts would not have existed anyway. What may be more to the point is that the introduction of European culture and incipient industrialisation, regardless of its advantages, upset the balance of power in West Africa and aggravated already serious tribal tensions. The civil war and all its attendant miseries can thus be seen as the unintended outcome of colonial administration.

In many ways, the pattern of Belgian colonialism was quite different from that of the British. The territories under Belgian jurisdiction that likewise became successor-states were governed differently but, nevertheless, suffered in similar ways from tribal and factional dissension. In Ruanda, for example, they instituted a most complicated electoral system and a five-level administrative hierarchy which, though well-intentioned, did little to ensure stability in this poverty-stricken state in East Central Africa. There had been clear tribal divisions between the dominant Tutsi peoples, who only comprised about 10 per cent of the population, and the indigenous Hutu agriculturalists long before the Belgians arrived on the scene. Tutsi control had existed since the sixteenth century, and the Belgians took over the mandate in 1919 from the Germans who had held it (together with Burundi) since 1890. Colonial administration did nothing very much to equalise what almost amounted to a caste situation. The Hutu seemed to acquiesce in their own subservience until 1959 when the Tutsi kingdom was overthrown by the Hutu who declared Ruanda a republic in 1961. This was recognised by the Belgian authorities in 1962, and in that same year a series of minor but murderous incidents gave rise to a general massacre of some 1,500 or so Tutsi whose property was then confiscated by the Hutu. In 1963–64 a further series of massacres took place involving some 10,000 people which some commentators (e.g. Kuper, 1977) have described as tantamount to genocide.

The experience of Burundi was not dissimilar. Again, most of the population were Bantu Hutu, together with other tribal minorities, whilst the dominant people were the Nilotic Tutsi who comprised about 14 per cent of the population, but in this instance the stratification system was much less rigid than in Ruanda which gave some promise for the future. Burundi, too, was under successive German and Belgian mandates until 1962, and in 1964 its union with Ruanda was also dissolved. By 1965, however, relations between the tribal groups had deteriorated to the point where they were trying to intimidate each other by policies of terrorism and counter-terrorism. In 1966, the hereditary ruler (the Mwami) was deposed by his son who, in turn, was overthrown in a military *coup* in which a captain (later General) Micombero set up a republic with himself as president. In 1972 he assumed absolute powers, and fighting broke out in earnest. In the 1965 incidents, the Tutsi had killed perhaps as many as 5,000 Hutu who were regarded as enemies of the authorised government. In 1972, the Hutu retaliated in force. This, in turn, precipitated massive reprisals in which perhaps 100,000 were slaughtered. Since this time, there have been further *coups d'état*, but actual bloodshed has been fortunately kept to a minimum.

Despite the understandable protests of the anti-colonialists, there is little doubt that in this case, colonialism exerted a restraining influence on the mutually hostile tribal elements. On the other hand, the Belgians can be justly charged with sins of omission in that they did little to develop these territories which, admittedly, have poor natural resources. Where wealth is limited, there will always be a struggle for whatever happens to be going, and what happens to be going is *power*. Such a situation could only emphasise rather than minimise already existing tribal tensions.

The situation in the main Belgian successor state, the Congo, was different again. The Congo (later the Republic of Zaire) was first explored by the Portuguese late in the fifteenth century. It survived as the kingdom of the Kongo into the nineteenth century – the 'scramble for Africa' period – when it became, in effect, a personal fiefdom of Leopold II of Belgium. His rule was officially recognised by the European powers at the Conference of Berlin (1884–85), and in 1908 became formally known as the Belgian Congo – a highly desirable colony rich in mineral resources, especially diamonds and cobalt.

The Congo became independent in 1960, during the hey-day of African decolonisation. It was a large state comprising many tribal groups with their own sectional interests, and almost immediately after independence its troubles began. The Belgians had administered the province quite successfully in economic terms, albeit with a good deal of paternalism that has been seriously criticised by some contemporary writers (e.g. Legum, 1961). Its development was such that at the time of independence, industrial production was high, health care was progressing, literacy was higher than in any other African colonies (42 per cent), but there were no Congolese doctors, and not one African officer in the entire military set-up (Johnson, 1983: 514). The Belgians' mistake was to leave the Congo with undue haste, under pressure from the United Nations, leaving the country ripe for the inevitable power struggles that ensued. Pent-up resentments against whites unleashed a series of killings in Leopold-ville by mutinous military units. It was the same tragic litany of rape, torture and butchery which the authorities were either too lax or too late to prevent. The Belgians sent troops to quell the uprising, and were roundly condemned by the UN who supported a new pretender, Patrice Lumumba. At much the same time, Shaba province (formerly Katanga) took the opportunity to secede under the leadership of Moise (later, President) Tshombe. In economic terms it was the most advanced of the provinces and the move was seriously resisted by the central government which had come under the leadership of the self-styled General Mobutu, a one-time NCO, who, with Western help, eventually made a presidential fortune.

As with Nigeria and Ruanda–Burundi, no one knows just how many died in the Congo as the result of general anti-colonial antagonism and specifically focused internecine hostilities. These have sometimes been glossed over as the inevitable formative traumas of new states, somewhat analogous to those of Europe when emerging from the Dark Ages. But the parallel is rather facile. If anything, the successor states should have learned from Europe's mistakes; instead, they have often been the scenes of death and misery on an unimaginable scale. In fact, those that we have considered here are – apart from Nigeria – among the lesser contributors to the decolonisation death toll. To do full justice to the catalogue of atrocity, it would be necessary to examine the cases of Amin's Uganda, Sukharno's Indonesia and the Khmer Rouge's Cambodia, not to mention the running sores in the Sudan, El Salvador, and so on. It is all very well to attribute this to poverty exacerbated by colonial administration, especially poverty side by side with relative wealth. But is it all as simple as this? It is true that the ambitious poor *do* become the rebellious poor, but the poor also readily become pawns in power struggles which frequently leave them as badly off as they were before. Colonisation often didn't do much for either, except to introduce them to the *possibilities* of a better existence. Before colonisation they were the wretched, ignorant poor; now, often under Western educated leaders, they have progressed to become the wretched, enlightened poor.

Our last case, that of Vietnam, presents us with an interesting comparison, not only because we are dealing with a Far Eastern territory as opposed to an African state, but also because the Vietnam situation combines both the anti-colonial war with post-colonial (some might say, *neo*-colonial) conflict.

The ancient kingdom of Nam Viet was conquered by the Chinese and remained under their control, off and on, until the fifteenth century. It was not until early in the nineteenth century that a united Vietnamese Empire was established, and when the French subsequently conquered the territory, they added Cambodia and Laos to form the Union of Indo-China in 1887. A non-Communist movement for independence was formed in 1927, and in 1930 the Vietnamese Communist Party was begun in Hong Kong, mainly at the instigation of Soviet-trained Comintern agents. This soon came under the control of Nguyen Ai Quoc, later the Vietnamese leader Ho Chi Minh, who had been in charge of the Comintern's Far Eastern Bureau in Shanghai. By the outbreak of World War II in 1939, there were a number of nationalist and religious groups seeking recognition. But this was set back the following year when, with the fall of France, the French were 'persuaded' to sign a treaty allowing a Japanese military presence in Indo-China which in 1942 became a full occupation. This was challenged by the Chinese who recruited both nationalist and Communist groups in the war against the common enemy. These groups had their eyes on eventual independence, so there was a great deal of playing off of one group against another in order to seek a potential advantage.

As the war progressed, and the Japanese position deteriorated, as a last-ditch expedient of their unsuccessful Co-prosperity Sphere campaign, they declared Vietnam, Laos and Cambodia 'independent'. This was only six months before the end of the war, and it was at this point that the murderous struggle for power began to take shape.

In September 1945, Ho Chi Minh proclaimed the Democratic Republic of Vietnam in Hanoi, and with the aid of his organisation, the Viet Minh (formed in 1941), he began to co-opt or eliminate his nationalist rivals. Within three weeks, the French, with British cooperation, were back in Vietnam, and in six months had re-conquered southern Vietnam and Cambodia. They reached a temporary understanding with Ho Chi Minh who was still pre-occupied 'neutralising' the power of his political opponents. But before the end of the year sporadic guerrilla war had broken out against the French.

After the Communist takeover in China in 1949, the Viet Minh began to receive supplies of material which enabled them to step up their war against the French. The following year, the USA sent considerable aid to the French, but, by this time, they had become further embroiled with

the Chinese and their allies in Korea. Meanwhile, the Viet Minh, following the example of their Chinese mentors, were consolidating their hold
on the North by a campaign of terror, intimidation and 're-education'.
Intellectuals, landowners ('criminals') and village leaders were the main
victims of the regime; many thousands were executed and imprisoned in
the attempt to communise the countryside. By 1954, and their defeat at
Dien Bien Phu, the French had had enough, and began negotiations to
end the war. The agreement which was made in July, but not signed by
either the Americans or the South Vietnamese, led to the withdrawal of
the French, gave the Communists the North down to the 17th Parallel,
and guaranteed the independence of Laos and Cambodia. This was not
altogether to the liking of the North Vietnamese who force-marched
some 5,000 peasants to the North for political and military training,
whilst vast numbers of refugees fled south.

In 1955, the Republic of Vietnam was proclaimed in the South, and
in the following year the remainder of the French forces left the country.
This was the signal for the Viet Minh in Hanoi to implement a resolution
of the Vietnamese Political Bureau to begin an armed struggle to take
control of the South; a plan that was to be backed up with programmes
of political and physical intimidation.

Insurgency began in 1957 through the agency of the Viet Cong, a
somewhat perjorative term that the Americans used for members of the
South Vietnamese Communist Party. They instituted a carefully orchestrated campaign of subversion, combining persuasive propaganda with
terror and assassination. Much has been written about the Viet Cong's
abilities as guerrilla fighters, but perhaps too little attention has been
given to their facility for propaganda warfare which was directed towards
undermining the confidence of government personnel as well as 'educat-
ing' the public. In time the Viet Cong established a vast network of
committees, cells and front organisations in order to engage the population in active support for the revolutionary cause. Executive decisions
were largely the prerogative of the PRP (People's Revolutionary Party)
which, in turn, received its general directives from COSVN (Hanoi's
Central Office for South Vietnam). But everyday operations were in the
hands of the NLF (National Liberation Front) who worked through
various district committees, and had a parallel structure to the PRP. By
1969, it is estimated that the NLF had about 40,000 cadres working for
it, and that their activities effectively blurred 'the line between the political and the military [in its] blanket condemnation of all establishments
[and its attempts] to harness the alienated' (Pike, 1969: 9). All was
designed to incite unrest and, if possible, generate a popular uprising in
government controlled areas.

Party control over the military activists, the Viet Cong, was, according to a Party directive, 'absolute, direct, and complete' (quoted in Greig, 1973: 73). This control was delegated by a Central Military Affairs Committee to the regional military affairs committees and political commissars attached to each guerrilla unit. The cell system had many functions. It gathered 'taxes' to ensure that funds and supplies were available to support the military units, and it also carried out clandestine information-gathering operations with members moving surreptitiously between urban and rural areas as part of the tactics of infiltration. All this enabled the Viet Cong to continue its work of subversion and sabotage.

The networks were extremely sophisticated, and revolutionary zeal was certainly not confined to the guerrillas themselves. A great deal of help was given by various women's associations in recruiting personnel for the Viet Cong; they were also effective in organising welfare and medical aid for the activists, many of whom were women. The youth associations, some of whose members were trained in the North, were also mobilised in the service of the 'revolution', and some were even employed in well-advertised suicide missions which were often preceded by horrific rituals reminiscent of Japan's kamikazi. Particularly effective, too, was the ideological indoctrination which interiorised every branch and facet of the overall campaign, emphasising, in true anti-colonial fashion, the decadence of the South and its imported Western values.

The American involvement in Vietnam escalated in 1961 when President Kennedy decided to increase radically the number of 'advisors' that were sent to assist the government in the South to counter the growing influence of the Viet Cong. Similar moves were made by both sides in Laos where Communist forces had become extremely strong. By 1963 American aid was needed to shore up the rather shaky régime in the South. More units were engaged as the scale of warfare increased. The Viet Cong's clever guerrilla tactics were proving extremely effective, and in growing frustration the Americans decided to take the war directly to the North by bombing selected targets – but all to little avail. The Americans now knew that they had either got to come to terms quickly or settle for a full-scale war. In 1965, President Johnson proposed that negotiations should begin to end the war, and offered one billion dollars for developmental aid. When this was refused – indeed, denounced – by Hanoi, the Americans began to bring in troops on a large scale, and air-raids were continued on the cities and the countryside on an on-off basis until almost the end of the war.

Much has been made of the American bombing offensive, especially against helpless and hapless civilians. The use of napalm and defoliants too has been rightly criticised, though they were hardly the means of attempted genocide that some have depicted (e.g. Kuper: op. cit.). This is to confuse massacre with genocide (see Carlton: 1990). Coverage has also been given to the atrocities perpetrated by the Americans, particularly in their search and destroy missions. Most notable – and least excusable – are those that took place at My Lai against totally defenceless elderly men, women and children, and which ended in a travesty of justice. Of the 47 men arrested, only one was eventually convicted. Few can now offer any good reasons for these acts. It is true that in this kind of insurgency situation it was often impossible to tell friend from foe, but this surely cannot mean that *everyone* must be treated as your enemy? To resort to mass killing in these circumstances simply betrays lack of craft and deficiency of intelligence. It is a pacification policy that is only one remove from that of taking and executing hostages.

What has not been given so much attention are the massacres carried out by the Viet Cong. These have been so de-emphasised that in some texts (e.g. Kolko, 1987) the very worst of these, at Hue, is just not mentioned at all. This most infamous of Viet Cong atrocities took place during the North's Tet offensive in 1968. Within twenty-four hours, attacks were made on 36 of the South's 44 provincial capitals, but most of these were successfully repulsed within a week. Saigon took longer, and the city of Hue was particularly bitterly contested. It was not recaptured for several weeks – a feat that was treated disparagingly in the US press (Santoli, 1985: 346). The events at Hue attracted surprisingly little attention abroad, but they actually qualify as some of the most horrific in the whole Vietnamese war. Once the NLF had captured the city, execution squads toured the streets searching for those who were regarded as enemies of the revolution. These people were hauled before hastily convened courts and given a perfunctory 'trial'. Those convicted were – as usual – police officials, civil servants, intellectuals, teachers and religious leaders, and so on, in other words, those who might question what was happening and who could therefore influence public opinion. The customary sentence for such presumption was almost invariably death, and not uncommonly death for the victim's families as well. The situation became even worse once the Communists looked like being ousted from the city; anyone who could identify secret members of the Viet Cong were in serious danger, and many were executed. In the months following the return of the US and government forces, mass graves were discovered at various places both in and outside the city, the largest being in some sand dunes near the South China Sea where around 800 bodies were found. In all, about 3,500 bodies were discovered, with some 2,000 other people unaccounted for. It makes one wonder how much similar treatment was meted out to other undesirables after the American withdrawal in 1973.

The decision to end the war has long been depicted as a humiliating defeat for the government forces and an ignominious sell-out by the Americans. Indeed, it is not infrequently maintained that the USA actually lost the war. This needs serious qualification. It is, of course, nonsense to say that they could not have won the war *militarily*. Their overwhelming fire-power and inexhaustible resources could have ensured a military victory if they had wished to achieve it. In fact, the losses to the North Vietnamese forces were astronomical, losses which they could not have sustained indefinitely. As for the US bombing offensive, the North Vietnamese had no really effective defence against these raids, and terrible as this strategy was for the North, it was only American restraint that prevented the wholescale destruction of the cities. But it was a war the Americans could not win in *political* terms. It is true that the Communists did not achieve the popular uprising they hoped for, but there was a great deal of sympathy for their cause in the South where the USA was trying to bolster an already discredited regime. Perhaps Robert Taber is right when he says that 'in the modern era it is not possible to colonize or to govern profitably or to keep a subservient native government in power – in other words, to exploit – without the consent of the exploited. To kill them is self-defeating. To enslave them is, in the light of modern political and economic realities, impractical where it is not impossible' (Taber, 1970: 152).

# CHAPTER NINETEEN

# Aggression and Moral Responsibility

The central question underlying our entire discussion is why do people commit atrocities? Is it to do with the way people are, or is it to do with the circumstances in which they find themselves, or possibly some combination of these? Are they 'naturally' violent and aggressive, or is their brutality the result of fear or frustration which have been generated by external factors? And whatever the reasons, can they then be held morally responsible for their actions?

Let us first of all consider the argument that it is all a question of nature rather than nurture. The most fundamental and determinist theories maintain that aggression is genetically based. It is reported that brain damage, electrical stimulation, excess of testosterone (male hormone) and low levels of estrogen can make *some* people act more aggressively (Davidoff, 1980: 368–9). But this tells us only that the 'drive' has some kind of physical basis, and that there is endocrinal activity when people are aggressive – it tells us nothing about what actually triggers violence, or what determines the *forms* and *levels* of violence. Other writers opt for instinct theories and argue that the problem lies in the individual psyche. Freud, for example, thought that people were born with an instinct to kill and destroy. He maintained that people 'are not gentle, friendly creatures wishing for love, who defend themselves if they are attacked', and held that the desire for aggression was part of our 'instinctual endowment' (Freud, 1957: 85–6). The studies of the Austrian ethnologist Konrad Lorenz, led him to agree with this idea that the capacity and even the desire to hurt others is fundamental to our natures (Lorenz, 1966). His view is that aggression is one aspect of the fighting instinct which humans have developed in order to survive. It is related to the mating instinct in that reproduction is facilitated by the union of the strong and the cunning, in short, those that have learnt to survive.

Another set of contenders are those who favour theories of aggression which hold that violent acts occur when people are thwarted or irritated in some way by *external* conditions. This would apply quite directly to many of the situations that we have discussed, especially where atrocities occur in the heat or aftermath of battles. This view is closely related to the idea that aggression is a kind of catharsis – that people need to give vent to their pent-up emotions otherwise they may develop certain forms of unpleasant neuroses. Freud toyed with the idea that expression is preferable to repression, but was quick to add that these feelings must be canalised, if possible in beneficial or harmless ways. The main snag with such a theory is that the responsibility for personal behaviour is conveniently shifted to some external source – perhaps because some theorists wish to see human nature in the best possible light. Also it implies that where practicable, all offending obstacles should be removed so as to obviate or, at least, reduce the likelihood of frustration. This has important implications for government, education, parents and the like, and discounts the contrary view that the overcoming of obstacles may be necessary for human development.

Equally plausible are those theories which put the blame on society rather than the individual. The learning theorists maintain that we model our behaviour on others. So, if we witness aggression or suffer aggression ourselves, we too are likely to be influenced in such a way and may also become aggressors (Strauss et al., 1979). There is a great deal of experimental work to support such hypotheses, though some of it is ambiguous (e.g. on the effects of TV violence) and much of it inconclusive (e.g. in relation to pornography and sex crimes). The key question that is left unanswered is why some people respond positively and others adversely to the same stimuli. Why, for example, will a few of those who see a film about a plane destroyed in mid-air by a bomb, go out and make hoax telephone calls to the police and to the airlines, while for most viewers the film has been no more than entertainment? Or, more pertinent to our discussion, why can a few who see 'Rambo' movies wish to emulate their anti-hero, while for the vast majority it is all so much improbable rubbish? Learning theories also tend to disregard the fact that a significant proportion of those involved in atrocities have never actually learned to *commit* atrocities; indeed the atrocity in question may have been their first and only time. These theories, therefore, do not answer the problem – if, indeed, there is any convincing answer.

There is one additional observation that should be made regarding learning theories: they do seem to receive some empirical confirmation from the fact that there are some societies that do not appear to act aggressively – the Zuni and the Pueblos of New Mexico, the Semai of Malaysia, etc. But the societies in question are very rare and invariably small-scale, undeveloped (or underdeveloped) societies. They do not represent the norm even among societies of their own type. Many undeveloped societies were excessively aggressive, as we saw from our example of South African tribal society. Furthermore, some of these traditionally pacifistic societies such as the Pueblos, could become uncharacteristically non-pacifistic when sufficiently provoked by would-be conquerors.

So much for the theories, but what about the actual *exercise* of violence and aggression? This brings us to war which is, of course, the most institutionalised – and perhaps most ineradicable – form of violence and aggression, and the occasion for most military atrocities. As far as we know, war is as old as mankind. Nothing has really changed except the technology. The warrior is one of the first identifiable social categories known to civilisation. The emotions, anxieties and rationalisations of the warrior/soldier were essentially similar for an Athenian at Marathon in 490 BC as they were on the Normandy beachheads in 1944. The only real difference is that in modern warfare death can come suddenly and without warning from an unknown, and perhaps unknowable, source. 'Battle, the central act of warfare, is a unique event in which ordinary men willingly kill and die as though those extraordinary actions were normal and acceptable' (Dyer, 1986: 4). Changed weapons and tactics have made no basic difference to this. Except in a few primitive societies where hostilities sometimes took the form of a non-lethal game, war has always been about killing as quickly and efficiently as possible. Consider the following from a Roman army training manual: 'A slash cut rarely kills . . . because the vitals are protected by the enemy's weapons, and also by his bones. A thrust . . . however, can be mortal. You must penetrate the vitals to kill a man' (quoted in Cottrell, 1961: 83). Other than the fact that we are here thinking about swords rather than bayonets, what really changes? The only essential difference is one of scale and efficiency. Alexander invaded Persia with perhaps 40,000 men; about the same number were killed on the Somme in 1916 in one battle alone. And during the last two years of World War II, over a million people were being killed each month (Dyer, 1986: 3).

The reasons and justifications for war do not fit neatly into any particular categories (Carlton, 1990). The motives for war are often hopelessly confused, and this takes no account of the disparity between the rationales of the political leaders, the higher military echelons, and the PBIs (Poor Bloody Infantry) who actually fight the wars and who, most likely, are there just because they are there. Wars may result from sheer economic necessity, though more frequently they are quests for what Andreski calls 'ophelimites', desired things, booty, land, wealth, women, etc. (Andreski, 1968). This does not have to involve massacre, but often does so when invaders want permanently to dispossess others of their property. War may, on the other hand, be pursued for quite different reasons: the search for status, or as an expression of individual prowess, or as a sign of nationhood in that it tests a people's mettle. Failing all these motives – or perhaps intermeshed with them – wars may be fought *as a kind of ritual*, as with many of the classical Greek city states which had their regular campaigning seasons, or they may actually be fought for *ritual reasons*, or what war-leaders believe or claim are ritual reasons, which are not at all the same thing. This too can precipitate massacre, especially where the victors feel themselves to be under what to us must seem an incomprehensible constraint to make thank-offerings to the gods. As we have seen, human sacrifice was common in the ancient world and even the Roman Games may have begun in this way. This ideological dimension is one of the most fascinating and least examined aspects of the principles and practices of war.

If we press the psychologists for some kind of an answer to the problem as to why people commit atrocities, we find that they tend to adopt a neutral, non-moral stance. Seemingly mindless brutality is not uncommonly euphemised as anti-social behaviour and those that manifest these unpleasant traits are seen as being maladjusted or as 'sociopaths'. Psychologists commonly speak of 'abnormal behaviour' but find this very hard to define. Normally the term connotes *defective cognitive functioning* where the intellectual abilities such as reasoning and perceiving are, in some way, impaired. It also connotes *defective social behaviour* – behaviour that would be commonly described as deviant – and *defective self-control* – a term that could be applied to most of us at some time or another. The underlying difficulty with this kind of analysis is that it fails to define exactly what distinguishes normality from abnormality. How are we to assess the *degree* of maladjustment or disturbance, and are we thinking in quantitative or qualitative terms? Add to these unanswered questions the additional issues raised by the cultural factors that distinguish people and practices, and the problem intensifies.

Some practitioners, in trying to be a little more specific, write of people who have an 'anti-social personality disorder', as though it were some kind of clearly identifiable disease. Those so afflicted are said to be not unsociable – they may even be pleasant and charming – but are said to be quite incapable of serious emotional attachments, largely indifferent to the feelings of others, self-centred and manipulative, and, above all, seemingly devoid of all sense of guilt or remorse (LeFrançois, 1983: 462). This is all very well as a characterisation of a particular kind of individual, but is it any more than this? One is bound to ask whether these terms are any more than mere labels – descriptions rather than explanations. As they stand, they tell us nothing, and simply seem to minimise the gravity of the situation. As the acerbic Thomas Szasz once said to his students about a particular psychiatric patient, 'Has she got an illness called depression or has she got a lot of problems and troubles which make her unhappy? . . . Does the psychiatric term say more than the simple descriptive phrase? Does it do anything other than turn a person with problems into a patient with a sickness?' (quoted in Davidoff, 1980: 479).

Many psychologists are more discriminating; they feel uncomfortable about ascribing unusual behaviour to some kind of abnormal functioning and this would even apply to such extreme acts as participation in atrocities. They would argue that these acts are clearly *deviant*, but deviant is not synonymous with abnormal. Admittedly, we are still puzzled by the responses of those classified as psychopaths such as some serial killers who appear to murder simply because 'they feel like it' (Carlson, 1987: 628–9). But these are truly exceptional cases. As far as we can judge, those involved in atrocities do not come into this category. 'Certainly not everyone who is a criminal should be categorized as having an anti-social personality disorder . . . It is important . . . that the label . . . is applied only to those whose whole life-style is typified by such characteristics' (Darley et al. 1986: 588). Our case histories have shown that this does not apply, in general, to those guilty of atrocities. In fact, the opposite would appear to be the case; it is particularly disturbing to find that, by and large, atrocities are not committed by exceptional human beings, but by 'ordinary' people, albeit in extraordinary situations.

There is some evidence to suggest that tendencies to violence in some individuals can be controlled or modified by drugs and, more controversially, by neurosurgery. Brain operations of this kind have been called into question because of the uncertainty of the consequences. After all, our 'maps' of the brain are still extremely crude and we are still not sure exactly how the multiple circuits work; the long-term results could be both embarrassing and catastrophic. The corollary of this is that there is no clear evidence that people can be made into unfeeling killers by psycho-chemical or other techniques, although there is reason to believe that it has been tried (Watson, 1978: 35–7). Mercifully, the Manchurian Candidate scenario which posits that an individual can be programmed to kill is still – hopefully – some way from us.

As there is nothing really new about war, so there is nothing really new about atrocity. Our studies have shown us that, yet again, it is simply the technology that has changed. Modern society has merely substituted the uncertainties of the indiscriminate bombing raid for the certainties of the sword in the belly or the knife in the throat. One of the earliest artefacts of civilised society, the Narmer Palette of Ancient Egypt, depicts a conqueror, possibly the king, who forcibly united Egypt's Upper (southern) and Lower (northern) kingdoms (*c.* 3100 BC), standing triumphantly over the decapitated corpses of his defeated enemies. In the following millennium, we have the despatch of Enna-Dagan, commander of the forces of the Syrian city-state of Ebla (little known until the excavations from 1964 onwards), who carried out campaigns in the Lebanon and against Mari, a city-state situated in what is now northern Iraq. The letter says, 'I besieged [the towns] and I vanquished the king of Mari . . . I heaped up piles of corpses in the land of Labanan . . .' and goes on to claim that he left thirty sets of corpses, and was later awarded Mari for his efforts (Bermant and Weitzman, 1979:

160). Can there be anything essentially different about ancient and modern massacres? Certainly the *motives* are very similar even if the *mode* changes.

Earlier civilisations were often awesomely cruel. Consider the boast of Shalmaneser III of Assyria who in his conquest of the mountain peoples of Uratu (modern Turkey) says that he dyed the ground with their blood as though it were wool, and that he impaled the defenders on sharpened stakes and stacked their severed heads against the walls (Piotrovsky, 1969: 47). Or that of another Assyrian conqueror, Sennacherib, who when he took Babylon (680 BC) – that most famous and oft-devastated of ancient cities – said, 'I levelled . . . its houses . . . destroyed them and consumed them with fire. I tore down . . . the outer and inner walls, the temples and the ziggurats [temple towers] built of brick, and threw the rubble in the Arahtu Canal. And after I destroyed Babylon, smashed its gods and massacred its population, I tore up its soil and threw it into the Euphrates so that it was carried by the river down to the sea' (Welland, 1982: 147). This attempt at the complete obliteration of a city and its inhabitants compares well with, say, the sustained Allied bombing of Hamburg and the fire-raids on Tokyo during World War II. Indeed, it is interesting to ask exactly what purpose total destruction serves. In the case of Allied area bombing, there is little doubt that it went on far beyond the point where it served any significant military purpose; 90 per cent of all the bombs dropped on Japan, for instance, were dropped in the last five months of the war, when the final outcome was beyond reasonable doubt.

It is here that we should think of the distinction between the '*tactical atrocity*' which is perpetrated for some assumed or actual purpose, as with, say, the killing of prisoners who cannot be 'kept', and the '*military atrocity*' which may have no such purpose, and is often committed on impulse (Watson, 1978: 175). Useful as this is, it tends to break down when one considers the kind of atrocities that are committed primarily to intimidate others, for example, would-be resistance fighters. These are 'tactical', in one sense, but are they really necessary, especially when they involve the murder of the innocent, as with, say, the shooting of hostages, or revenge killings such as those at Lidice and Oradour?

We are regaled in the media in our own time with a depressing litany of atrocities which share certain common features with the historical incidents we have discussed. Whether committed in face-to-face situations or at a distance, one factor recurs time and time again – depersonalisation, the turning of the enemy into a non-person. It is usually important that opponents are thought of in impersonal terms – not as people but as 'targets', 'terrorists' and 'rebels', whose deaths are necessary as punishment or as an example, or as a prerequisite for 'pacification'.

Above all, they are to be seen as inferior and terms such as 'Bosche', 'slants', 'gooks' and *untermenschen* all encourage these modes of thought. Nowhere is this better seen than in the Nazi atrocities during World War II. In a now famous psychological study of SS killers, Henry Dicks found that they displayed tendencies to extreme anxiety, had previously had poor relations with their fathers and expressed little emotional attachment to their mothers. They were intolerant of tenderness and evinced signs of 'anti-social sadism' (Dicks, 1972). It is important to ask just how revealing this kind of study is. Is it any more than the kind of vague quasi-Freudian 'analysis' that would look well in a popular journal but hardly merits serious investigation? Dicks is identifying biographical factors which, by implication, are held to be causative influences. It is always possible to construct all sorts of unlikely and meaningless correlations between chosen sets of variables. In this instance there may be no relationship at all between these antecedents and the perpetration of the atrocities in question. There are plenty of people who display varying combinations of such characteristics who do not become mass murderers. In addition, Dicks goes on to identify in these men features which conduce to the typical 'authoritarian personality'. This model, popularised by T. Adorno, has been ably criticised and no longer stands up to serious scrutiny, not least because it tends to minimise the fact of human learning capacities for focused aggression and the indoctrination factor in prejudice. Dicks also maintains, from his indepth studies, that in prison these men were among the best behaved inmates, and, in general, were mild-mannered, non-impulsive, over-controlled people who could be very aggressive once they gave way to anger. This seems to be a disconsonant conclusion considering the highly systematic and coldly impersonal nature of the Nazi extermination programme in which they were involved. But it does tend to support the contention that given the right circumstances, the right cause and the right authoritative voice, people can be induced to kill on command (Milgram, 1972).

If it does take a particular type of personality to commit atrocities, we must take care not to divorce this from the social context of the particular massacre in question. As we have seen, circumstances certainly alter cases as far as atrocities are concerned. Furthermore, we should not confuse the issue of the personalities of the killers themselves with the personalities of those who *order* the killings – a point brought out particularly well by the 'final solution' programme. The bureaucrats, intellectuals and hosts of minor officials who were either directly or indirectly involved in the killing industry were happy to let others do the grisly work for them, but were perhaps incapable of carrying out the crimes themselves – a fact which, of course, makes them no less culpable in moral terms (Carlton, 1992: Excursus).

Perhaps no one is *absolutely* incapable of perpetrating atrocities, although some people are obviously more likely to respond to the appropriate conditioning than others. This at least, is the theory underlying reported research programmes designed to test which soldiers do not value other people's lives and are, therefore, potentially ruthless killers (NB the work of Sigmund Streufert for the US Navy reported by Watson, 1978: 179–83). In some ways, however, it is the sheer ordinariness of those involved which makes their actions so disturbing. This is evidenced by the confessions of many Vietnam war veterans. These studies have shown that, by and large, those involved in atrocities, though under considerable stress, were not opiate users – a common problem in Vietnam – and were more likely to be decorated for heroism than others. Many of them talked freely about their parts in some truly horrific atrocities, including the subsequent mutilation of the dead, such as cutting off genitals, breasts, etc. As far as we can tell these were run-of-the-mill GIs who were caught up in a particular group situation and acted with uncharacteristic savagery. What any one of them would have done left to themselves is anybody's guess. The conclusion is unavoidable that perhaps we are all potential criminals.

A somewhat different aspect of the same problem was highlighted in the immediate aftermath of the failed bomb-plot to kill Hitler at his HQ at Rastenburg on 20 July 1944. In Berlin, a number of the key conspirators were rushed down to a courtyard lit by the headlamps of vehicles, and peremptorily shot before the SS could arrive to interrogate them – something that might have been acutely embarrassing for those that were party to the plot and who tried to cover their tracks by ordering the execution of their fellow officers. What is interesting here is that the execution squads were not made up of hardened SS personnel (who stopped the killings when they arrived) but were almost certainly composed of orderlies, clerks, waiters and so on, who happened to be carrying out their routine tasks at the time (Goodspeed, 1962: 199). As we have seen from Milgram's study it was a case of the right order from the right person for the right reason – who argues with a general who orders you to kill 'traitors'?

So everything turns on the question, are those who commit atrocities special kinds of people, or are we all potential murderers? And if we are, in what ways can we be held responsible for our actions?

The very concept of moral behaviour implies some degree of moral responsibility, and this, in turn, presupposes both freedom of choice and the capacity to make rational judgements. As Kant has argued, '. . . unless the moral will is free either to do or not to do what the moral law prescribes, morality itself [must] be regarded as an illusion' (Aiken, 1957: 39). Here Kant is taking the view that morality ('practical reason') is not primarily addressed to the resolution of intellectual doubts regarding, say, political or religious verities, but to irresolutions of the will. Moral behaviour, then, assumes at least some measure of moral culpability.

But how free are we? Are we really in a position to make valid moral judgements? Indeed, how rational are we? (It is patently a weakness of the Utilitarian 'greatest happiness principle' that it assumes that humans have the ability to make rational, dispassionate decisions as to what will bring about a greater balance of pleasure over pain.) The question of freedom, or lack of it, necessarily raises the old but still pertinent issue of determinism versus free will. The problem of whether or not we have genuine moral freedom is something that must be faced by those who insist that we should take moral imperatives seriously. For determinism implies that we have a kind of moral (mental?) infirmity for which there is no ultimate cure. Indeed, an extreme determinist might argue that the question is irrelevant because we just are what we are – no one is really to blame for anything.

Determinism can be defined as 'the belief that everything that happens has a cause or causes, and could not have happened differently unless something in the cause or causes had also been different' (Carr, 1965: 93). In other words, given the necessary pre-conditions there will be a particular effect, and, therefore, if we knew all the pre-conditions, everything – including human behaviour – would be predictable. Experimentally, especially in the physical sciences, reproduction of this kind is often possible, but this is rarely so in the human sciences because not all the pre-conditions can be re-established; and then there is always the extra factor, the memory of the earlier experiment or occasion, which 'neutralises' the whole procedure. Determinism, then, is concerned with antecedents, with causes and effects, and is not to be confused with fatalism – the *'que sera sera'* idea that everyone has an unavoidable 'fate'. This really has no place in a scientific discipline. Nevertheless, the conviction that whatever will be will be still informs a great deal of quasi-religious thinking.

What we are asking here is to what extent are our believed voluntary actions completely determined by inherited genetic factors, or by our personalities as they have been formed by past actions and feelings, or because of an intricate complex of current conditions? Are we mere bio-social automata or are we free, volitional beings? Because, if we are not, we cannot be held to have moral responsibility. William James once posed the problem quite graphically when he wrote that 'our whole feeling of reality, the whole sting and excitement of our voluntary life depends on our sense that in it things are really being decided from one moment to another, and that it is not the dull rattling off of a chain that was forged innumerable years ago' (quoted in Koestler, 1956: 95). But is this sting and excitement an illusion? And, if so, is it a necessary illusion? Freud suggested that we were self-deceived, but maintained that this self-deception was important because it enabled the individual to function within the restrictive confines of an alien society (Stafford-Clark, 1967). Whatever the belief, the result, of course, is much the same. Unconsciously and emotionally, we *act* as though we are free, even where that freedom expresses itself as violence.

It follows from all this that there has to be great uncertainty as to whether we can be said to be either free or unfree. Thus, we return to the primary concern of our discussion – have we moral responsibility or not, especially in relation to violence and aggression? From whence does this proclivity for aggression derive? Is it a legacy of primeval times? Should we attribute it to our basic animal natures which some might interpret as 'original sin'? Is it something humans will hopefully outgrow when they reach psycho-social maturity? Must we assume that until that far-off state of hypothesised mutual goodwill, humans are not entirely accountable for their actions? Is it society that is at fault in the way it formulates its codes, or is every offender *ipso facto* 'sick' because his bio-social profile renders him incapable of coherent moral behaviour? Obviously, we have to distinguish here between compulsion and causation and just what constitutes compulsion and causation, especially in relation to atrocities. Few authorities dispute that there are some people who appear not to have the psychological capacity for making normal distinctions. They seem unable to make what society regards as rational, moral judgements. But if the psychotics and the psychopaths, however defined, are treated as rare exceptions, what are we to make of the human proclivity for aggression? In particular, how are we to explain the insanity of massacre which is aggression in its most gratuitous form?

The whole issue of freedom and moral culpability raises these many unanswered – and perhaps unanswerable – questions. The exact relationship between the two is still uncertain and in operational terms still needs a great deal of fine tuning. But surely the fact that we have responsibility for our actions cannot be seriously questioned. As Kant has argued the sense of moral constraint is a singular feature of being human. We may feel a sense of 'ought' and 'ought not' about *different* things, but we all feel a sense of obligation about *something*. No reductionist arguments can satisfactorily account for this normative compulsion. Certainly the teaching of the world's great religions is that we have moral responsibility and the appeal of these religions is based upon the assumption that without free will – however that is construed – there can be no free response.

People who commit atrocities are not all psychopaths. Their biographical profiles are such that they must still be held to be morally responsible for what most would presumably regard as totally irrational acts. How then are such people to be judged? Can we possibly take the Emotivist view that all moral prescriptions are pseudo-statements and, therefore, meaningless because they tell us nothing about the properties of the acts, only that they are regarded with approval or disapproval? Or are we to take an Absolutist view – as is quite common with many religionists – that there are some moral principles which are 'indelible' and true for all time? And is a detached scientific view possible? As Arthur Koestler has put it: 'The aim of the historian, the psychologist [and] the social scientist is to explain social behaviour by the interplay of cause and effect, by unravelling the conscious and unconscious forces behind the act ... Their aim is to trace and measure, not to judge. Nevertheless, moral judgements seep into all our reactions and determine social behaviour ... praise and blame ... whether justified or not scientifically, are essential to the functioning of society. Man cannot be deprived of the illusion that he is master of his fate, nor [can he] be deprived of moral indignation ... when he sees people [gassed] by the million. Fatalism and ethical neutrality may be the only correct philosophy, yet they are denials of the brave and pathetic endeavour of the human species' (Koestler, 1956: 96–7).

# Appendix:
# Massacre and the Occult

The occult is not only a matter of considerable controversy, but through the ages has generated hostility and persecution. It has been argued that belief in witchcraft, for instance, is one of the great fears from which mankind has suffered, and that it has taken its toll literally in blood (Parrinder, 1970). It is estimated that the Inquisition burned some 30,000 witches, and that perhaps as many as 200,000 suffered in Europe between c. 1450 and c. 1750 (Robbins, 1964). The last witch to be burned in the UK was in Scotland in 1727, but the final repeal of the Witchcraft Act, which concerned not only the practice but also the *pretence* to practise witchcraft, was not until 1951. Parrinder's statement may seem to be rather exaggerated and florid, but it is largely borne out by the evidence. It should be noted that the emphasis here is on the *belief* itself – true or false – not on the *practice* of witchcraft, as such. It has also been maintained that there is a current resurgence in both belief and practice, and that this may be largely attributed to a decline in the influence of orthodox religion (Haining, 1972). In modern transitional societies, particularly in Africa, this has often meant a return to earlier forms of witch-belief which have become syncretised with elements of non-indigenous religions (Mitchell, 1965). However, in Western society the occult tends to involve a fashionable dabbling with exotic cults (Cross, 1968). It is not the intention here to trace these modern trends, but rather to discuss the nature of some beliefs, and the theories which are advanced to account for their persistence and functionality.

The all-encompassing but nebulous term 'the occult' covers a multitude of beliefs and practices, but most notably witchcraft. Any treatment therefore must involve a brief discussion of what this implies. A particular feature of the occult is that it necessarily involves dissonant and contradictory claims to knowledge. These are either associated with *anomalous objects*, that is things which do not conduce to ordinary experience such as UFOs, apparitions, fairies, etc., or to *anomalous processes*, that is beliefs or claims which relate such objects to human experience, as in witchcraft. Marcello Truzzi maintains that the occult connotes an esoteric knowledge which is revealed only to the initiated. This is typically one of the main characteristics of 'a cult' as normally defined by sociologists of religion. Furthermore, says Truzzi, it implies a belief, often undefined, in supernatural powers which are at the disposal of those human agents who possess the necessary capacities for invocation (Truzzi, 1971).

Such a definition begs a number of preliminary questions. Should the occult be seen as an arcane or secret science, a view that seems to be implicit in the teachings of much modern 'white witchcraft'? (Wilson, 1971). In this, there are shades of Sir James Frazer who postulated that magic (meaning the occult?) could be distinguished from religion in that it was blatantly manipulative in intent and practice whilst religion was characterised by supplication and resignation. In effect, magic was a kind of pseudo-science whereby primitive man attempted to control the unseen powers that he did not understand (Frazer, 1957). This raises the problem of whether the occult is related to a scientifically amenable natural order, and this in turn, poses the supplementary question of exactly what should be subsumed under the umbrella term 'occult'? At the present time it appears to include all sorts of pursuits from the bizarre sexually-oriented antics of self-styled witches during the summer solstice (Johns, 1969) to the more academic concerns of parapsychological investigation. It really goes without saying that it is this overlapping of the trivial with the serious that – to the public mind – brings the very idea of the paranormal into disrepute.

The specific phenomenon that may be termed the witch 'experience' has a universal distribution. This does not mean that it is found in every society, but that it is found in every *type* of society. It was a feature of some historical societies (note, for instance, references in the Old Testament scriptures, for example, 1 Sam. 28) but by no means all. It is particularly common in many pre-literate societies, especially in Africa, but it is interesting that it is not found in some of the most primitive of those societies, notably among the Bushmen of the Kalahari. On the other hand, it was prevalent in some advanced societies such as those of medieval and post-medieval Europe where witch-trials were still being held in the late eighteenth century. It is experiencing something of a revival in modern societies, albeit in somewhat sterilised forms.

Although witch beliefs and practices vary a great deal in time and place, they do tend to exhibit certain common features:

1. *They usually have strong moral connotations.* Philip Mayer points out that the witch-myth recognises an opposition of moral values (Mayer, 1970). The 'peculiar power' is traditionally seen as evil, unnatural or even bestial. In effect, it constitutes a reversal of the norms of society, and a violation of its taboos. Hence it is interesting to note the counter-claims of certain modern practitioners who insist

that with the aid of nature-spirits their 'white witchcraft' is positively beneficial to society.

2.  *It is not unusual to find that the power of the witch is believed to be specifically located.* It may therefore either be held that it is peculiar to particular individuals and is manifested on appropriate occasions, or that it is a power which is potential in every member of the community and can be exercised in certain conditions. In many societies, it is believed that the identity of the witch can be established by oracular or 'practical' means (i.e. experimental tests). Yet in both forms of the belief no material connection can be empirically demonstrated between those individuals who have the power, and the benefits or sufferings they are supposed to have caused.

3.  *Witches are commonly credited with uncanny powers or characteristics.* They may be thought to fly; this was a widely-held view in medieval Europe where witches had to hasten to keep their unsavoury compacts with the Devil. Or it may be believed that they can change their form at will; among the Navaho, for instance, this was thought to take a werewolf form (Kluckhorn, 1962). Witches are almost invariably adults, and not infrequently women – a view traditionally held, for example, among the Nupe of northern Nigeria. Some people are thought to be witches because of some particular property they possess. As we shall see, among the Azande peoples this was referred to as *mangu* a mysterious substance that each has inherited (Evans-Pritchard, 1937). On the other hand, it may be that the witch is to be identified by a sign or mark, or some strange physical characteristic. In medieval Europe, a simple birth-mark or tattoo could be construed as a 'Devil's Mark', and the more fanatical witch-finders were even prepared to look under the eyelids of suspects or shave their pubic hair in order to find a mole or anything that would confirm their suspicions (Trevor-Roper, 1967).

A witch case almost invariably begins with an unexplained incident – perhaps an accident, an illness, or possibly a calamity of some kind. A member of the victim's family or social group will then make a witchcraft accusation against the person who is supposed to be exercising these powers. Divination then follows through the mediation of a witchdoctor or witchfinder who may, as in many African tribes for example, have an institutionalised role in that society. The oracles will then be consulted, the standard tests applied and where appropriate the person will be punished in the prescribed manner.

Nobody seriously disputes the 'witch experience' insofar as this connotes witch *beliefs*. What is in doubt is to what extent people actually *practise* the 'black arts' (it is here that a line should perhaps be drawn between witchcraft and sorcery which is generally acknowledged as the attempt to manipulate unseen powers for *evil* purposes). Between the wars, colonial legislators were very uncertain about the matter. There were severe penalties in Northern Rhodesia, Kenya, Tanganyika, Nigeria and Uganda for anyone practising, or even pretending to practise, witchcraft, or even, in some cases, witch-finding. But the recognition of the *idea* of witchcraft did not necessarily imply a belief in its powers, and even witchcraft confessions were not always regarded as valid. As Howells points out, experientially it is very difficult to know how to distinguish between the effects of spells and those of suggestion (Howells, 1948). Observers were quite prepared to accept that certain kinds of misfortune and perhaps even death could be attributed to powerful suggestion. But the existence of a witchcraft Ordinance in these territories put the onus of 'proof' on the accused because the law failed to define what it was that the prosecution really had to prove.

The European experience was rather different. In the medieval and post-medieval periods the practice of witchcraft is well-attested. People were actually members of covens and really did perform elaborate rituals and cast spells often for ostensibly evil purposes. But to what avail is open to question. Practitioners might justly be accused of witchcraft but what did this really mean? Any evidence of causality is lacking; there seems to be no provable connection between a spell and its avowed consequences. So why have people persevered with witchcraft beliefs and practices?

A number of theories have been advanced to 'explain' the witch phenomenon, especially by social scientists. Anthropologists, in particular, are inclined to see witchcraft in terms of its functionality and have consequently proposed various types of *structural theory* to account for it. These maintain that witch beliefs arise as the result of tension and dislocation in structural formations such as families, groups, etc. Pressures build up within small claustrophobic groups, and these are said to give rise to frustration and bitterness which, in turn, generate witchcraft accusations. It is when people become important to one another in *many* ways in a complex of multi-strand relationships that accusations are said to be most common. Hell can be other people. So, it is argued, life can sometimes become intolerable in unalterable face-to-face situations. It is in circumstances such as these that resentment spills over into accusation and recrimination.

This is the theory in its most unelaborated form; but it does have more sophisticated variants. These suggest that accusations tend to be made in any one of three structural situations.

1.  When the accused individuals are doing what society requires of

them but where there is some conflict of interest. For example, in a traditional African matrilineage when a husband may want to take his wife and sisters from the control of his mother's brother.

2. When the accused individuals are exceeding the demands of society, that is those who are too rich or too powerful to be attacked directly.
3. When the accused individuals do not measure up to the expectations of society, as with the stranger or that stereotype of the witch, the much-maligned aged crone who lived on the outskirts of the medieval village.

Interesting and suggestive as these ideas are, they are so highly generalised that they can cover any and every contingency. A more enlightening approach has been taken by another anthropologist, S. F. Nadel. In a now famous monograph, he asks how two neighbouring societies that are similar in culture and customs can be so different in their attitudes to witchcraft? In effect, Nadel is saying that the presence of witchcraft stems from the fact that people cannot or do not live up to the norms of society, yet cannot or will not openly rebel against them. This interpretation is vague and unsatisfactory inasmuch as it could apply to almost any society in almost any connection. Nadel shows *how* witchcraft is manifested, and in which directions it is made, but does nothing to explain witchcraft, *per se* (Nadel, 1952).

Also popular in the social sciences are *psychological theories* of witchcraft. W. Howells, for example, takes the view that for many peoples, witchcraft is merely an interesting diversion, and he cites the instance of a young wife living away from home in her husband's patrilineage who soothes her wounded feelings by telling her own family that her father-in-law is a witch. As Howells puts it, 'it allows a satisfactory indirect attack against an object of hostility, but it kept simply as gossip' (Howells, 1948).

Closely allied to this approach are what might be called *cathartic theories* of witchcraft. These see witch accusations as tension-release mechanisms which provide an emotional catharsis for those concerned. This 'safety-valve' approach is exemplified by the work of Clyde Kluckhorn on Navaho society. He maintains that in situations where pressures are brought about by perpetual subsistence living and the threats of whites to their traditional way of life, witchcraft acts as a safety-valve for all the accumulated antagonism. This kind of theory could be very plausibly applied to the notorious Salem witch trials of 1692 (Bednarski, 1970) and the 'devils' case at Loudun in 1634 (Huxley, 1971) where the accusations had strong religious-cum-sexual implications. Both resulted in waves of allegation and persecution, and in the latter case, the execution of an almost certainly innocent priest.

A particularly popular approach to the problem of 'explaining' witch-craft is that which sees the witch accusation as a blame-shifting mechanism. These *scapegoat theories* can be shown to have considerable relevance in all sorts of historical situations. Concrete hostilities and animosities are sometimes canalised or deflected against selected social scapegoats. Huxley also stresses this when he states that 'most societies have chosen whipping-boys to absorb their exasperations, tensions and frustrations' (Huxley, 1971). Then, lapsing into a more psychological mode, he goes on to argue that witch-hunting (and perhaps witch-role acceptance?) are manifestations of 'herd-intoxication'. He categorises it with the use of drugs and a pre-occupation with 'elementary sex' as a form of 'retrogress-ive self-transcendence'. Witch-hunting, for Huxley, is simply just another way of trying to escape from the insulated self.

Complementarily, there are theories of witchcraft which centre on the need for *social control*. Witch beliefs can act as very potent mechanisms of control, and it is noteworthy that in small, nomadic societies these beliefs are often absent, presumably because it does not take much to keep a tiny struggling band together. It is not that difficult to maintain a measure of cohesion with groups that live on the margins of subsistence. This could be contrasted with the situation in some centralised tribal societies, for instance, pre-colonial Zulu society where witch-finding was a terrifying and highly ritualised affair, especially where it involved notables within the king's entourage. If a person was accused of exercising witchcraft against the king's family or his *indunas* or particularly himself, there was no appeal and no mercy. The accused was pinioned by the executioners, and rods were hammered into his anus until he was dead, and a detachment of warriors was sent to his kraal to execute his family and confiscate his herds (Ritter, 1958). In these circumstances, it is difficult to avoid the suspicion that witch-finding was used as an aid to political power; to eliminate rivals and undesirables, and to enrich the nobility at the victim's expense.

In some ways, one of the most rewarding approaches to this whole question is to be found in *cognitive theories* of witchcraft. What is so interesting for the social analyst is that for those that accept them, witch beliefs constitute a closed intellectual system. Those who 'believe' are often quite aware of the natural order of things, but for them the *context* of misfortune may be more significant than its intrinsic nature. They may well be prepared to admit that a person is ill because they have been attacked by an undetectable virus, but the question remains, why this particular virus and this particular person at this particular time? To say, as we tend to do, that it's just 'bad luck' is hardly a description, and is certainly not an explanation. To resort to an interpretation of events involving supernatural agencies can therefore be just as cogent for the believer who inhabits the charmed circle of superempiricism.

Take, for example, the well-researched case of the Azande. For these people, witchcraft had important structural and cathartic functions. Close agnates were never accused, and commoners never accused members of the tribal aristocracy; either of these would have brought unnecessary and unwanted disruption to the current social order. On the other hand, the accused were those who had a relationship of some significance with their accusers; indeed, they were often members of the same household. The system was thus 'self-correcting' in that the number of accusations was kept down by fears of a possible boomerang effect – the suspicion that it may take one to catch one.

The Azande believed that witchcraft was the explanation for every mishap that could not be accounted for in any other way. The belief was that every person had the inherent capacity to be a witch; this could be activated, perhaps unconsciously, when some suppressed animosity was present. It follows, therefore, that if that person were subsequently accused of witchcraft they could not effectively protest their own innocence.

This is all somewhat reminiscent of the actions of Freud's 'resentful Id', and perhaps comes closer to 'explaining' the presence of evil as the expression of a corrupt and self-interested nature than as the product of daemonic possession. The former emphasises inner personality factors whilst the latter stresses the influence of external, malevolent forces. In their own ways, the Azande are not only trying to account for the vagaries of the natural order, but are also trying to understand something of their own often unpredictable behaviour.

The view of witchcraft as a knowledge-system is underlined by the European experience. Trevor-Roper (the present Lord Dacre) stresses the bizarre beliefs which became the bases of the accusations in the witch trials of the sixteenth and seventeenth centuries. He writes of 'ill-advised ladies' lubricated with 'devil's grease' (taken from the rendered-down bodies of murdered infants) who eased themselves through cracks in doors and windows to make their way to compacts with the Devil (Trevor-Roper, 1969). The whole thing has marked sexual overtones. The Devil, who is physiologically versatile, was thought to be an incubus for she-witches, and a succubus for males. Thomas Aquinas reconciled these seemingly contradictory ideas by hypothesising diabolic absorption/discharge functions – in effect, a kind of metaphysical hermaphroditism. There was a willing acceptance by many of their 'guilt', indeed, in many cases the accused were unable to say whether they were guilty or not. It was only in this post-medieval period that the entire daemonic thought structure developed. This constituted a merger of traditional witch-beliefs with the elaborate daemonology of religion and it is this that distinguishes European witch-beliefs and practices from their counterparts in tribal societies. Together they became a formidable, institutionalised force which may have been exaggerated and systematised to counter the waning authority of the church.

Whatever the accuracy of this diagnosis, today the West is confronted by its own peculiar versions of the witch-craze. These take two main forms. The first, so beloved of the popular press, is witchcraft as *esoteric cult*. This can range from the midnight cavortings of self-proclaimed initiates, fresh from their covens, complete with diaphonous shifts and ritual impedimenta, to the more raucous activities of young counter-cultural satanists who practise their craft within the general ambit of the pop world. The second, and far more serious, concerns those situations in which witchcraft, and particularly witch-hunting, can be used as a *social metaphor*. Many societies, as we have seen, have found the persecution of selected groups to be a convenient mechanism – one might almost say indispensable expedient – for the maintenance of control. And this may then be justified in terms of a believed historic mission. As Adolf Hitler expressed it: 'The National Socialist movement has its mightiest tasks to fulfil . . . it must condemn to general wrath the evil enemy of humanity [Jews] as the creator of all suffering' (Hitler, 1943). The imperatives of control can always be validated by the appropriate ideology. And this had added force if it is given a superempirical dimension.

How can we account for the continuing 'presence' of witch beliefs – indeed, perhaps the occult generally – in modern society? Given our increasing capacity for rational explanation, the evident resurgence of the non-rational seems both anachronistic and unnecessary. Perhaps this resuscitation of the occult should be seen as a vain yet understandable striving for autonomy in an apparently mechanistically-ordered world. A world in which comprehension has come to mean scientific know-how. A world in which the language of science has become increasingly removed from that of the laity, and where the more esoteric concerns of science now belong to a different universe of discourse. The devotee is thus disillusioned and alienated. He wants to order his own existence. He wants to free himself from the deterministic shackles of scientific explanation, not appreciating that the only certain thing about science is its ultimate uncertainty. He would like to negotiate his own individuality and liberate himself from those commanding voices that tell him how to order his thinking, his living and his society. Yet in trying to trace an atavistic path back to a believed, older reality, he has returned to a dark age of the mind. The devotee craves an emancipation of the spirit, only to be bound by the confining parameters of formulaic superstition.

# Bibliography

Acton E. *Russia*, Longman, London, 1986.

Adkins A. *Moral Values and Political Behaviour in Ancient Greece*, Chatto & Windus, London, 1972.

Aiken H. *The Age of Ideology*, Mentor, New York, 1957.

Alderson A. *The Structure of the Ottoman Dynasty*, Oxford University Press, London, 1956.

Andreski, S. *Military Organisation and Society*, RKP, London, 1968.

Aristophanes. 'Birds' in *The Complete Works of Aristophanes* (Edited by M. Hadas), Bantam Press, New York, 1971.

Arrian *The Campaigns of Alexander* (trans. Aubrey de Selincourt), Dorset Press (in association with Penguin Books), New York, 1986.

Auguet R. *Cruelty and Civilization*, Allen & Unwin, London, 1972.

Barber N. *Lords of the Golden Horn*, Macmillan, London, 1972.

———— *The Week France Fell*, Day Books, New York, 1979.

Becker P. *Rule of Fear*, Panther Books, London, 1964.

———— *Path of Blood*, Penguin, Harmondsworth, 1979.

Beevor A. *The Spanish Civil War*, Orbis, London, 1982.

Behr E. *The Algerian Problem*, Penguin, Harmondsworth, 1962.

Bell P. *The Origins of the Second World War*, Longman, London, 1986.

Bermant B. and Weitzman M. *Ebla*, Weidenfeld & Nicholson, London, 1979.

Blanch L. *Pavilions of the Heart*, Weidenfeld & Nicholson, London, 1974.

Boak A. and Sinnigen W. *A History of Rome to AD 565* (5th Edition), Macmillan, New York, 1965.

Bourne P. *Men, Stress and Vietnam*, Little, Brown & Co., New York, 1970.

Bower T. *Blind Eye to Murder*, Paladin, London, 1983.

———— *Klaus Barbie*, Corgi, London, 1985.

Bowle J. *A History of Europe*, Heinemann, London, 1979.

Calvocoressi P. and Wint G. *Total War*, Allen Lane, London, 1972.

Carcopino J. *Daily Life in Ancient Rome*, RKP, London, 1940.

Carlson N. *Psychology* (2nd Edition), Allyn & Bacon Inc., Boston, 1987.

Carlton E. *Ideology and Social Order*, RKP, London, 1977.

———— *War and Ideology*, Routledge, London, 1990.

———— *Occupation: The Policies and Practices of Military Conquerors*, Routledge, London, 1992.

Carr, E. H. *What is History?* Penguin, Harmondsworth, 1965.

Cassels L. *The Struggle for the Ottoman Empire*, Murray, London, 1966.

Ceram C. *Gods, Graves and Scholars*, Gollancz, London, 1952.

Charques R. *A Short History of Russia*, English Universities Press, London, 1959.

Fr. Chirkovsky N. *An Introduction to Russian History*, Vision Press, London, 1967.

Cohan A. *Theories of Revolution*, Nelson, London, 1975.

Collins R. *The Medes and Persians*, Cassell, London, 1974.

Conquest R. *Inside Stalin's Secret Police*, Macmillan, London, 1985.

Cook, J. M. *The Persian Empire*, Dent, London, 1983.

Cottrell L. *The Great Invasion*, Pan, London, 1961.

——— *Penguin Book of Lost Worlds Vol. 1*, Penguin, Harmondsworth, 1966.

Covensky M. *The Ancient Near Eastern Tradition*, Harper & Row, New York, 1966.

Crawford M. *The Roman Republic*, Collins, Glasgow, 1978.

Dank M. *The French Against the French*, Cassell, London, 1978.

Darley J., Glucksberg S. and Kinchla R. *Psychology* (3rd Edition), Prentice-Hall, Englewood Cliffs, N.J., 1986.

Davidoff L. *Introduction to Psychology* (2nd Edition), McGraw-Hill, New York, 1980.

Davidowicz L. *The War Against the Jews 1933–45*, Holt Rinehart & Winston, New York, 1975.

Davies J. 'Towards a theory of revolution', *American Sociological Review*, Vol. 27, No. 1, February 1962.

Dicks H. *Licensed Mass Murder*, Tavistock, London, 1972.

Downing D. *The Devil's Virtuosos: German Generals at War 1940–45*, New English Library, London, 1977.

Dunning A. and Ballard C. (Eds) *The Anglo–Zulu War: New Perspectives*, University of Natal Press, Pietermaritzburg, 1981.

Dyer G. *War*, The Bodley Head, London, 1986.

Ehrenberg V. *From Solon to Socrates*, Methuen, London, 1968.

Elliot G. *Twentieth Century Book of the Dead*, Penguin, Harmondsworth, 1973.

Ellis W. *Alcibiades*, Routledge, London, 1989.

Emery W. *Archaic Egypt*, Pelican, Harmondsworth, 1972.

Fine J. *The Ancient Greeks*, Belknap, Harvard, 1983.

Finley M. I. *Slavery in Classical Antiquity*, Heffer, Cambridge, 1964.

——— *Ancient Sicily*, Chatto & Windus, London, 1980.

——— *Ancient Slavery and Modern Ideology*, Pelican, Harmondsworth, 1980.

Fortune G. and Fortune W. *Hitler Divided France*, Macmillan, London, 1943.

Fotion N. and Elfstrom G. *Military Ethics*, Routledge, London, 1986.

Frankfort H. *The Birth of Civilization in the Near East*, Anchor, New York, 1950.

Freud S. *Civilization and its Discontents* (trans. J. Riviere), Hogarth, London, 1957.

Frye R. *The Heritage of Persia*, Sphere Books, London, 1976.

Galbraith J. K. 'New World Order', *The Guardian*, March 27 1991.

de Gaulle C. *The Call to Honour*, Collins, London, 1955.

Gerwith A. *Reason and Morality*, University of Chicago Press, Chicago, 1978.

Ghirshman R. *Iran*, Pelican, Harmondsworth, 1978.

Ginsberg M. *On the Diversity of Morals*, Heinemann, London, 1956.

Goebbels H. *The Goebbels Diaries* (Ed. L. Lochner), Hamish Hamilton, London, 1948.

Goodspeed D. *The Conspirators*, Macmillan, London, 1962.

Grant M. *Gladiators*, Penguin, Harmondsworth, 1971.

Greig, I. *Subversion*, Stacey, London, 1973.

Grigg J. *1943: The Victory That Never Was*, Eyre Methuen, London, 1980.

Gutteridge W. *The Military in African Politics*, Methuen, London, 1969.

Hadas M. (Ed.) *The Complete Plays of Aristophanes*, Bantam, New York, 1971.

Hanson V. *The Western Way of War*, Hodder & Stoughton, London, 1989.

Harden D. *The Phoenicians*, Pelican, Harmondsworth, 1971.

Hastings M. *Bomber Command* (2nd Edition), Michael Joseph, London, 1980.

———— *Das Reich*, Michael Joseph, London, 1981.

Herodotus *The Histories* (trans. Aubrey de Selincourt), Penguin, Harmondsworth, 1972.

Hilberg R. *The Destruction of the European Jews*, Quadrangle Books, Chicago, 1971.

Hohne H. *The Order of the Death's Head*, Pan, London, 1969.

Hopkins K. *Conquerors and Slaves*, Cambridge University Press, Cambridge, 1978.

Hospers J. *Human Conduct*, Harcourt, Brace & World, New York, 1961.

Hoyt E. *Japan's War*, Hutchinson, London, 1986.

Huart C. *Ancient Persia and Iranian Civilization*, Routledge & Kegan Paul, London, 1927 (reprinted 1976).

Hunt A. 'Bombs long gone', *The Guardian*, 10 August 1989.

Infield G. *Secrets of the SS*, Military Heritage Press, New York, 1981.

Irving D. *The Rise and Fall of the Luftwaffe*, Futura Publications, London, 1976.

———— *The Destruction of Dresden*, Macmillan, London, 1985.

Johnson P. *A History of the Modern World*, Weidenfeld & Nicholson, London, 1983.

Kagan D. *The Archidamian War*, Cornell University Press, Ithaca, 1974.

———— *The Peace of Nicias and the Sicilian Expedition*, Cornell University Press, Ithaca, 1981.

Kirby W. *The War Against Japan*, HMSO, London, 1969.

Kochan L. *The Making of Modern Russia*, Pelican, Harmondsworth, 1967.

Koestler A. *Reflections on Hanging*, Gollancz, London, 1956.

Kolko G. *Vietnam: The Anatomy of a War 1940–75*, Unwin, London, 1987.

Kramer S. *The Sumerians*, University of Chicago Press, Chicago, 1963.

Kuper L. *The Pity of It All*, University of Minneapolis Press, Minneapolis, 1977.

———— *Genocide*, Penguin, Harmondsworth, 1981.

Lansing E. *The Sumerians*, Cassell, London, 1974.

Leach J. *Pompey the Great*, Croom Helm, Beckenham, 1978.

Leakey L. *Defeating Mau Mau*, Methuen, London, 1954.

Leakey R., Bulzer K. and Day M. 'Early Homo Sapiens remains from the Omo River region of Southwest Ethiopia', *Nature*, No. 222, 1969, pp. 1132–38.

Lee S. *The European Dictatorships 1918–1945*, Routledge, London, 1988.

LeFrançois G. *Psychology* (2nd Edition), Wadsworth Publishing Co., Belmont, California, 1983.

Legum C. *Congo Disaster*, Penguin, Harmondsworth, 1961.

Levin N. *The Holocaust*, Schocken Books, New York, 1973.

Lewis R. *Everyday Life in Ottoman Turkey*, Batsford, London, 1971.

Liddell-Hart B. *History of the Second World War*, Cassell Books, London, 1970.

Lorenz K. *On Aggression*, Methuen, London, 1966.

McKee A. *Caen: Anvil of Victory*, Pan Books, London, 1966.

McNeill W. *A World History*, Oxford University Press, London, 1979.

Meggett M. *Desert People*, University of Chicago Press, Chicago, 1960.

Milgram S. *Obedience to Authority*, Tavistock, London, 1972.

Morris D. *The Washing of the Spears*, Sphere Books, London, 1969.

Mountfield D. *The Partisans*, Hamlyn, London, 1979.

Muller H. 'The limitations of Greece' in J. Claster (Ed.), *Athenian Democracy*, Holt, Rinehart & Winston, New York, 1967.

Novick P. *The Resistance Versus Vichy*, Chatto & Windus, London, 1968.

Oliver R. and Fage J. *A Short History of Africa*, Penguin, Harmondsworth, 1966.

Olivova V. *Sports and Games in the Ancient World*, Orbis, London, 1984.

Olmstead A. *A History of the Persian Empire*, University of Chicago Press, Chicago, Reprinted 1970.

Overy R. *The Air War 1939–45*, Europa Publications Limited, London, 1980.

Paine L. *The Abwehr*, Robert Hale, London, 1984.

Payne R. *The Roman Triumph*, Pan Books, London, 1962.

Perham M. 'Reflections of the Nigerian Civil War', *International Affairs*, No. 46, April 1970.

Pike D. *War, Peace and the Viet Cong*, MIT Press, Mass., 1969.

Piotrovsky B. *The Ancient Civilization of Uratu*, Barrie & Rockcliff Cresset Press, London, 1969.

Powell A. *Athens and Sparta*, Routledge, London, 1988.

Preston P. *The Coming of the Spanish Civil War*, Methuen, London, 1978.

Rawls J. *A Theory of Justice*, Harvard University Press, Cambridge, Mass., 1971.

Reitlinger G. *The Final Solution*, Thomas Voseloff, South Brunswick, 1968.

———— 'The SS: The alibi of a nation', *Arms & Armour*, London, 1981.

Revill J. *World History* (2nd Edition), Longmans, 1962.

Ritter E. *Shaka, Zulu*, Panther Books, London, 1958.

Roberts B. *The Zulu Kings*, Sphere Books, London, 1977.

Rodzinski W. *The Walled Kingdom*, Fontana, London, 1984.

Saggs H. *Civilization before Greece and Rome*, Batsford, London, 1989.

Santoli A. *To Bear any Burden*, Abacus Books, London, 1985.

Sartre J. P. 'On Genocide', *Ramparts*, February 1968, pp. 37–42.

Schapiro L. *Government and Politics in the Soviet Union*, Hutchinson, London, 1967.

Service E. *Profiles in Ethnology*, Harper & Row, New York, 1978.

Seidel G. *The Holocaust Denial*, Beyond the Pale Collective, Leeds, 1986.

Seth R. *The Executioners*, Tempo Books, New York, 1970.

Slim W. *Defeat into Victory*, Cassell, London, 1956.

Smith C. 'Cruel march to the tomb', *The Observer*, 29 July 1990.

Smith H. *The Russians*, Ballantine, New York, 1976.

Snyder L. *The War: A Concise History 1939–45*, Robert Hale, London, 1962.

Stafford-Clark D. *What Freud Really Said*, Pelican, Harmondsworth, 1967.

Strauss M., Gelles R. and Steinmetz S. *Behind Closed Doors: Violence in the American Family*, Anchor, New York, 1979.

Sullivan M. *The Arts of China*, Cardinal, London, 1973.

Sykes C. *Orde Wingate*, Collins, London, 1959.

Taber R. *War of the Flea*, Paladin, London, 1970.

Taylour W. *The Myceneans*, Thames & Hudson, London, 1983.

Tedder Lord *With Prejudice*, Cassell, London, 1966.

Theal G. M. *History of South Africa 1795–1875* (5 vols), George Allen & Unwin, London, 1908.

Thomas H. *The Spanish Civil War*, Penguin, Harmondsworth, 1977.

Thompson L. *1940*, Collins, London, 1966.

———— (Ed.) *African Societies in Southern Africa*, Heinemann, London, 1969.

Thucydides *The Peloponnesian War* (trans. Rex Warner), Penguin, Harmondsworth, 1972.

Toynbee A. *Armenian Massacres: The Murder of a Nation*, Hodder & Stoughton, London, 1915.

———— *Experiences*, Oxford University Press, London, 1969.

Tucker R. *The Just War*, John Hopkins University Press, Baltimore, 1960.

Vogt J. *Ancient Slavery and the Ideal of Man*, Basil Blackwell, Oxford, 1974.

Wakin M. (Ed.) *War, Morality and the Military Profession*, Westview Press, Boulder, 1979.

Walzer M. *Just and Unjust Wars* Pelican, Harmondsworth, 1980.

Watson P. *War on the Mind*, Pelican, Harmondsworth, 1978.

Wavell, Stuart, *The Sunday Times*, 22 July 1990.

Webster C. and Frankland W. *The Strategic Air Offensive Against Germany*, HMSO, London, 1961.

Welland J. *By the Waters of Babylon*, Hutchinson, London, 1982.

Wells C. *The Roman Empire*, Fontana, Glasgow, 1984.

Wheeler M. (Ed.) *A Book of Archeology*, Cassell, London, 1957.

Whitehouse R. *The First Cities*, Phaidon, Oxford, 1977.

Woolley L. *Ur of the Chaldees*, Penguin, Harmondsworth, 1954.

Worsley P. *The Trumpet Shall Sound*, Macgibbon & Key, London, 1968.

Xenophon *Recollections of Socrates* (trans. A. Benjamin), Bobbs-Merrill, New York, 1965.

———— *The Persian Expedition* (trans. Rex Warner), Penguin, Harmondsworth, 1978.

———— *Hellenica* (trans. Rex Warner), Penguin, Harmondsworth, 1979.

Yap Y. and Cotterell R. *The Early Civilization of China*, Weidenfeld & Nicholson, London, 1975.

Young P. *World War 1939–45*, Arthur Barker, London, 1966.

## Reading for the Appendix

Bednarski J. 'The Salem Witch Scare viewed sociologically' in M. Marwick, *Readings in Witchcraft and Sorcery*, Penguin, Harmondsworth, 1970.

Cross C. 'The Witches ride again', *Observer Magazine*, 1 December 1968.

Evans-Pritchard E. E. *Witchcraft, Oracles and Magic Among the Azande*, Clarendon Press, London, 1937.

Frazer J. *The Golden Bough*, Macmillan, London, 1957.

Haining P. *Anatomy of Witchcraft*, Souvenir Press, London, 1972.

Hitler A. *Mein Kampf*, Houghton Mifflin, New York, 1943.

Howells W. W. *The Heathens*, Doubleday, New York, 1948.

Huxley A. *The Devils of Loudun*, Harper & Row, New York, 1971.

Johns J. *King of the Witches*, Pan, London, 1969.

Kluckhorn C. *Navaho Witchcraft*, Beacon Press, New York, 1962.

Mayer P. 'Witches' in M. Marwick, *Readings in Witchcraft and Sorcery*, Penguin, Harmondsworth, 1970.

Mitchell J. 'The meaning in misfortune for urban Africans', in M. Fortes and G. Dieterlen (eds), *African Systems of Thought*, Oxford University Press, London, 1965.

Nadel S. 'Witchcraft in Four African Societies', *American Anthropologist*, Vol. 54, 1952.

Parrinder G. *Witchcraft, European and African*, Faber and Faber, London, 1970.

Ritter E. *Shaka, Zulu*, Panther Books, London, 1958.

Robbins R. *Encyclopedia of Witchcraft and Demonology*, Neville, London, 1964.

Trevor-Roper H. R. *Religion, Reformation and Social Change*, Macmillan, London, 1967.

———— *The European Witch-Craze of the 16th and 17th Centuries*, Pelican, Harmondsworth, 1969.

Truzzi M. 'Definition and Dimensions of the Occult', *Journal of Popular Culture*, Winter 1971.

Wilson C. *The Occult*, Mayflower, London, 1971.

# Index